I0056860

UNFAKED

LIFE IS SO MUCH EASIER WHEN
YOU JUST SHOW UP AS YOU

LAURA PICCARDI

'Honest, refreshing and 100% on point. Many times while reading *Unfaked* I thought it was talking directly about me! I guess that's why I found it so empowering and helpful – because I was able to transport myself into the story and take all the learnings I specifically need for my life right now. *Unfaked* isn't another "one-size fits all" solution – Laura has cleverly shared her advice and strategies in a way that allows you to make it your own, which means you're much more likely to get the results you want, because you're in the driving seat. I'll definitely be recommending this book to every woman I know.'
Catrina O'Brien – Senior Retail Development Manager, Mattel Inc

'*Unfaked* lays bare the thoughts and emotions we, as ladies, all have but don't talk about. Like Debs, I've always been an all or nothing kind of woman, but *Unfaked* made me quickly see that there's a better way to do life – and it does so in such an entertaining, engaging and relatable way. For once I didn't feel like I was being talked at or told what to do – Laura makes you feel like you're getting advice from a trusted friend, which is really powerful. I can't recommend *Unfaked* highly enough to all the busy women out there.'
Christina Doyle – Head of Client Strategy, ELMO Cloud HR & Payroll

'Until recently, I felt overwhelmed, scattered and like I was constantly playing catch up – in both my work and my personal life. I was plagued by a permanent sense of guilt – trying to be all things to all people and exhausted from 'doing all the things' but still feeling ineffective. Laura and the Uppy framework helped me realise my own unique priorities, how my own thoughts had been impacting me achieving these and what I could do to adjust my mindset to make a positive change. She has helped me become aware of myself again and the important part I play in driving the productivity and success of my own day. I feel empowered and my productivity is much improved too. I'm now doing the right things instead of ALL THE THINGS!'
Nicky McEnery – Marketing Director & Entrepreneur

'*Unfaked* provides valuable and practical advice for women with a hectic life. The insightful tips can be easily applied to assist in managing everyday situations to cultivate ongoing happiness and a healthy work–life balance. Thanks Laura for a useful and entertaining guidebook.'
Sylvie Dimarco – Deputy Company Secretary, Perpetual Ltd

'When I met Laura I was at my wits end. I was working very long hours, eating badly and felt stressed and overwhelmed most of the time. I was in a cycle that I couldn't seem to get out of, and had no strategies on how to manage my stress. After working through the Uppy framework I now find myself in a place where I'm calm, in control and living a happier, healthier life. Working with Laura was fantastic and overall a lot of fun! Having been through everything herself, she can identify with the many challenges we women face, and that in itself was very comforting, knowing she truly understood some of my struggles. She has truly changed my life for the better.'
Lyndsey Henderson – Director, My Mobile Physio

'Laura is amazing. I've got my Uppy on – and then some – thanks to this incredible woman. I'm now taking care of ME, which I'd forgotten about and pushed aside amongst the busyness of my life. I've reprogrammed my brain and made the subtle changes I've needed to take my life UP to the next level, and prime me for success in all aspects of my life.'
Madeleine Webb – Business Strategist & Entrepreneur

I'd like to say a MASSIVE thank you to my parents, my biggest cheerleaders, for always being there for me with the most unbelievable support. And also to my gorgeous husband Matteo, for being my solid rock and safe place, and always allowing me to be Uppy by loving me just the way I am.

First published in 2019 by Laura Piccardi

© Laura Piccardi 2019

The moral rights of the author have been asserted

All rights reserved. Except as permitted under the *Australian Copyright Act 1968* (for example, a fair dealing for the purposes of study, research, criticism or review), no part of this book may be reproduced, stored in a retrieval system, communicated or transmitted in any form or by any means without prior written permission.

All inquiries should be made to the author.

A catalogue entry for this book is available from the National Library of Australia.

ISBN: 978-1-925648-86-7

Project management and text design by Michael Hanrahan Publishing

Cover design by Peter Reardon

Disclaimer: The material in this publication is of the nature of general comment only, and does not represent professional advice. It is not intended to provide specific guidance for particular circumstances and it should not be relied on as the basis for any decision to take action or not take action on any matter which it covers. Readers should obtain professional advice where appropriate, before making any such decision. To the maximum extent permitted by law, the author and publisher disclaim all responsibility and liability to any person, arising directly or indirectly from any person taking or not taking action based on the information in this publication.

CONTENTS

A note from the author   ix
Preface   xi
01   Meet Debs   1
02   Buckle up   43
     Cause vs Effect   47
     Presence   49
     Stages of learning   53
     Talking to key people   55
     Non-negotiables   58
     Uppy Scale   60
     Balance   63
     Actions   65

03   Who's in there?   67
     Mind fuckery   67
     Good times   70
     Find themes   72
     Uncover values   73
     Define values   77
     Timeline   79
     To dos   84
     Take control   86
     Actions   90

04   What do you want?   93
     Internal GPS   93
     The dream   96
     Get SMART   97
     Aligning with others   99
     One year from now   102
     Goal game plan   105
     To do or not to do   109
     Visualise   112
     Actions   116

05	**How the health are you?**	**119**
	Choose your response	122
	Power of your mind	127
	The stress response	129
	Track	141
	Eat	144
	Move	146
	Step back	148
	Actions	163
06	**What's your story?**	**165**
	Beliefs	166
	Back story	168
	Belief brief	175
	Possibilities Process	186
	Change the story	189
	Actions	194
07	**Who do you see?**	**199**
	Vulnerability	200
	Labelling	202
	Actions	216
08	**Take the reins**	**219**
	Take control	220
	Change the meaning	223
	Blueprints	227
	Rapport	236
	Actions	245
09	**Hello again**	**247**

A NOTE FROM THE AUTHOR

———————

G'day! I'm Laura Piccardi, the author of *Unfaked*. I would firstly like to say a massive thank you for picking up a copy of my book and joining the Unfaked revolution. This has been an absolute passion project for me and something I'm unbelievably proud of, so I'm extremely happy that I get to share it with you, and hopefully make a bit of a difference in your life.

I wanted to quickly tell you a little about me, and how I came to write this book – because although this is a story, it's very much based on fact. Debs' story is an amalgamation of the lives of pretty much every woman I've ever met. If I know you, there may be points in the story where you think I'm talking specifically about you…and I guess in a way I am, but I'm also specifically talking about most other women I know too. You see, although this is Deb's story, it's also your story – because it's actually the same story for all of us.

Of course there's a big piece of me in this book too, because I've most definitely walked Deb's path. But I found that when I was looking for answers, I couldn't find anyone who spoke to me in my language. Or helped me to really understand what was going on in my body at a fundamental level, and indeed how my mind was driving it all. Once I finally did understand all of that though, by spending a shitload of time and money figuring it out by myself, that's when my life and health really started to turn around. They say knowledge is power, and for me that was most definitely the case – it gave me the power to take the right action consistently…which is the only way to create long-term change.

So from then on I vowed to help as many people as I could gain this same understanding, and give them the power to change their lives too. And I realised the best way to do that is to present it in a real, practical and relatable way. I'm over people being told what to do all the time – 'Be the best version of yourself in 5 easy steps', 'Get the body you want in just 90 days' – if that shit worked, we'd be seeing a decrease in the statistics of lifestyle-related disease and levels of distress, but in reality it's the worst it's ever been.

Well I've made it my mission to make a massive dent in these stats, and while I've been doing that successfully as a coach and speaker for many years, it's now time to take it to another level and reach more people with this extremely important message – that the only thing you need to focus on in order to have the health and life that you want, is to simply:

Be you, the real you and nothing but the real you.

Happy Unfaking x

Ah, P.S. You'll notice throughout the book, Debs talks about specific worksheets and resources she uses to guide and support her. You can access and download all of these at www.uppy.com.au/unfaked

PREFACE

I can't believe I'm actually doing this. When I wrote all this stuff I never thought in a million years that another human being would lay their eyes on it. I'd spent my entire life trying to hide the real me. I'd become a master chameleon – just like the lizard I would constantly change myself to fit in with different surroundings and situations, based on who I thought I 'should' be, because I'd always figured that the 'real me' wasn't good enough. But having gone through everything I have in this past year, I've realised that the real me isn't actually that bad … in fact, I've even grown to love the bitch! And I realised that by sharing my story, warts 'n' all, I can actually help others like me, and like you, to do the same – to step out and be the real you and nothing but the real you. Because when you do that, nothing but good shit happens. You stop hiding and you start living. You forget about looking over your shoulder in constant fear that you're going to get found out for having absolutely no freaking idea what you're doing, and you start looking forward – towards everything you truly want and everything you truly deserve. This is the place where true health and happiness come out to play … when you unfake yourself, and just be.

We've learned to believe that life happens to us, rather than for us, and consequently we relinquish all responsibility for our thoughts and actions, and just get taken along for the ride – we do the same shit day in and day out, constantly searching for answers and the next quick fix, but still nothing changes. We pin all our hopes for happiness on external sources. It's always something we will have and never something we just are – 'I'll be happy when … I've lost 10kgs, I've got that promotion, I get married, I buy that car, I go on that holiday, I fit into all the clothes in my wardrobe again'. Well, guess what? I've had all of those things in my life (some more than once) and eventually I got to the point where I was more miserable than I'd ever been. My health had gone to shit, I was constantly tired, consistently bloated, I had regular bouts of anxiety, I couldn't think clearly, I never felt content, and even though I had a lot of people around me I was incredibly lonely. To the world I looked like I had it all, but behind closed doors I was slowly dying inside.

Okay, I know that sounds really dramatic. But now that I've seen the other side of things I realise just how sad and unnecessarily stressful my life was. Now I know that I control the shots in my life and that I'm the creator of everything that happens to me, it's like I've woken up and I'm not afraid anymore. I'm not afraid of failing, I'm not afraid of being rejected and I'm not afraid of showing up as me – the real me and nothing but the real me. It doesn't mean that only good things happen to me and everything around me is rainbows and unicorns, but it means I respond to the world very differently so I'm able to take control of the way I feel and I'm able to live the life I actually want.

I now have enough energy to get through the day without having to rely on coffee, and then still have enough in the tank when I get home from work to enjoy some personal time with myself and my loved ones. I no longer get regularly bloated to the point where I look pregnant, and I've actually dropped 6 of the 10kgs I've been trying to lose for the last few years. My periods are finally coming regularly each month – and without the crippling cramps and emotional extremes. My thinking is a lot clearer, my memory has improved and I now have a general level of calm about me, rather than constantly feeling anxious, with a tightness in my chest.

I don't put as much pressure on myself to please everyone and be perfect all the time, so I'm setting more meaningful and realistic goals, which means I'm not constantly beating myself up for not achieving the unachievable. And I don't fuck myself over like I used to by self-sabotaging with food, shopping and procrastination binges.

I could go on and on, but let's just say that finally I feel content with myself and my life, and as a result I finally feel like life is happening for me … and it feels really bloody good.

If you're thinking this all sounds a bit wanky, you wouldn't be alone in that. I thought that way too, for a very long time. And that's why I've made this decision to share my soul with you. You see, I'm just a normal woman trying to make it in this crazy thing we call life. I'm exactly like you, and I have the exact same thoughts and worries as you – in fact most of us do. No-one had ever explained life to me and how it really works, at least not in a way that actually got through, so I just kept on keeping on and trying to make the best of what I'd got. No-one, that was, until I met a woman who actually spoke to me in my language and cut out all the crap and just got real. I realise now that I'd heard most of the things she said many times before, but no-one had ever helped me to really cut through all the surface level bullshit and get to the heart of the matter, and no-one had ever helped me to make it relatable to real life. Every day I would see all these positive messages and posts on social media and in my inbox about 'being the best version of yourself' and 'living your best life', but I would always think, what the fuck has that got to do with me? I figured it was something other people did, people with more time. I didn't think it was possible to have or be any of those things while building a successful career and trying to set the future up for myself and my family. Turns out, the things they were saying were incredibly valuable, they just weren't getting through to me. But my wish, is that by me sharing this with you – real woman to real woman – you'll start to hear what you need to hear. And you'll start to realise that having the life you want is actually much easier than you think … and everything you need in order to have that is inside you.

If I'm honest with you, I'm still really scared about putting all of this out there for the whole world to see. I'm sure you'll appreciate when you read through my inner most thoughts and fears, and see how they played out in my physical wellbeing, behaviours and indeed my life, why it's such a terrifying act. But I'm at the point now where I figure someone's got to do it. Like it or not, we ladies have all got the same shit going on. You might think you're the only one in the world going through it, but I assure you you're not. And in that lies an unbelievable untapped power. For some reason, we've all decided that we just need to keep calm and carry on, on our own. We think that if we let anyone else in on our dirty little secret (that we can't actually be everything to everyone, and juggle all the things at the same time, while maintaining the perfect body and having the ideal life), we'll be cast out as a complete failure and be forced to live the rest of our days fat, miserable and alone. Ironically however, by continually trying to do the impossible – keep calm and carry on, on your own – you're heading for the exact destination you're so desperately trying to avoid. Think about it: we ladies have never had more opportunities and we've never had more resources available to us, yet we just keep on getting more unhealthy, more stressed and more unhappy. We're obsessed with showing the world how busy we are, because we think that means we're successful, but in doing so we're running ourselves into the ground. I remember once being told that the definition of insanity is doing the same thing over and over, and expecting a different result. Well, we've been trying over and over again to make it on our own and it just ain't working, ladies. So I hope by me putting myself out there, I can inspire you to start putting an end to this insanity and empower you to try something different – to know who you really are and what you really want, and stay true to that no matter what. And to speak up and seek support when you need it. I finally did and it changed my life. Unfortunately, I had to hit rock bottom in order to find all this out, but hopefully, with the help of my journey, you don't have to.

So I'd love for you to take from my journey whatever you need. You'll see that I've done a few summaries along the way – that was so I could organise things in my brain and remember the important stuff, but you might find it useful as a bit of an action list for things that you can take away and apply in your life. I've personally gone back through my journal many times and each time it's taught me something new. It's kind of become my guide book for how to do life, so you may find it works that way for you too. I reckon it's useful to read through the whole book first so you understand what's ahead, and then go back and work through it slowly and methodically.

As you'll see, the strategies I learned were designed in a particular order to allow the different concepts to be introduced at specific times, so they can logically build upon each other and be slotted easily into real life. So I recommend sticking to the format at first so you can get the most out of it, as I did, and then dipping back in to the different sections when you need to, and when you're ready to take it up to the next level.

As you'll learn fairly early on, the key to real and long-term change is to do little things often and build upon them, so that they become a natural part of your life. So I urge you to go through the process at your own pace and allow yourself to nail each aspect before you move onto the next. There's no right or wrong, so just stay true to what feels right for you. And please remember that slow and steady really does win the race here – as you'll see, I adopted quite a lot of the strategies fairly quickly (I think because I was so desperate to get out of the hole I'd put myself in), but then didn't put enough time into making some of them stick, so when push came to shove I reverted to my old ways of thinking and behaving, and I had to go back through the process again. So while it can seem like a pain in the arse in the short term, I can tell you it's most definitely worth putting the work in, because it will save you an abundance of time in the long term. And just a heads up: some of my entries and explanations can be a little epic at times (so much so I think I started to get RSI in my hand at one point!) but that's kind of why I think this will work for you – because you get to work through everything in real time and in real life. I encourage you to scribble, highlight, draw, fold pages down – whatever you can and need to do in order to get fully involved in the process. I've not released this book so that you can *learn* something; I want you to *be* something. And the only way you can do that is to *do* something.

So are you ready? Then let's bloody do this!

Debs x

MEET DEBS

April 19th

Okay. So I went to a conference earlier this week for professional women and one of the guest speakers reckoned that writing in a journal saved her life. Sounds a bit over the top if you ask me, but I guess I'll give it a go since nothing else is working for me at the moment. I feel so lost, and I can't talk to anyone about it. Everyone thinks I'm this high-powered executive with all my shit together, but that couldn't be further from the truth. Underneath this exterior, I'm freaking out. I constantly feel like I'm out of my depth, especially after this promotion, and it's only a matter of time before people start to realise that. So I feel like I'm always looking over my shoulder and working even harder to cover my tracks and make sure I don't get found out for the complete fraud that I am. I mean, seriously, why the hell did they make me a director? I'm pretty sure it's because they know I've dedicated my life to my career, and they know I'll work every hour of every day to deliver results if I have to. I'm sure there are people who are more qualified than me for the role, but maybe because I work so bloody hard, they figure they can just make me their bitch and rely on me to always be there.

Have I just made a massive rod for my own back? I know that's how I've always operated in the past but I just don't think I can keep it up any more. I'm so tired all the time, and my body is going to shit. I can't believe how much weight I've put on this year – last week I wore a skirt without tights cos the weather was so nice, and I actually got thigh rub so bad I ended up having to sneak into the bathroom with my lip balm and grease them up just so I could walk to the train without looking like I'd shit myself. I can't remember the last time I actually felt sexy. I dread having to get naked in front of Steve. I know he says he married me for the person I am, but I was 10kgs lighter then – surely there'll come a point where he realises he needs more than what I can offer him?

Oh God, it's so exhausting trying to keep this image up, but I've worked so hard to get to where I am so I'm not about to compromise everything by 'talking about my feelings' and letting people know what's really going on. I'd get eaten alive by the people at work – especially those male chauvinistic pricks on the board. Hell no, I'm not giving them the satisfaction of thinking I can't cope with playing at their level. This is the level I've been working towards my entire career, and I can't afford to let my guard down now. So I guess you, dear journal, will have to be my friend and listen to all the craziness that goes on inside my head. Good bloody luck.

Am I even supposed to write this sort of shit in here? I have no fricking idea what I'm doing. I should be polishing my stupid preso for tomorrow but I'm so tired I really can't be arsed. I'm in way over my head with this role. I just hope I can fake it enough to keep fooling everyone. Oh Christ, it's just gone past midnight. This is probably not how journaling is supposed to go is it? Aren't I supposed to get all inspired and find the answers? The only answers I have right now are that I'm knackered and I'm screwed for tomorrow. I have to say though, I do feel slightly better having got that rant out of my brain. No answers, but a little less anxiety. I'll take that. Okay, I need to stop procrastinating and wasting time. Bye. Thanks. Good night … how do you even sign off on these bloody things?!

April 20th

OH. MY. GOD. I went to put on my best 'I've got my shit together' outfit this morning, ready for my first big preso in this new role, and I could barely do the fucking zip up on the skirt. I couldn't believe it – I was in a rush, having hit snooze five times after another restless night, so I pulled up the zip with an almighty force and then as it passed the top of my hips, about a quarter of the way from its final destination, a little piece of my muffin top got caught in it. Oh GOD, I'm flinching again just thinking about it. It was SO painful. And the worst bit was I had to suffer in silence, even though I wanted to yell every swear word under the sun, because Steve was still asleep and already pissed off with me because I woke him up when I came to bed late last night … again.

It hasn't been that long since I last wore it, and I've been really good with my eating lately … what the hell is that all about? Luckily I managed to prise my flab from the jaws of the zip, and then safely get it to the top by lying on the couch and sucking everything in as hard as I could, but I was far from comfortable. I didn't have time to find another outfit, so I ended up chucking a looser fitting jacket on to hide my gigantic muffin top, but then I was overheating all morning so had to keep subtly wiping the drops of sweat from my upper lip without anyone seeing. It was so awkward – I had to wait until they turned their head slightly, and quickly wipe it with the back of my hand like a ninja before they caught me. Nothing screams incompetence like a sweaty upper lip. FUCK YOU, MUFFIN TOP. WHY ARE YOU HERE? I haven't eaten carbs at night for over three weeks now, but I feel like I'm getting fatter. HOW IS THAT EVEN POSSIBLE? I felt like everyone could see the rolls of fat spilling over the top of my skirt, it was so embarrassing. How can they take me seriously as a leader and trust me to look after the growth of the company if I can't even look after myself? I really hope that stupid jacket did the job. I need them all on board with me if I've got any chance of getting through this.

April 22nd

Shit. It's Steve's birthday today. I know our rules are when it's your birthday the other one has to do whatever you want in bed, but I just can't face it right now. I'm so tired and I feel so gross. What if he wants me to get on top? He'll have a full frontal of my belly flopping about all over the place. That's not sexy in any way. I just can't suck it in when I'm in that position. What if he does see that and he can't get hard? That would ruin me. I know I'm not as thin or attractive as when we first got together, but surely he can see I'm trying to get back there? This is totally stressing me out. What the hell am I going to do? He's already pissed off with me for working so much. If I can't even give him this, maybe it'll tip him over the edge? I don't know what I'd do without him. ARRRRRR, why am I being such a bitch? There's too much in my brain to be able to deal with this right now.

Okay, there has to be a way that I can avoid having sex without him feeling like I'm neglecting him. There HAS to be. What if I had some sort of medical condition? But what medical condition could I have that wouldn't lead him to think I've been messing around? That's the opposite of what I want him to think. Oooh what about a pap smear? Maybe I could tell him that I'm having a pap smear tomorrow and they advise no sex within 24 hours as it could affect the results? That sounds viable doesn't it? Okay, done. I know I'm going to hell for this but I'll make it up to him. As soon as I've dropped a few kilos, I'll totally be back in the game.

April 23rd

Luckily Steve bought the pap smear story, so I dodged the bullet there. It's made me realise, though, that I really do need to sort myself out and lose this weight – I can't handle the guilt of being a terrible wife, and I really need my team to respect me. It won't be long before they start noticing that I'm wearing the same shit over and over again – there's only so many combos I can create with my limited array of muffin-top-disguising clothes, but I refuse to buy new stuff until I drop a few kilos. Just the thought of having to try something on in the next size up makes me feel sick. Fuck it, this is doing my head in, I need to do something. What was that flyer I saw the other day for a bootcamp? I'm sure it said I could have the body I want in 12 weeks or something? Bit longer than I'd like, but I'm sure if I smash it I can get there quicker. I've done it before, so I can do it again. I just need to be good for a few weeks and I'll be able to wear the clothes on the left side of my wardrobe again. Then I'll be happy. Oh man, I'm soooo ready to be happy again. Okay, where's that bloody flyer …? Perfect, there's a group at the park down the street. Shit, it starts tomorrow – where the hell is all my exercise gear? God, I hope there aren't loads of skinny fit bitches there.

April 24th

Bootcamp – done. Couldn't walk up the stairs this afternoon without hanging onto the handrail and I'm tired as all hell tonight, but no pain, no gain right? It's good to be back. That's all I've got for today … over and out.

April 25th

I can't believe I've managed to write in here for almost a week – I definitely thought I'd get bored of it after a couple of days, but it's actually quite nice to get all this shit out. There's no way I could say this stuff to another human being, they'd definitely think I'm crazy. Maybe I am? I mean, seriously, who else thinks like this? Anyway, I won't stay long again tonight as I have to get up early for bootcamp in the morning. I'm so happy I'm not the fattest or most unfit person there – I was really stressing about that.

May 10th

Whoops – I just re-read my last entry where I said how good I was for writing in here consistently, and now it's been two weeks and I haven't even picked up my pen. I've just been too tired and haven't wanted to do anything after work except crash on the couch and then crawl into bed. Even brushing my teeth has been an effort some nights … not only because I'm so tired but also because my muscles are so bloody sore from boxing and swinging weights around that it's hard to lift my arm higher than my belly button. Don't get me wrong, I am enjoying bootcamp but it's really full on. And the annoying thing is I'm not losing any freaking weight! In fact, sometimes I feel even fatter cos my stomach bloats like crazy. I can't understand why – it's like this monster starts to grow inside of me and tries to escape via my gut, but when it can't get out it just keeps expanding, and expanding, like a giant balloon … except it never fucking pops. I wish I could stick a pin in it and ease the pressure, it's so uncomfortable. And then that's all I can think about. It completely consumes me.

Whenever people talk to me, all I'm thinking is, can they see it? What will they think? I don't know how I engage in conversation most of the time, because I'm not paying any attention when I feel like that. And it's so hard to concentrate on my work. I swear it takes me three times as long to do anything because I can't keep my mind on the task at hand. In the break of a meeting yesterday I even had to undo a couple of buttons on my pants because it felt like they were cutting off my blood supply and I couldn't breathe properly. I've been bootcamping consistently for two weeks – surely I should be feeling a bit thinner and fitter by now? It just doesn't make sense.

I read something in a magazine earlier (when I should have been putting together a presentation for the sales conference ☹) about losing weight being 70 per cent nutrition and 30 per cent exercise, so I guess that's maybe where I've been going wrong? I haven't been really bad, but I have been eating a bit more again lately. I figured that was okay, though, because I needed the energy for all the exercise? But regardless of that, I've been busting my arse four mornings a week at bootcamp and doing extra hikes at the weekend, so surely that should do something for me?

Anyway, the magazine had a diet plan in it which looked pretty good so I think I might try that. The article said something about how I need to eat more protein to build up my muscle and if I do that I'll burn more fat. I'm nervous that might make me bulky though? Surely I want to strip down not build up? I don't bloody know! I've tried eating like this before, cutting out as many carbs as possible, but I always end up falling off the wagon and eating my entire weekly allowance of carbs in one night. It's like I can only be all or nothing – I'm fine when I don't have any carbs or bad stuff at all, but as soon as I have just one little naughty thing I think, 'Fuck it', and I figure I might as well keep going since I've already ruined it. I've never actually followed a proper plan though, so maybe it'll work this time. I guess it's worth a crack – the article had some woman in there who had lost 30kgs after doing it, so surely it must be a good one. And I only need to lose about 10 to 15kgs so it should be even easier for me. I'll go to the supermarket and stock up on food at the weekend and start on Monday. Happy bloody days.

May 11th

Fucking hell, what a week. I'm soooooo glad it's over. After-work drinks could NOT have come quickly enough today – I was GAGGING for a wine. As soon as that smooth red velvety liquid hit my lips, I felt my entire body relax and the week start to melt away. Not for long though – I think I may have overstepped the mark with a team member and taken a joke too far. The others were taking the piss out of him because at work he likes to follow his set routines and gets upset if something changes, so they were asking if he's like that when he's having sex too and if he always follows the same routine when pleasuring his partner. Everyone was laughing, including him, until I started to do an impression of his 'pleasuring routine'. Slowly the laughs started to fade and a pretty intense awkwardness filled the air. It's so freaking difficult sometimes to know where the line is between being part of the team and being their boss. I swear to God if anyone else had done that they would have thought it was hilarious. How could I have been so stupid? I just got wrapped up in the moment – for once I wasn't worrying about what they were all thinking and was just enjoying being one of them, so I let my guard down. Well that's the last bloody time I do that. Have I just completely screwed up any respect I've earned so far? I shouldn't have had those last two wines. What was I thinking? That was so fucking unprofessional. I have to remember that I'm their superior and I can't be one of them.

I do miss being one of them though. I miss the days where I could just be stupid and joke around, and not have to have my professional hat on all the time. Now I have to be the one they look up to. I have to show them that I'm responsible and in control. I shouldn't let them see me this way. In fact, I shouldn't even let Steve see me this way – I'm drunk … my eyeliner has taken up residence in the corners of my eyes, I've got a few random dribbles of red wine down my blouse, and for some reason my right bra strap just WILL NOT stay up. I can't believe I'm even writing in here right now. But if I don't, then who the fuck else am I going to talk to? I can't let anyone else see that I'm freaking out and have no fucking idea what I'm doing. Keep calm and carry on, right? Fuck that. I'M REALLY FREAKING OUT HERE. I need chocolate. That's the only thing that will save me now. The diet doesn't start until Monday anyway.

May 12th

Urgh, I'm so hungover. There's not a chance in hell I'm going for my hike today. I need to do some work anyway, as I buggered about yesterday reading that magazine and spent too long trying to put out fires with the sales team – incompetent dickheads. Thank GOD Steve is going out for the day so I can sit on the couch in my period pants and not feel guilty for working on the weekend. I'm going to need snacks to get me through the day. Can I go to the supermarket in my PJs? I reaaaaalllly don't want to put my bra on. I'll definitely see someone I know if I do that though, won't I? Oooh, I know. I'll put on my active wear – that way if I do see someone, the lycra will fool them into thinking I've been exercising and I'm all virtuous and shit. I can chuck a cap on too so I don't have to put as much make-up on. Why am I even writing all this down?

* * *

Okay, I'm back, and mission accomplished. I saw one guy who works upstairs in IT but I managed to hide behind a promotional stand of biscuits on the corner of an aisle until the coast was clear. I reckon that was fate – I never would've thought to get biscuits, but they're delicious. They're exactly what I wanted in my mouth, I just didn't know it. I've decided I'm going to allow myself to eat what I want today and not feel guilty about it, and then I'll smash this diet on Monday. Right, I'm signing out – time to get comfortable and get some work done.

* * *

Hmmmmm, so I just put my period pants and PJs back on and it made me realise that I haven't actually got my period yet. I'm pretty sure it should have been here by now. I've looked at my calendar and I can't remember exactly when my last one was, but I'm pretty sure it was around the time of my last big preso at work, because I remember having to eat a heap of painkillers to numb the deep cramping pain in my uterus to get through the day … and that was one month ago. I don't think I'll freak out just yet as I'm not 100 per cent sure … but I am a little bit nervous. I should totally write this shit down so I know for certain. Why don't I do that? I'm so rubbish with stuff like this. With work I'm an organisational maniac, but I just get so busy and pre-occupied with getting through the day that I forget about all this personal crap. Arh, whatever, I've got work to do – I'll figure this out later.

* * *

I'm back again. I just had a big fight with Steve and I don't know what to do about it. I'm currently sat in the bedroom, having walked out crying. I know I should go back in there and sort it out, but I just can't. I'm too angry and upset – I know I won't be able to say what's going on in my head and I'll probably end up blurting out something I regret, so it's just better if I don't say anything. I don't see why I should anyway, he's the one that was in the wrong – he should come to me. I mean, how dare he judge me like that. I spend my entire life being judged, with people just waiting for me to fuck up; I certainly don't need that at home too.

And I knew he had an issue with my body. This confirms it. Can you believe he had the nerve to ask me about my diet while I was eating a piece of chocolate – he might as well have just said, 'Stop eating chocolate, you fat bitch.' I know I'm a fat bitch. I don't need him to tell me that. The worst thing was he seemed completely oblivious to how much he'd hurt me. When I asked him why he wanted to know, he said it was because he wanted to help me if he could – oohh, right, I understand. You want to help me lose weight so I don't embarrass you when we go out, don't you? I know he was embarrassed when we went to Jonathan's birthday party a few weeks ago. I tried so hard to get out of going as I had nothing to wear and I couldn't bear the thought of spending an entire evening pretending to be happy and living the dream, when in reality I was feeling completely uncomfortable and self-conscious. I even pretended to be sick, but the guilt of letting everyone down got the better of me. So I eventually threw on my long maxi dress that hides everything, even though I know Steve hates it and says it looks like I'm wearing a sack, and reluctantly went along. I guess he figured it was just better if he wasn't seen with me though, as I hardly saw him all night – he fucked off into the living room with the men as soon as we walked through the door, and left me to fend for myself with the women in the kitchen. And now he actually expects me to believe that he wants to help me because he wants me to be 'happy'. Bullshit.

Anyway, I told him the diet plan was on the fridge if he really was that interested, so he said he'd have a look at it later and then just carried on watching TV – as if nothing had happened. I sat there seething for ages – I wanted to tell him I knew the real reason he wanted to 'help' but I was so angry I couldn't talk. In the end, I couldn't contain it any longer and I burst into tears. He looked surprised that I was upset! I don't understand how it's possible to be THAT clueless. Does he really not understand what he's done? He asked me what was wrong, but if he can't see it for himself, then why should I tell him? He needs to be more aware of what he does and how it makes me feel, and he should know that being so insensitive about my weight would upset me. I just said don't worry about it and came in here. Maybe if he has some time on his own, he'll be able to think about what he's done.

What a crappy end to the day. And now I can't even finish the bloody chocolate cos I'm stuck in here. Nice one, Steve.

May 14th

Steve eventually came into the bedroom on Saturday to talk about what had happened. It turns out he really is that clueless. He still maintains that he genuinely does just want to help me so I can be happier – he reckons he hates seeing me being so hard on myself and knows how busy I am, so if he can make it any easier for me then he'd love to help. He also said that sometimes he feels useless – because he sees me as such a strong, independent woman he thinks that I don't really need him, and I can get by just fine on my own. So he thought if he could help me with this, it might be his chance to step up as my husband and look after me a bit.

If that is true, that's really quite sweet. But also really far from the truth. I would literally be nothing without him. Actually that's not true – I'd probably be a morbidly obese alcoholic. I love to live to the extremes – my default mode has always been all or nothing – so without him as my solid rock, I'd go completely off the rails. Doesn't he realise that the reason I'm doing all this is to set us up for the future? I want us to have a nice lifestyle, where we can afford to have what we want and do what we want, but that shit doesn't come cheap. I figure if I just put in all the work now we can reap the benefits later. I just want us to be happy – that's why I work so hard and demand nothing but the best. I didn't realise he felt that way – I do need him, I need him more than he'll probably ever know.

I'm only realising all of this in hindsight, mind you. At the time when we were chatting, I just did my usual silence thing. It's so weird. Whenever I get into a situation like that where I'm expected to open up, I do the opposite – I clam up and shut down. I can hear the words in my head but I just can't make them come out of my mouth. I guess I'm just so scared that he'll think I'm being stupid, or crazy, or irrational. I mean, if he ever read any of this journal, I'm sure he'd probably try to get me committed. I can't let him see this side of me – a terrified and weak little girl isn't exactly sexy, is it? So rather than say any of these things, I just let him talk and then told him everything was fine.

Anyway, to cheer me up, he suggested we go out to my favourite Italian restaurant for Sunday dinner, since it was my last chance to eat good food before I started my diet. We had a lovely night, actually, but I think I probably went a bit overboard. I don't know when I'll be able to eat like that again, so I figured I should probably get it all in while I could. Oh my GOSH it was SO DELICIOUS though! We started with bruschetta with the juiciest tomatoes I think I've ever tasted and the most amazing platter of meats and cheeses. Then we shared a pappardelle with ragu that melted in my mouth like butter, and a risotto that was so creamy I wanted to rub it all over myself! And don't even get me started on the gelato – I went all out with three flavours of pure heaven: salted caramel, coconut, and vanilla with crushed up brownie pieces in it. WTF! Why can't I just eat that stuff all the time? I definitely can't though, I feel like SHIT today. My stomach is so bloated and hard I look six months pregnant (hopefully that is just the food and not the reason I haven't got my period! Eek, I shouldn't joke about that!) and my head feels really fuzzy like I have a hangover, but I only had one glass of wine. Is a sugar hangover an actual thing? Maybe it's that?

Anyway, it's game on with the diet now so hopefully I'll feel better soon. Had scrambled egg whites and ham for breakfast, and have a can of tuna and rice crackers for lunch – I'm feeling pretty good about it. I didn't make it to bootcamp this morning as I felt too rubbish so I'll try and do something tonight after work to make up for it.

May 21st

So I've done one week on the diet and I have to say I'm feeling quite good. I think eating the fuck out of everything last weekend was probably not a terrible thing because it's made me motivated to be good now and give this a real go. I've been back to bootcamp every day too, and I think my skirt this morning actually felt a little bit looser – I could fit my little finger between the waistband and my gut without having to have it surgically removed. I'm pretty hungry and tired, but I think it's just the adjustment period to my new way of life, so I'm sure it'll pass soon. It's worth it, though, or at least it will be when I look good again and get my life back.

May 24th

Had a great meeting with the team today. I think they're starting to like me. Well, except for this one girl – Julie – who seems to be completely unimpressed with everything I do. I know she got on really well with her last manager, and I know I have some pretty big shoes to fill, but everyone else seems to be coming round. For some reason I just can't get her to warm to me. Don't get me wrong, she's really good at her job and gets everything done to a very high standard, but I want her to like me! There, I said it. I know that sounds really childish, and I know I have to accept that not everyone will like me, but I'm still struggling to make my peace with that. I work so freaking hard and do everything I can to give these people the best opportunities, so the least they can do is pay me some respect. Maybe I should have a chat with her and try to find out what her problem is? No, bad idea. I can't be dealing with the uncomfortableness of a conversation like that. I could just give her more one-on-one time so she can see I'm really invested in helping her? But then the others might think I'm favouring her. Urgh, managing people can be so bloody exhausting. I know I signed up for this and it's part of the deal when you move up the ladder, but sometimes I just wish I had less responsibilities and fewer things to juggle.

I remember my Dad often used to say, 'It's tough at the top' – bloody right it is … tough and lonely. It's alright for them because they can just come to me when they need help or don't know what to do, and I'm always there with support and encouragement. But who do I have? If I ask for help, people will think I can't manage. I can't show weakness like that. People expect me to have all the answers, and to be honest that's the way I like it. I like being known as the woman who gets shit done, and the woman who makes shit happen. It makes me feel good. If anyone found out that I'm winging it most the time, I'd be ruined. So asking for help is simply not an option. I've come this far on my own, I just need to suck it up and keep pushing on. This is what I've been working so hard for all these years. It's what I've always wanted.

It's funny, it really is what I've always wanted – I thought once I got to this level I'd be happy, but something still doesn't feel quite right. I can't work out what it is, but I still feel like something's missing. There's definitely more pressure with this role than I thought. I guess I was thinking that being this next step up would give me more flexibility and I could finally get a bit more balance in my life, but actually I have even more to prove now, and the stakes are even higher. I have to be so careful that I don't do something wrong and I don't let my team down. I feel like all eyes are on me, and certain people are just waiting for me to fail. Hopefully once I settle in a bit more, things will be easier and I'll feel more content.

It would help if I wasn't so bloody tired all the time though. I've gotten into the habit of having four coffees a day now – one when I wake up, one when I get into the office, one mid-morning and one in the afternoon to get me through the rest of the day. That diet plan says coffee is okay as long as I don't have lots of milk, and I drink mine black, so I don't think it's messing with my weight loss, but I do kind of feel like I'm relying on it, and I'm not sure if that's good for me. I'll try cutting it back down when I'm more settled too. I can't deal with that right now, I've got enough on my plate – not literally, though, sadly … I'm freaking starving!

May 27th

I am SO ready for the week. Had a really nice day with Steve today – he dragged me away from my computer and took me out for the day. The sun was out and it wasn't too chilly so we went for a lovely long walk in the bush and had lunch at this cool new healthy café in town. I have no bloody idea what I ate, it was some kind of 'nourishing bowl' with all sorts of green and pickled stuff in it, but it was bloody tasty, and I'll tell you what – I did the best shit of my life this afternoon! Steve chose that place because he wanted me to enjoy myself without ruining my diet. He's so bloody thoughtful. How did I end up with such a good guy? I really don't understand how or why he puts up with so much of my crap sometimes … but I'm really pleased he does. I am trying to be better and more considerate. It's just been a crazy few years. I've been under a lot of pressure, and had a lot to prove to get ahead in this stupid career. I know I shouldn't take it out on him, but when I'm so tired and busy it's so much harder to be patient and loving.

It was interesting though, at the beginning of the day. We went to grab a coffee on our way to the walk, and as we sat in the café Steve was talking to me and then he stopped mid-sentence and just said, 'Where are you?' I was a bit confused initially – 'I'm sat in a café drinking coffee with my husband' was my sarcastic response. But then he said, 'I know that's where you are physically, but where are YOU?' He said he felt like he was talking to a mannequin – like I was an empty shell and my body was there but my mind was somewhere else entirely. He could see in my eyes I wasn't paying attention – apparently they were slightly vacant and glazed over. I do know I can do that sometimes – in fact, I kind of thought I was the master of it. I can be looking at someone and nodding or agreeing at the right times, but I'm not actually listening to a word they're saying. And afterwards I won't remember anything that was said – kind of like when you're driving along and then think, *How the hell did I get here?* I guess because Steve knows me so well I can't get away with it with him. He actually told me he notices I do it quite often – he's been letting it slide up until now, because he knows I've been busy with work, but apparently today he'd had enough. He said he wanted to spend the day with his wife, and if she wasn't going to show up, we would just go back home.

He was pretty direct, which isn't really like him, but I have to say I kinda liked it. He was right last week – I do try to be independent almost all of the time, but I really quite liked the feeling of him taking charge for a while. For once, I felt like I didn't have to have all the answers and I didn't have to drive the situation. I could just chill out in the back seat and let someone else take the wheel. It was so lovely. I put my phone on silent and then left it in the car for the rest of the day, and committed to giving Steve and the day my full attention. We agreed that when I did wander off, Steve could let me know with a code word – so a few times he yelled 'GOOSE' and it brought me right back! Don't ask me why that was the code word, but it worked! I felt more connected to Steve than I have in a really long time – we laughed, we played and we talked a lot of crap – it felt like the old days, before life got too serious. For so long now I've been feeling like I'm just a shadow of my former self. I thought I'd lost that Debs, but maybe she is still there?

Anyway, after today I'm feeling a bit more refreshed and prepared for the week. And with all my meals planned out and my exercise gear packed and ready for bootcamp in the morning, I think it's going to be a good week.

May 31st

So much for a good week. I've had two members of the team 'off sick' so I've had to pull three late nights to try and get everything prepped for the big pitch to the new sponsors tomorrow. This is exactly what I didn't need. I was finally feeling like I was on track but because of this bullshit, I've only made it to one bootcamp and my diet has gone out the window. I've managed to be good during the days but then when I've had to stay late, I've ended up eating chocolate and chips from the bloody vending machines – I haven't had time to pee, let alone figure out where to get something healthy to eat. I tried to just stick to my back-up tuna and rice crackers, but I swear if I have to eat one more can of fucking tuna I'm going to throw myself out the window. I've tried every flavour you can think of – tomato and onion, tomato and basil, lemon and pepper, lime and pepper, sweet chilli, spicy chilli – and I just can't do it anymore. I'VE HAD ENOUGH. I feel so dirty when I eat tuna straight from the can as well – it's like I've regressed to a savage beast and have no respect for myself. There has to be another way to lose weight and get my body back, surely to fucking God.

Anyway, I can't think about it right now – I have to get this prep done and smash the pitch out of the park. I know there's going to be a lot of eyes on me for this one, so I can't fuck it up. This is such a good opportunity for me to show them that I do actually know what I'm doing, and I do deserve to be where I am … even though, let's face it, I actually don't. Fake it till you make it, right? I'll get back on the wagon after Friday. Hopefully I won't have done too much damage, given that I've been good during the day. I'm so anxious right now anyway I must be burning off more calories than normal – my heartrate is going about double the pace.

Arrrgh, I'm procrastinating so much. I need to stop writing about all this bullshit and get on with my work. I'm going to screw this up for sure. I just don't know if I can do it. What if I don't land this deal? Why did James and Kelly have to be sick THIS WEEK. Are you fucking with me, universe? That's the only explanation for this shit fight I'm in right now. What have I done to deserve this? I'm a good person. I always pay my bills on time and throw my rubbish in the bin. Can't you just give me one little fucking break? I guess it's my fault for giving my team as much responsibility as I did. I thought it would get me a quicker buy-in with them and help me to gain their loyalty and respect, but that was clearly a mistake. I've always known that if I want something doing properly I should just do it myself, but I was so pre-occupied with trying to get them to like and respect me, I dropped the ball. How well liked am I going to be now when I let the entire team down? Nice one, Deb. FUCK – I'm still procrastinating. I'm going.

* * *

Okay, I don't know what just happened but it's really scared me. I spent the last twenty minutes in the toilet freaking out. I felt like I couldn't catch my breath and my heart was beating out of my chest. I was sat at my desk and had a massive wave of emotion come over me – I felt completely overwhelmed and tears started streaming down my face. I ran to the toilet before anyone saw and just couldn't stop crying. I was trying to mop up the tears as they came out so they didn't ruin my make-up and make it obvious that I'd been upset, but I had to give up and concentrate on my breathing as I felt like I was losing control. I sat on the toilet and tried to take big breaths, but it was like there was a brick on my chest restricting my lungs from taking in too much air. I kept telling myself to stop being stupid and to calm down, but I just felt completely powerless. Eventually I managed to bring myself back – funnily enough, I started thinking about Steve and imagining he was there, and it made me feel much more at ease and able to get a handle on my breathing and heart rate.

Oh man, I wish he really was there. I've literally never felt so alone. WTF was that? Is this a sign that I really am in over my head? Am I finally coming unstuck? I wish I could go home. But I've just got too much to do. Arrrgh, listen to me – I sound so pathetic. I've been in much higher pressured situations than this before and I've been fine. This was just a random occurrence, and I need to stop reading into it. Now pull yourself together Debs, and stop wasting time.

June 1st

Thank FUCK the pitch is over. I actually think it went pretty well, all things considered. The feedback from above was positive and the sponsors asked some good questions, so I think they were engaged and impressed with what I had to say. It just sucks that we can't find out their decision immediately so I'm going to have to stress about it for another week. Anyway, it's time to get back on the wagon – I'm feeling pretty crap about this last week. I mean, it could have been worse – like I said, I was good in the days, so it's not like I was eating bad stuff all the time, but still I shouldn't be eating anything like that until I'm back to where I want to be. Bootcamp again on Monday and back to the diet. I just need to figure out what I can eat during the day if I don't have tuna. Problem is, I don't have enough time to prepare actual meals for the whole week and the tuna was super handy. Maybe I'll have a look at some of those meal delivery things. I think Michelle said you can get low carb ones so maybe that would work? Whatever, I'll figure it out tomorrow. Tonight I must drink wine and relax.

June 2nd

SHIIIIIIIIIIIIIIIIIIT – I've just realised I STILL haven't got my period!!!!!!! With all the shit that's been going on, I totally forgot all about it. That's potentially almost three weeks late now. That's not okay. Oh GOD, surely I can't be pregnant? Gosh, our sex has been so sporadic and sparse lately – don't tell me on one of the rare occasions we did do it, Steve actually hit the bullseye? When was the last time? Could it have been during prime time? Let me think … ah, yes, it was after David and Emma's wedding. I remember because I'd been drinking all day so clearly didn't care about my disgusting body. So that was six weeks ago. Wow, has it been that long? How has Steve not burst by now? We used to do it every day back in the early days, and even after that it would definitely be at least once a week. Oh shit, could he be getting it somewhere else? If he wasn't, surely he'd have been all over me by now, even with my body the way it is? Fuck. I can't believe this is happening. And what if I'm now carrying his child? I don't even know if I want a kid but I definitely know I don't want to bring one up on my own. I see all my friends with kids and it just looks so full on – and they're all still with their partners (although I'm not sure some of them should be).

Okay, think, think, think. Six weeks ago was a bit before halfway through the month so I don't think it could have been in prime time. So if I'm not pregnant, what the hell is going on? I guess I better do a test to make sure. Should I tell Steve there might be a chance? That could turn him off me even more. I'm not sure if I need that pressure. If it does turn out to be positive, I think I'll need time to process it by myself and figure out what to do. I know getting married and having kids is what we're supposed to do, but is that what I really want? I guess I've just always thought I could figure it out later, but what if later is now? It's true that I'm not getting any younger, and now that I'm staring forty in the face, could this be my last chance? But do I want it to be my last chance? I've finally managed to get to where I've always wanted to be, and a child could ruin it all. This is such a head fuck! Okay, I think I'll just take a test and then tell Steve later – if I need to. There's no point in worrying him unnecessarily, and I need to keep an eye on his movements for a while anyway and see what he's up to. I'm not ready to discuss it all if I don't have to. Plus I need to focus on work at the moment.

June 3rd

I'm shitting myself. Bought the test but am too terrified to take it. What if it's positive? What if it's not? I'm so confused right now. Well, I need to pee and it's getting late so I guess it's now or never. Here goes …

June 4th

IT WAS NEGATIVE!!!! I was so overwhelmed by it all I forgot to come back and write in here yesterday and went immediately to celebrate.

It was weird when I saw that one little line appear in the window of the pregnancy test. I don't think I took a breath for the whole three minutes after I'd peed on it, and then when it appeared I couldn't for the life of me remember what one line meant – even though I'd read the instructions about a million times. I had to rummage through the bin with one hand while I clasped the pee-coated, toilet-paper-wrapped stick in the other to find the box and check what the fuck one line meant. Ahhhhhhhhh, negative. The weird bit though, was I then started to cry uncontrollably. I couldn't work out if they were tears of sadness or joy, but they just wouldn't stop streaming down my face. I still don't really know now what that was all about.

I was definitely relieved, so there was a big element of joy, but also it's got me wondering if I would actually be able to get pregnant if I wanted to … and that thought makes me really sad. I've always figured that if and when I decided the time was right, it would just happen. But maybe I don't even have a choice anymore? Last time I saw the doctor she very kindly told me my eggs are now in decline because of my age, so maybe it is too late anyway? I think what makes me feel the worst about not having kids is how much I'll be letting mum and dad down. I know they would be so ridiculously overjoyed if they had grandkids, so who am I to deny them that gift? Am I just being totally selfish? I know Steve has said he's not bothered about having them, but when I see him with all our friends' children, he just seems so happy and content. Has he changed his mind but he's too afraid to bring it up with me? Will he start to resent me at some point for not giving him something he actually did want all along? And what about everyone else – what will they think? Will they think there's something wrong with me if I don't reproduce? Will they take pity on me? And will there be this big elephant in the room whenever we're together, because they think I'll get upset if we talk about it? Am I destined to be an outcast for the rest of my life? Jesus, there's so much pressure.

June 5th

Back to bootcamp this morning. It was good but everything just seemed so hard today for some reason. And now I'm STARVING. I have found an excellent solution to my tuna dilemma, however – I was chatting to Michelle yesterday and she's been having these protein shakes some girl at her work told her about. They're perfect – there's like 3g of carbs and 28g of protein in each one, so if it really is true that building muscle with protein helps you burn fat, these shakes could be the answer to all my prayers. Why haven't I heard about them before? They sound like a working woman's dream! She gave me one to try for lunch today, and it was pretty delicious too – cookies and cream flavour. It was like drinking a melted gelato – HELL, YEH!

Imagine being able to lose weight while drinking something that tasty. I'm definitely on board with that. Michelle brought me a few more round tonight to get me through the next few days until the box she's ordered for me arrives. What an awesome friend. She's always there when I need her, and she always seems to know the answers. I just don't know how she does it – three kids, a husband and a successful business … oh, AND she looks amazing. And here's me – working for someone else, 10kgs overweight, no kids and little to no desire to have sex with my husband. Wow! When I put it like that, I make myself sound like quite a catch, hey? Anyway, I'm sure with picking up bootcamp again and getting my diet right with these shakes, I'll finally start to see results, and then I can feel sexy enough again to get my relationship back on track.

June 7th

I just realised I got so caught up in the baby debate the other day I forgot to try to figure out why I haven't got my period. I just don't know what other explanation there could be for it. I'm thinking I might actually have to go the doctor to check there's not something seriously wrong. It's been almost four weeks now since I should have got it. It's been late before, but never this late. Maybe while I'm at the doctor she can also give me something for my ridiculous PMT. I know every woman gets it but this seems extreme – sometimes it makes me feel like everything is so hopeless I just want to go to sleep and never wake up. And I hate how I get with Steve – I get so irritated by EVERY little thing he does, and then I get angry, and even sometimes when I look at him I feel nothing at all, like he's a stranger rather than the love of my life. It's like a switch is flipped in me a week or two before I get my period and I become an irrational, emotional maniac (more so than usual), but then as soon as I get my period – BAM – I'm back to normal (whatever that is). How fucked is that? It really messes with my brain, and makes me feel like an out of control crazy bitch. I don't know how to explain it to Steve though. I guess it must be related to my hormones because it seems to happen in line with my period, but surely they can't completely change my personality and the way I feel about Steve?

Oh, and of course, there's the unbelievable pain once I do get my period. The pain doesn't come every month but, when it does, it makes up for the months it didn't show up. It's like someone is pushing all their bodyweight down on my uterus and every now and then tying it all up in knots. Try dealing with that while addressing a room full of 500 people. If only they knew what was really going on. I should probably talk to her about my tiredness too, because it's really annoying and making everything so much harder. Sometimes it almost feels like my body is tingling where it's trying to run around and find every last piece of energy that may be hiding in every nook and cranny. But at the same time I feel like a deadweight and I have to consciously focus my attention on each body part just to get them to move. I feel so lazy when I'm like that – I just don't want to do anything but lie on the couch and watch trashy TV. Hardly the behaviour of a successful career woman, right? Only by guzzling coffee can I manage to drag my arse to work and get through the day, but I'm definitely nowhere near as efficient and it's really difficult to get the thoughts straight in my head – basically because it feels like my brain has been replaced with a big grey rain cloud. I think I'm pretty good at hiding it from my colleagues – actually, I seem to have become a bit of a master at putting on a shiny façade – but little do they know I'm actually dying on the inside. Well, that might be a bit dramatic, but it's really shit and I feel like I have no control over it.

That's settled it though – I need to head to the doctor and find out where my period is, and get some drugs to sort all this other stuff out. I'm SO over it. Night.

Oh, PS – we won that sponsorship deal I pitched for last week. ☺

June 9th

This last week has been good. I've been going really well on the shakes and have made it to bootcamp every morning, so I really feel like I'm back on track. AND, I GOT MY PERIOD!!! The doctor is sending me to a specialist, though. She wants to put me back on the pill but wants to see what they say first. It's so annoying having to keep taking time off work to go to all these bloody doctors' appointments. I'm going to have to stay later and maybe work more on the weekend to make up for it, which Steve won't be happy about. Maybe I should get him a gift or something to soften the blow? It might earn me a few brownie points and buy me some more time until I get through this crazy period. Actually, talking of time – I know he's had his eye on that new Omega watch so perhaps I could get him that. Oooh, no, I have the perfect idea – I'll get him a flight to go visit his brother down south for the weekend. He hasn't seen him in ages – he'd love that. I can tell him I thought he would like some one-on-one brother time, and then that way I get the house to myself to get on with all my stuff. Everyone's a winner. Sometimes I surprise myself with these genius plans.

June 14th

So I went to see the specialist and get the results of all my tests this morning. Turns out I have polycystic ovaries and I'm possibly insulin resistant – which explains why my period was all over the place, why I get such crazy PMT and why I've been struggling to lose weight. I can't believe I'm almost forty years old and I've never known this before! My periods and weight haven't always been this bad, though, and I figured every woman had their issues at that time of the month, so I just had to suck it up and get on with it. It was so humiliating when I went in to see the specialist. Well, first I had some girl who must have been about half my age shove a camera up my hoo-hah (all I could think was, *I bet your eggs haven't even reached their prime, let alone started to be in decline*), and then the specialist made me lift up my top so he could measure the girth of my belly. Perfect. That's exactly what I felt like doing when I was already feeling vulnerable and violated.

So I stand there while he reaches a tape measure around my 'girth' (that's such a disgusting word), and then he proceeds to tell me that I'm carrying too much weight around there. Umm, tell me something

I don't know, genius. According to him, even though the blood glucose test I took the other day came back in the normal range, excess weight around the gut is a classic sign of insulin resistance, so he's prescribed me some pills to help sort it out and advised that I do go back on the pill. Apparently, these insulin pills (I think they're called Metformin?) will also help me to lose weight … FUCK, YEH! He said they might make me feel a bit nauseous at the start, but whatever – if they'll get rid of my 'girth', I can totally put up with that!

June 15th

This is kind of gross, but I haven't pooed for five days now. It's starting to stress me out – my stomach has been constantly bloated and uncomfortable for the last three days and I keep getting random pain. Seriously, what is going on with my body? I'm trying to do my best to lose weight and get healthy but the world just keeps slapping me in the face. And to top it off, I think I'm getting a sore throat. I've tried coffee to help get things moving, but think I drink too much for it to have that effect any more. Next I'm going to try prune juice – Michelle reckons that always helps her when she gets backed up. I also thought I'd order a spicy curry for dinner tonight. Steve loves curry anyway, so that'll make him happy. (He doesn't have to know it's because I need to clear myself out!) If that doesn't work, I'll have to get some laxatives or something – this shit (literally!!) needs to go.

June 18th

After two more days of nothing I had to call in the big guns. I bought a natural laxative from the pharmacy and took the maximum dose before going to bed with lots of water. Let's just say it worked. Maybe a little too well – I'm pretty sure there's absolutely nothing left inside of me now. I know it's disgusting, but no-one's ever going to read this, and the whole situation has been quite stressful so I need to talk about it somehow.

The annoying this is, with all this health crap I've had going on, I've been pre-occupied and feel like I've dropped the ball a bit at work. Gary sent me back the proposal I'd been working on with lots of silly mistakes marked up, which is NOT okay. I need to be more diligent and make sure I don't submit anything to the bloody CEO of the company except perfection. It's already hard enough trying to convince him he made the right choice by promoting me into this role, so why do I insist on making my life even more difficult by producing sub-standard work? I was so embarrassed when he called me into his office to discuss the proposal. I don't know why but I always feel really intimidated when I'm around him. I think I just feel completely inferior. He's so much more educated than I am, and he's so good at what he does. I could never be as good as him. I'm always so conscious when I'm speaking with him of not saying something stupid or sounding dumb. I must have re-run our conversation over in my brain about a million times. Did I say the right things? What does he really think about me? Does he think I'm completely incompetent?

I need to raise my game and stop letting my personal shit get in the way. Now I'm on these pills, hopefully I'll start to feel better anyway. The specialist was right about the nausea though – it's worse in the morning, but I've been finding a little hit of sugar helps to ease it. I've not been having a lot, just a couple of biscuits or half a muffin, and I don't think I'll need to do it for much longer – I just need to get through this initial bit and then I'll get back to just having my breakfast shakes. Anyhoo, I best get back to my work – it's now 9 pm and I'm still at the office. I didn't get everything done that I wanted to today, but it'll make my life so much easier for the rest of the week if I just put the extra time in now.

* * *

Okay, so it's now 10:40 pm and I'm in a cab on the way home. I had to write in here because I feel terrible. I'm really angry with myself. After my last entry I got back to my work, but it was all data analysis and I'm really bad with that stuff – that was where I'd made most of my mistakes in the last proposal to Gary. I'm so worried I'll get it wrong again. I was going over and over the same set of stats to check and double check I was doing it right, but after a while my brain felt like it wanted to explode. Well, maybe not explode – I think overflow would probably be a better description. It felt like a coffee cup in one of those machines at the service station when you press the wrong button and liquid just keeps coming out, and the only way to salvage your coffee is to grab the cup and run. I felt like I needed to grab the cup and run, so I thought I'd give my brain a break with a few minutes on the internet looking for some new work shoes – I need some with a lower heel that still look sharp but are more comfortable to wear all day when I've done too many squats at bootcamp and my weary legs can't deal with the instability of a high heel.

Anyway, fast-forward half an hour and I'd bought three pairs of shoes, two handbags, a bra and two work blouses. I'd spent $850! It was like I'd gone into some sort of twilight zone – I went down a hole and didn't emerge from it until I'd pressed submit and received the notification to tell me my order would be with me tomorrow. Why do they make it so easy! And why do I always do this when I'm tired and stressed? Steve will kill me if he sees another delivery arrive, especially since I just told him last week we couldn't afford to go on that ski trip next month with our mates. Truth is, I don't want to go on that anyway – can you imagine the embarrassment of everyone seeing how uncoordinated I am, not to mention the humiliation of having to squeeze into a ski suit. No freaking way.

Anyway, back to the shopping. I guess I can send it back? But the damage is already done. I've still wasted all that time and now I'm wasting all this headspace worrying about it. Why did I do it? I have to say, though, I did feel better while I was doing it. It was like I could switch my brain off just for a little bit and get lost in the internet. I think that's why I love scrolling through Facebook and Instagram so much, too. I get to escape for a while and be part of a different world. Steve is always telling me off for being on my phone in bed. He thinks that's the reason I don't sleep very well – he read some bullshit article about how using technology before bed can affect your quality of sleep, but I really like the escape. Sure, seeing how wonderful other people's lives are does make me a bit angry sometimes, but it's generally just a good distraction. And it takes me ages to get to sleep anyway, so what else am I going to do?

Anyway, back to this current issue. Maybe I can work from home tomorrow morning so I can intercept the delivery and send everything back before Steve has any knowledge of it happening. And I'll make a promise to myself not to do it again. Ah, shit, just pulling up to the house and none of the lights are on – looks like Steve's gone to bed before I'm home again. I really am a crappy wife.

I wonder if he's left me any dinner – I'm starving.

June 19th

I'm gutted. Turns out it was probably those shakes messing with my stomach and making me constipated. Michelle called me last night to say she'd been speaking about my situation with someone (I hope she didn't use my name) and apparently a few other people have had that reaction too. Why doesn't it include a warning on the freaking box? It's so annoying because they were so bloody convenient. Now what? With work ramping up before our annual conference, I have even less time to worry about what to put in my mouth. Maybe it's time to try those healthy meal deliveries – that was my plan before the shakes any way. I hope they can deliver them quickly though, cos I have nothing in the fridge and I've got a full-on week coming up.

In other news, Steve has been working late quite a bit these last couple of weeks. He doesn't usually do that so I'm wondering what's going on. He says he has some big project on but I'm not sure. We've been pretty distant with each other lately, but to be honest I've kind of been okay with that because it's given me a bit of space to focus on making up the time I had out at the doctors. We've barely seen each other since that nice day out we had at the park, and when we do we feel more like housemates than lovers. Has he finally had enough? Have I finally pushed him over the edge? I've been so lost inside my head these last few months with all the work stuff, and even more so lately with this added health crap, that I haven't really noticed how he's been around me. But now that I think about it, he definitely hasn't been touching or kissing me as much. Is it because my head has been elsewhere, or is it because I've let myself go and he doesn't find me sexy anymore?

It's so frustrating because I'm trying so hard to get back to where I was when we met but it's so bloody difficult. I don't understand it – in the past whenever I wanted to lose a few kilos, I'd just lay off the carbs for a bit and ramp up the exercise and it would drop off me, but now I feel like all that is just making me fatter. How am I going to win his affection back looking like this? I don't know what to do. If he's found someone else that will totally destroy me. It took me so long to feel comfortable with him, thanks to my trust issues from that dickhead Dan and our fucked up relationship, but what if I was wrong? I was wrong about Dan so maybe I've been wrong about Steve too? I mean, can you really ever trust someone 100 per cent? I know that I want to, but there's enough evidence from the past to prove that I shouldn't.

Oh my God, listen to me – I'm actually going crazy. Steve is so kind and loving, there's no way he could do something like that to me. Is there? He knows what I went through with Dan so he couldn't let me go through that again. I think it must just be that I haven't been paying him enough attention lately and maybe that I don't turn him on like I used to. That's not enough for him to stray from our relationship, though. No, I'm just being stupid. I need to get my shit together and stop letting these thoughts distract me. I said I was going to make more effort but I still haven't gotten round to it. If I can get all this prep work done for the conference next week, I can take him out for the day on Sunday and spoil him – I'll show him that I do really care about him and appreciate him. And I'll even let him bring back the GOOSE code word to make sure he gets my full attention.

June 20th

Got my first delivery of the healthy meals today – thank God they let me slip in a last-minute order. Lunch was little lamb sausages with sweet potato. I was a bit unsure as I thought they were supposed to be low carb and sweet potato is pure carbs, but I went with it as it felt like I hadn't eaten a decent meal in days. It's been so hectic at work trying to pull everything together for this bloody conference I haven't had time to prepare anything, so I've had to get my team to grab me stuff when they've gone out for lunch. Mostly that was fine because they got me salads, but for some reason I've been getting really hungry in the late afternoon. Usually a diet coke and some chewing gum has helped to get me through, but then by the time the evening's arrived it's like I've lost all my self-control and a 'beast' is unleashed.

It doesn't help that I've been in the office by myself at that time, so I haven't had to maintain my image in front of anyone. Sometimes I feel like a crack addict – as soon as one piece of sugar hits my lips, I can't stop thinking about where I'm going to get my next hit. I told myself I was allowed one sweet treat per night – after a long day, I needed the sugar for energy, plus I felt like I deserved something nice – but one turned into two, then three and before I knew it I was sat among a desk full of empty wrappers with a painfully bloated belly, hating myself. The stupid thing is that it didn't happen just once. I've done it for the last three nights. I didn't write about it in here because I was too embarrassed even to tell you, journal, but it's all just become too much for me to handle. I kept telling myself I wouldn't do it again, but then once the sun went down and everyone else had gone home, out came the beast. I just couldn't stop. Each time I said to myself, 'just one more', but then I kept thinking about eating another one while I was trying to get on with my work and it was distracting me, so I figured it was just easier to give in so I could concentrate and get my shit done. Somehow the self-loathing after didn't seem as bad as the trauma of trying to fight it in the moment.

Seriously, what is going on with me? It's like I've lost all self-control – I'm either buying shit I don't need or eating the fuck out of everything as soon as I'm left on my own. I feel like I'm always trying to hide a guilty secret. It's making me paranoid – I'm terrified someone will find out, and then tell everyone else. Imagine that – a shopaholic, binge-eating boss. Wow, how inspiring is that? I feel like it's given my confidence a bit of a knock as well actually – this morning before my team meeting I felt quite anxious. I felt like they'd be able to see right through this bullshit image and see me for what I really am – sad, weak and pathetic. I'm going to have to pick my game up even more now to make up for this and ensure they have no reason to doubt my ability to get shit done and lead them. Hopefully now these meals are here I can contain the beast and get back on track. I can't live with this extra burden on my shoulders. It's really getting me down and making it so much harder to just 'keep calm and carry on'.

June 26th

Urgh, I feel DISGUSTING. I have not managed to contain the beast – well, not completely anyway. I can't believe how horribly I'm failing at this diet thing. Plus I haven't been to bootcamp in over a week, thanks to the stupid conference (which actually went pretty well, luckily). It's probably not even worth carrying on with it now – next week I have another huge presentation, so that's the whole week out, and then I have to do the entire team's performance reviews so I need to prepare for those, do them and then action the outcomes. I've got no fucking chance of 'getting the body I desire' now, so I might as well just give up.

I really thought I would do it this time, and I was going so well at the start, but it's been so much tougher than I anticipated cos I've just been so busy and had so much weird stuff going on with my body. Talking of – my sinuses have now gone out of control. I've been managing them for ages with my nasal spray – usually a few regular squirts of that keeps them clear, but that's not even working at the moment. I probably should have asked the doctor about that, actually, during one of my visits. I'm sure it's not normal to rely on nasal spray the way I do. I've been doing it for so long, though, I guess I've just accepted it as normal, so I didn't even think to mention it to the doctor. I can't believe I'm going to have to present to the whole company with this stupid thick head and stuffy nose – I'll probably end up heavy breathing down the microphone in between words. Awesome. That's exactly what I want people to be focusing on while I deliver the most important presentation of my career so far.

And those tablets the specialist gave me haven't done anything for me. I haven't lost any weight – in fact, last night when I got on the scales I was 2kgs heavier than the night before. How is it even possible to put that much weight on in ONE DAY? If something doesn't happen soon I think I'll just stop taking them. They seem like pretty hardcore drugs, so if they're not making me better, what's the point. I was speaking to Jen about it the other day actually, and she said she was diagnosed with polycystic ovaries a few years ago but she just manages it by making sure she lives a healthy lifestyle. She was getting really heavy periods, struggling to lose weight and had weird excess hair where she shouldn't (thank fuck I don't have that!), but apparently all of it's considerably better since she's been paying attention to her exercise and diet. I am paying attention to my exercise and diet, though, so why is nothing getting better for me??

Mind you, it must be a lot easier for Jen – she doesn't have as much pressure as I do so she probably has more time to exercise and cook healthy meals. In fact, she's got a pretty bloody easy life in comparison. Easy, but mediocre. Don't get me wrong, she's my friend and I love her, but I just don't know how you could be happy knowing that you haven't reached your full potential. She seems to be content just cruising along as a standard employee in an art studio, with no aspirations to climb the ladder or even go freelance and have her own thing. She says she likes to just rock up to work, do what she loves (create shit) and have no other responsibilities. I would go CRAZY if that were me. I want more for myself. I need more for myself. Getting to my death bed and knowing I just settled would be a complete failure as far as I'm concerned. I just can't comprehend how you can be happy if you're not striving for the best. Anyway, one thing she has got me on is her ability to manage this polycystic ovary crap, so I guess she wins on that front. Let's see how I go for the next couple of weeks.

I really need to sort this over-eating thing out too. It's even harder when I'm so tired because half the time I don't even realise I'm doing it until it's too late. It's the same scenario as the internet shopping (which I successfully managed to return by the way – well, except for one pair of shoes and the bra, which I really needed). It's like I go into some sort of trance and I don't come out of it until I've well and truly fucked myself over. And I swear this tiredness is making everything take twice as long, which means I'm having to stay even later to get it all done. When will all of this end? Am I EVER going to get on top of it all? My to-do list seems to constantly be getting longer, not shorter. That list is supposed to make my life easier but all it's doing right now is making my anxiety worse, as I never feel like I have enough time to do everything. I just wish there were more hours in the day. Then I'd be able to have it all – a successful career, plenty of quality time with Steve, and time to do something for me once in a while. I'd be able to go for walks in nature, and do something creative again. (I used to love painting and making little trinkets for the house.) I'd be able to chill out and listen to music or even go to some more live gigs with Steve. I'd be able to feel like I had control over my time, rather than it having control over me. I'd feel free, not stuck. I just don't want to wake up one day and realise that the decisions I made today were wrong and I can't have the life I want. What if I get sick, or Steve gets sick? What if I get made redundant? What if we don't have enough money? I feel like I'm in a whirlwind and I'm always chasing my tail. What if I'm getting it all wrong and all of this was for nothing?

July 10th

Wow, it feels like I only wrote in here yesterday but it's been two bloody weeks! I don't even know what's happened, it's all been so crazy busy. I pulled off the presentation – luckily, I drugged myself up so much a few days before and on the morning that my drippy nose and inappropriate mouth breathing didn't pose a problem. My presentation was actually received well by everyone, as far as I can tell. I've had a few compliments from people since, and the vibe among the team is super positive and motivated at the moment. There was one question I couldn't answer very well from one of the sales guys though, which pissed me off. I totally should have known the answer but it was about stats and, as I've said, I'm really shit with numbers. So when I tried to give my response it was like everything in my brain just disappeared – it was completely deserted, like one of those towns in an old western movie with no sign of life except a few pieces of tumbleweed rolling through it.

I'm pretty sure he only asked me because he wanted to make himself look good, and he has an issue with me being his superior within the company – perhaps if he focused more on doing his job properly and less on proving to everyone how big his dick is (figuratively speaking, of course) he could be where I am. He needs to suck it up and show me some respect. How dare he try to fuck me over with such an irrelevant question in front of the whole company? I should have known the answer, though – that's what really pisses me off. If I'd spent less time eating the fuck out of everything and more time memorising the stats, I would have avoided that embarrassment and been able to shut that prick down. I guess there's always next time, right? I won't forget about this – next time I'll be ready for him and anyone else who thinks I don't belong where I am. I CAN do this. I just need to be better prepared and stop letting my personal shit get in the way.

In other news, I've managed to get my eating a little bit more under control. The over-eating has still been happening, but I made sure I had some more healthy snacks available so it wasn't as bad. I've been having these low-fat wrap things with peanut butter (that diet plan I followed a while ago said peanut butter is good … although I'm not sure you're supposed to eat half a jar per night?!), packs of ham and turkey, and then when I really need something sweet I have these little protein bars I found in the supermarket that only have 2g of carbs in them, but taste like a proper chocolate bar. So at least when the beast does come out I shouldn't be doing as much damage. I haven't ordered any more of those meals for the moment – I kept forgetting to bring them to work and then it was too late to have them when I got home, so I just ended up throwing a lot of them away. I've been having these different crispbread things with cottage cheese for lunch too, which has been working quite well, although I still can't kick that mid-afternoon hunger.

I'm almost done with the performance review stuff now, and then I can focus a bit more again. I was telling Michelle what a massive fail bootcamp was and she reckons I should try going to yoga with her. I have to be honest, I can't think of anything worse – stuck in a room for an hour with a bunch of hippies, not being able to talk and feeling completely inadequate because I can't even touch my toes. I'm not sure Michelle realises how inflexible and uncoordinated I am. I'm pretty sure I'll be so embarrassing she'll never be able to go back there. She really wants me to go though, so I guess I'll just suck it up and make the effort since she's always so good to me.

Oh, I took Steve out on Sunday too. It was a really nice day and I think we re-connected a bit, but things still don't feel completely right. I thought about discussing it with him but I'm still no better at that. I think this is just the way I am – some people are good at talking about their emotions and some aren't. I guess we just can't change certain things – like the fact that I'm a perfectionist. That's how I was born and that's how I'll die – if it ain't perfect, it ain't good enough. Sometimes I kinda wish I wasn't quite so much of a perfectionist cos it makes me put a lot of pressure on myself and I'm constantly frustrated when others don't live up to my standards, but it's allowed me to move up the career ladder quicker than I possibly should have, and to smash some pretty impressive goals, and that's the shit that people will remember – if I'm not someone, then I'm no-one, and that's simply not an option for me.

July 16th

So. Yoga. It was pretty much everything I anticipated, if not a bit worse. I thought you were supposed to feel relaxed when you did it but I was anxious as hell – especially in the last bit when you have to lie there for five minutes just 'being still'. It was like the floodgates of my brain opened up during what I'm pretty sure were the longest five minutes of my life, and my mind started going about a million miles an hour. I was thinking about what I've done with my life, all the shit that's wrong in my life, all the shit I have to do, all the shit I haven't done, what I was having for dinner, what Steve could be up to at that moment, why my left arse cheek was so itchy … oh my GOD – you name it and I thought it during those five 'relaxing' minutes at the end. And what the hell is that chanting thing they make everyone do?

It's so weird. Was that supposed to be relaxing too? Maybe it would have been if everyone was in tune, but they were all over the place so the effect it had was more like the feeling you get when you hear fingernails running down a blackboard. People are obsessed with yoga, though – what am I not getting?

I'm pretty sure even if I did it three times a day for the rest of my life I would still NEVER be as skinny or bendy as the bitch taking the class – or as strong, for that matter. I don't understand how she was able to hold her entire body weight just a couple of centimetres off the floor while her legs were folded over the top of her arms. I'm still confused even now. I mean, sure, she has less body weight to lift than me, but her arms were about as thick as my middle finger so I'm surprised she's even able to lift up a cup of coffee. She probably doesn't even drink coffee anyway. I expect it's strictly green tea and chai for her temple of a body. Anyway, obviously I couldn't do any of the moves and I completely lost my balance three times … while I had both my feet on the floor. I'm sure everyone was watching me thinking what a poor excuse for a human I was. It was so embarrassing. Even the 60 year old on the next mat was more flexible than me! And the worst part was I didn't even sweat. How can you call something exercise if you don't break into a sweat? What a fabulous waste of time the whole thing was. Well, I've done it now, so at least Michelle can stop going on at me to try it. I can safely say yoga is not for me.

July 29th

Oh my GOD, I reaaaaalllllllyyy don't want to go to work tomorrow. These last two weeks have literally been the shittest two weeks of my life. I just can't face any more of it. Feeling like this has totally fucked up my day today too – it's Sunday and I was supposed to go out with Steve but I just couldn't be arsed. I knew he was going to try and make me be present with him but I swear to God if he'd so much as uttered the word 'goose' I'd have stabbed him with the bluntest object I could find. So now I've just completely wasted the day by lying on the couch and binge-watching crappy TV. I feel so guilty.

I still can't believe Gary just left like that. I mean, I understand why he didn't want to say anything before he handed his notice in, but when they marched him out of the office with absolutely no warning, I had no idea what was going on. As usual, everyone came to me to find out what was happening. The whole office was in a blind panic. No-one knew if he'd quit or been pushed, and of course then we were all shitting ourselves wondering if we'd be next. That's why I haven't written in here for a while – I've done nothing but put out fires for the last two weeks and I'm completely exhausted. It was SO frustrating that I didn't manage to get to the bottom of it until almost a week later. I just kept getting palmed off by the board, and then I had to keep palming everyone else off – I didn't want them to know that I was just as much in the dark as they were, so I kept making up bullshit stories to try and buy myself more time.

I totally get why he left – I knew he'd been feeling undervalued for a while, but show me a person in that company who isn't. Sure, we managers do our best to keep the teams engaged and enthusiastic, but they're not stupid; they know what's really going on. I'm so fucking over it. I hate all this political bullshit. Why can't I just do what I'm good at, and what I was hired to do, rather than wasting all my time and energy with this unnecessary crap? I try not to let it affect me personally but of course it does. My eating has been worse than ever – I've been missing meals during the day and then eating the fuck out of everything at night. And exercise just seems like a far off distant memory now. I'm back to the stress of mornings spent trying to find something to wear to hide my ever-growing muffin top, and evenings full of self-loathing and regret. Happy fucking days. Why is it, whenever I think I'm finally getting on track, something happens to push me right back off again? I swear the world is against me and is willing me to fail. Well, guess what world? Today you win. I can't even be bothered to have a shower, but I don't want Steve to know I've been lying on the couch in my own filth all day, so I'm going to have to drag my arse up soon so it doesn't look like I only showered for his benefit. Fuck. That's all I've got left in me.

August 1st

Today I think I hit rock bottom. I don't think I can ignore what's going on with me anymore. It's funny though, because nothing major happened – nobody died, I wasn't diagnosed with cancer, Steve didn't leave me – but what happened this morning put the fear of God into me. I hadn't slept well, like normal, and had spent most of the night thinking about everything that was going wrong at work. All the politics, why Gary left, the mistakes I'd made over the last few weeks and what I should have been able to do better. Thank God Steve was away so I could toss and turn without worrying about waking him. So then I dragged myself out of bed and went into the bathroom, as I do every day, for my morning wee and to assess the level of work and war paint needed to make myself acceptable for the outside world.

When I looked into the mirror this morning, though, all I saw was the shell of my body. I looked into my eyes and there was nothing there – it was like I was dead inside. I felt nothing. I searched for some kind of connection between me and my reflection but I was completely detached from myself, as if I was looking at a total stranger. I yelled, 'Who the fuck are you?' and then collapsed to the floor in tears. From my reaction you would think I'd seen a ghost or witnessed a murder – my entire body was shaking. I must have stayed on that bathroom floor for half an hour before getting myself together enough to go to work.

In that moment, I felt completely alone. I know I've felt that way before but this was different. This time I felt like I wasn't even there for myself. I felt like I'd been dropped into the middle of a desert with no compass, no water, no food, and no idea which direction to turn. I felt completely exposed, vulnerable and lost. And it scared the shit out of me. I know that I've isolated myself from my friends and even Steve lately, so I've been feeling lonely for a while anyway, but to lose connection with myself as well? That just took things to a whole new level.

It feels like my spirit has left my body and I'm now just a machine operating on autopilot. How did it get to this? Where has my spirit gone? Can I get it back? Or am I destined for a life of misery and solitude? There has to be more to life than this? Ahhhhh, I just don't know what to do.

August 5th

I feel like the last few days have been a blur. I still don't know what to do. I can't concentrate on anything, and I don't want to speak to anyone. Luckily I managed to work from home on Thursday and Friday so I could just get my head down and not have to deal with other people's shit, and thank God Steve is still away – I just couldn't face putting on a front for him either. I know I should talk to him about this, but to be honest I really don't know what to say – 'Oh, hi darling. How was your trip? By the way, I've completely lost my shit and I want to crawl into a hole and die. What shall we have for dinner?' He'd probably turn around and run – at least he would if he had any sense. Fucking hell, how did it come to this? I need to find a way out. I need to pull myself together. BUT HOW DO I DO THAT? Think Debs, think.

August 12th

I've spent the last week Googling everything I can think of to try and figure out how to get myself out of this hole, but all the information I found simply described some of my issues and didn't give any real practical solutions on how to overcome them. I don't need someone else to tell me what I already know; I need someone to tell me how to fix it. Surely I'm not the only person going through this? Where do the others go for help? They can't all keep calm and carry on, can they? It's so hard to know where to go when I don't have one specific issue. It's not like I've got a physical pain so I can go to the doctor, or a twisted ankle so I can go to the physio – I don't really know how to explain all the things I've got going on so I just don't know where to turn. I do think now, though, that I'm probably experiencing some sort of burnout – I think I've managed to self-diagnose that from the information … well that's good to know, but what the fuck do I do about it, people?

August 15th

I may have found my glimmer of hope among all this shit. I had to get to a meeting after lunch today so I shut down my laptop and jumped into the car. I was so deep in thought I did that thing where you arrive somewhere and have absolutely no memory of how you got there – I've still never figured out how that works. I realised I'd had some sort of talkback radio station on, which generally bores the living daylights out of me, but as I reached over to change it they introduced their next guest. You won't believe what she started talking about … freaking burnout! I swear to God I thought she was talking about me. Everything she described was what I've been going through – constant tiredness, bloating, weight issues, erratic periods, anxiety, feelings of not having enough time, being under constant pressure, perfectionism, and even feelings of isolation and loneliness.

Luckily I was early for my meeting so I could sit in the carpark and listen to her whole segment – and she seemed to have a good idea about how to fix all this shit. As soon as I got out of my meeting I Googled her website to get a better idea of who she is and how she rolls. I thought about it all the way home. Do I really need someone to help me sort my life out? It seems so ridiculous. I've overcome so many things on my own before, why can't I do it this time? I just feel like I'm failing miserably at life … I guess that's why I need help – I'm obviously clueless. I'm still worried to talk about my situation out loud though, in case someone finds out. I don't think I could live it down if they did.

Anyway, by the time I reached home I'd decided that I just needed to suck it down and call her. I figured a chat wouldn't hurt, and at least then I could make a proper decision once I had all the facts. I'm really pleased I did – we only talked briefly because I had to do a late conference call, but I definitely felt like she got me and my situation. We've scheduled a proper call for tomorrow so we have more time to go into more depth about where I'm currently at versus where I want to be in my life – and then of course how she can help me to get that. Luckily one of my meetings got cancelled in the late afternoon tomorrow, so I can head home early and talk in private. Man, I hope she can help me. I'm so over this.

BUCKLE UP

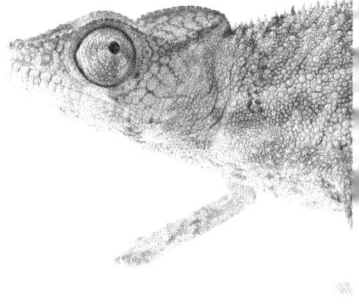

August 27th

Sorry it's been so long since my last entry. I had a really interesting/
eye-opening chat with Ellie, the chick from the radio, and it kind of
brought up a heap of stuff that put me even further into my hole.
Don't get me wrong; the chat was great and it was really helpful in
giving me some insight into where I'm at in my life, but it was also
super-depressing because it made me realise how much I've been
neglecting myself and how much that's affecting my physical and
mental health – and how much it's probably affecting Steve's life too.
God, I wonder how different his life would be if he didn't have to put
up with my shit all the time.

Anyway, I still wasn't sure whether to work with Ellie or not.
Everything she said totally resonated with me and I did feel like she
completely understood me and where I was at, but to be honest, I
was still so embarrassed at the thought of having to have a coach.
She called me a few days after our chat, and at first I said I wasn't
sure if I was able to commit to working with her at the moment,
because I have a lot of stuff coming up at work – but she could see
right through that. She didn't directly say that she knew it was my
pride holding me back, but she asked me a few questions that made

me realise just how much it was getting in my way. I realised it was better to suck it up and give it a go, rather than keep struggling on and probably end up in an even worse position than I'm in now. If the truth be known, I am still a bit embarrassed. I mean, seriously, how is it possible that I can manage massive teams of people and be entrusted to make critical decisions about other people's businesses and careers, but I can't even manage the simple things in my own life? Can you imagine what people would think if they found out? They'd never take me seriously again.

At this point though, working with Ellie seems like the best option to sort me out. I'm over feeling like shit and constantly doing the wrong things to try to make myself feel better. I remember one of my previous bosses saying the definition of insanity is doing the same thing over and over, and expecting a different result – well if that's the case, I am most definitely insane. I keep doing all these stupid diets and exercise programs, and I keep working myself into the ground with these crazy hours and putting all this pressure on myself to succeed … and I just keep getting further and further away from where I want to be. No, it's time to stop this insanity and do something different. It's time to put my big girl pants on and just go for it with Ellie.

Like I said, even in our initial chat I started to get some good insight into how I arrived at this place, just from the questions she was asking me – and, let me tell you, she asked me a lot of questions. She did say to me at the beginning that was what would happen. I was quite clueless about the whole coaching thing actually, but she explained that by her asking me questions it would enable me to find the answers myself, and therefore create a much deeper and stronger change because it will come from within me. I'm nervous I won't know all the answers, but apparently that's okay. She asked if I was happy to be open and just go with it even if I felt uncomfortable, because if I did I would unlock things from my brain I didn't even know were there, meaning the answers would present themselves. Of course, I agreed – I didn't want to seem uptight or let her down in the first consultation.

I'm pleased she told me all that upfront about the questions though, because I was a bit more prepared when the uncomfortableness did come. It was weird – it didn't even happen when she asked me any-thing particularly personal or deep. The question that actually made me the most uncomfortable was, 'How will you know when you're happy'. Fuck! That question cut like a knife. In that moment, I realised I couldn't remember when I last truly felt happy, or even what real happiness felt like. How can I know when I'm happy if I don't know what happy is? That's probably the bit that sent me down the hole actually. It was a really harsh realisation.

I realised that even on those few lovely days I had with Steve over the last few months, I still wasn't completely happy. Although I tried to be more present, and I definitely was at times, there were still always these little voices in the back of my head reminding me about all the things I needed to get done and judging me for how I looked and what I was doing. It's like my brain has forgotten how to be happy, because every time I try it just feeds me with thoughts and worries that drag me right back down. So when Ellie asked me that, it really upset me. All I could think was, *What have I become? And has it all been worth it?*

I tried to swallow my emotions because I didn't want Ellie to think I was crazy and wonder what the hell she was getting herself into. She promptly told me, though, that I'm not unique (charming!) and that actually I'm quite normal. She said that the sad thing is a sur-prising amount of people are going through the exact same thing as me – but we just don't know about it because no-one talks about it. Apparently the good thing about it being such a standard scenario, though, is that the way to change it is standard too; meaning that the same thing works for the majority of people. So she said she can pretty much guarantee that as long as I apply all of the principles and strategies that I'll learn by following her system (she calls it the 'Uppy framework'), and commit to sticking with it even when the going gets tough, I will be able to sort myself out, unlock my real health and happiness, and take my life to a whole new level. She went on to explain that 'Uppy' is a philosophy, based on years of experience both personally and professionally, and underpins everything she does. It's the key to living a truly happy, healthy and fulfilled life:

Uppy is you, the real you and nothing but the real you.

Ellie said that once you know who you really are and what you really want, and you have the confidence to stay true to that no matter what, you've unleashed your Uppy and life can be everything you want it to be. Apparently, everything we do will be focused on getting me to that place, and arming me with the tools to be able to stay there. It's nice to know there's an actual outcome we're shooting for, something semi-tangible in a very non-tangible situation. I'm still a bit sceptical if I'm honest – she made it all sound quite simple in the end – but once I've made a decision I'm all in, so I've told myself I'm going to commit to this, which means I guess I just have to trust what she says.

So then came our first actual session, which was super interesting – it was basically all about me getting myself prepared, and getting my mind set up. *Are you kidding me?* I thought. My mind is already set up and prepared for every eventuality that could possibly occur – that's half the reason I'm in this mess. Planning for all situations and possible scenarios is one of my special skills! Turns out, that skill will come in handy, according to Ellie, but apparently I just need to refine it a bit, so it's not quite so hectic and there's room for some other thoughts in my brain. She went on to explain a few concepts to help me with that and get me ready for this 'journey' I'm about to embark on.

Just as a side note: it really pisses me off when I see people on Facebook or whatever, talk about the 'journey' they've been on – especially when that journey just seems to have involved lying in the sun all day with the odd break to go to the gym. Am I really going on a 'journey'? Or am I just sorting my shit out – it doesn't seem quite so profound (or wanky) when you put it like that, does it? I guess if I say I'm going on a journey though, it makes me sound less pathetic. And if anyone does find out it'll fool them into thinking I'm just trying to better myself, rather than bring myself back from the brink of a breakdown. Okay, that's decided it, a journey it is – I'm going on a fucking journey baby!!

Anyway, as Ellie walked me through these concepts, they all seemed so obvious, but none of them had ever occurred to me once in my life. She was really happy that I write in here so regularly (well, somewhat), and asked me to keep with it – writing down my thoughts, and also adding in what I learn and take away from our sessions each time. She said keeping a journal is critical to my success, cos I'll be much more likely to value and remember what I need at that time, and I'll have something to reference in my own words when I look back and reflect. Plus I'll be able to track and measure my progress much more easily – now she was talking my language. So here's my summary of some of the stuff we talked about on getting prepared.

Apparently there are two different ways we can live our lives: at Effect or at Cause.

Effect

At Effect, we are reactive. We tend to blame other people or circumstances for the way we feel, what we experience and the situations we find ourselves in. We give up all responsibility and believe that things happen to us, rather than us making them happen. We rely on people and things that we can't control to make us feel good and achieve what we want, which ultimately leaves us feeling powerless and puts limitations on our lives.

Cause

At Cause, we are proactive. We take full responsibility for everything that happens to us and we consciously and consistently take action to create what we desire. When living at Cause, we believe that everything in life is a choice and that we are solely responsible for making those choices. Through that, we create our own opportunities. This means people at Cause tend to get more of the important shit done and live healthier, happier and more fulfilled lives – I guess they've unleashed their Uppy, right?

Oh my gosh, I am SO living at Effect right now … in fact, I think I always have. Ellie helped mc to see that I've been blaming work for my stress, tiredness and lack of time, I've been relying on Steve to make me feel secure in our relationship, and I've been pinning all my hopes of feeling good about myself on these different diets and exercise programs. I guess I've been living with a bit of a victim mentality, really, because I've always felt like I can't change a lot of the things in my life, and that's just the way it is. But Ellie emphasised that everything in life is a choice – up until now, I've been choosing to be a victim of my circumstances, but I can easily flip this approach around and choose to take full responsibility and therefore full control of my life.

'Easily' flip it around, she says. Ellie makes it sound so bloody easy – but if it were that easy, why haven't I done it before? Why is that not just the way I operate? She said I need to get some fundamental things sorted out before I can live at Cause more easily – I need to build better foundations for my life, so I know what's important to me and what I really want, and I need to uncover and unlock the thoughts, patterns and behaviours that have been holding me back. She assured me that this was all part of the process we'd follow on my journey towards unleashing my Uppy, and she'd take me through each stage as I was ready for it. I think this may test my patience a bit, cos I'm used to going into things full steam ahead and doing everything all at once. I like to see quick results – that's what motivates me to keep going. Mind you, that clearly didn't work with my recent attempts at diets and exercise, did it? I got to the point where I was seeing results and my clothes were starting to feel a bit looser, but then I fucked it all up by working rather than exercising, and eating everything I could get my hands on. Jesus! That was an epic fail. Ellie did pick me up on this at the start, though – she stressed that I'd get the best results by taking small consistent steps rather than trying to do it all immediately – slow and steady wins the race. So I do know I'll need to be patient … doesn't mean I have to like it though.

I asked her if it's actually possible to live your entire life at Cause, because to me that just doesn't seem likely. Apparently it's not, but the trick is to become good at catching yourself when you're living at Effect and then making the necessary changes to move to Cause. She said that often the reason we live at Effect so much is because we're living in the past or the future, rather than the present. We blame the things from the past for the way our lives are and we are today, and we worry about things in the future that may or may not ever eventuate. So we change our thoughts and behaviours now in an attempt to compensate for what's happened, and get ourselves prepared for every possible outcome that could happen (hmmm, sounds familiar). Either way, we have no control over any of these things, so giving our time and energy to them simply keeps us at Effect, because we get stuck in this loop of blame and excuses. Ellie said:

> *The only thing we can ever control is what's happening in the present moment.*

So the more we live there, the more we can live at Cause, and the more we can take control of our lives. I guess that makes sense. I'm often blaming the way dickhead Dan treated me for my insecurities with Steve, and I'm ALWAYS stressing about the future – will we get sick, will we have enough money, will something happen that will split us up, will we be able to have kids if we want them, will I get found out at work, will I ever have a bikini body??? Oh my GOD, I could go on and on and on. No wonder I'm living at Effect – I'm anywhere but in the present moment. Ahhhhhhh, that must be why I felt so much calmer when I committed to being present with Steve on those days out – even though it was only for a few seconds each time, when I was truly present the thoughts and worries disappeared, or at least got quieter, so I definitely did feel more in control and more content. Now I understand that was cos I was more at Cause. Hmmmmmm, how very bloody interesting.

Anyway, it's all well and good to say live in the present moment, but how the hell do you do that when there's so much to think about? I get how being stuck in the past doesn't work for you, but surely you can't just forget about the future and live moment by moment? How can you achieve anything if you don't have anything to strive for? Ellie reassured me that it's okay to have aspirations and goals, and wants and desires, but the trick is to just have them in your sights and then come back to the present moment, and concentrate only on what you can do right now to take you towards those things. Worrying about whether something will happen or not doesn't make it happen – or indeed prevent it from happening – only action in the moment does.

We talked about my persistent concern that people at work will find out I'm a fraud. Ellie helped me to see that worrying about being found out isn't going to prevent me from being found out … so we resolved that the only thing I can do is concentrate on each of the tasks at hand and do them to the best of my ability, ultimately ensuring I do my job to the best of my ability. If all this is true, then that's literally all I can do? Huh. I wonder if that's actually possible. I asked Ellie if this being present stuff had anything to do with mindfulness – I mentioned that we'd had a person come into work a few times to try to teach us how to be mindful, but I'd not paid much attention because I didn't really understand the point of it. She said that mindfulness is the practice of being consciously aware and in the present moment, so yes that was exactly what we were talking about. I don't know why that person at work didn't give us this kind of background information – the importance of being mindful makes so much more sense now, and I'm so much more motivated to do it.

Ellie said another nice way to think about mindfulness and being present is to approach things with curiosity. Curiosity? I didn't understand the significance of this at first, so Ellie asked me to look the definition up in the dictionary. It says, 'A strong desire to know or learn something'. Why is that so important? Well, apparently, if I can always look at a situation with curiosity, and so with the view to notice, know or learn something from it, I will always be able to see it for what it is, rather than getting wrapped up in my own thoughts or judgements about it and operating from my emotional brain with a clouded view of the situation. In short, I will be present. And as a result I will feel more calm and clear, because my mind won't be so full and my body won't be so stressed. Ellie said I can even use this with my own thoughts – instead of getting annoyed that I responded to something at Effect and not Cause, I can get curious and ask myself, 'What was the reason I responded in that way?' This allows me to come at it more from a learning and problem-solving point of view, and stay present rather than getting swept away to a time and head-space I can't control. And in doing so, I can discover different ways to respond when the situation presents itself again, meaning I can move forward in my life and have more control over how I feel.

Ellie gave me some other great questions to ask myself, to help me with the process of bringing myself back to the present moment and moving myself to Cause:

- 'What am I blaming or what excuse am I giving for the way I feel right now or the situation I'm in?'

- 'What can I do to take responsibility for the way I feel/situation I'm in?'

- 'What action can I take to get myself into the present moment and into the mood/situation I want to be in?'

I did have a little go at this when I was getting ready for work this morning. I could feel myself getting more and more pissed off as I tried to find something to wear that looked even vaguely okay, and I noticed that I'd started to beat myself up about my failed attempts to lose weight. Of course, this was nothing new – it was a standard daily occurrence – but this time I became more aware of the relation-ship between what I was thinking and the way I was feeling. Let me see if I can remember the thought process I went through as I asked myself those questions that Ellie gave me, because it was really quite interesting:

- *What am I blaming?* If only I hadn't fucked up all those diets and lost all my self-control, I wouldn't be feeling like shit right now.

- *What is my excuse?* It's just so fucking hard to do it when I'm so busy and have so many things to do. If only I had more time I'd be able to focus better on looking after myself and I wouldn't be such a fat mess.

- *What can I do to take responsibility?* I have chosen to prioritise work over my health, so I have chosen to be overweight and to feel like shit every morning … and in fact every day.

- *What action can I take to get myself into the present moment and the mood I want?* Hmmm, this was a tricky one. I told myself that I'm already taking action by working with Ellie, and even by going through this thought process I was taking responsibility for the way I feel, and therefore taking myself into Cause.

I do think I was at Cause for a moment, but then I caught sight of my gut in the mirror again and the thoughts all came flooding back. I didn't have time to work through it all again, so I just resolved that a lot more practice would be required to nail it and then I'd be able to live more naturally at Cause. Still, it was nice to get a glimpse of what it can feel like. And I'd say the fact that I managed to do it on my first go is definitely an awesome result, right? Ellie said you have to celebrate the small wins on the way to the bigger ones, so I guess that can count as one? Hell yeah, I'm taking that as one.

Wow, I think that has to be my most epic journal entry yet! That's definitely enough for one night – I'll write up some more stuff tomorrow. See ya.

August 28th

Fucking hell. Now that I've become aware of the whole Cause and Effect thing, I'm noticing it in everything I do … and I am most definitely 100 per cent at Effect. It's actually quite frustrating – even though I'm now aware of it, I'm still no good at doing anything about it. I get that awareness is the first step, but I want to live at Cause already. I feel like I've been handed a pen but I have no idea how to write – so what use is the freaking pen?! I just spoke to Ellie quickly, actually, to vent about this, and she reminded me that slow and steady wins the race. So, for now, I should just remain aware and make note of the particular situations and feelings that come up, and what I do in those moments. So then I can reflect on my responses, and get curious and proactive about what I can do to move myself more to Cause the next time. She stressed that during this process I should observe and not judge. Judging means I've slipped into the past or future, and therefore Effect, because I'm comparing myself and/or my situation to other things that are beyond my control and outside of the present moment. She said that, as with living in the past and future, judging doesn't change any-thing – only the action I take right now does. She advised me to simply *notice* what happens – not to judge it as bad or indeed good, simply get curious, remain neutral and see it for what it is.

Apparently this awareness and writing down of everything I observe is critical, because it gives us invaluable information to work with to progress me through the change process, and it allows me to learn how to take myself through it too – Ellie said her goal is to teach me how to coach myself, so I can become self-sufficient when it comes to working my way through issues and life in general.

Fair enough. Well in that case then, today I was *aware* that I ate two chocolate bars when I was stressed, I *noticed* that I responded passive-aggressively towards Rob (my condescending prick of a team member) because he questioned my decision about the new social media campaign, and I *observed* that I got in a mood with Steve because he didn't let me know he'd be home late and I didn't know where he was. How's that for awareness, Ellie?!

Anyway, let me explain the next concept for getting my mind prepared – that'll distract me for a minute from my impatience of not living fully at Cause already.

Stages of learning

I actually did know all about the four stages of learning because I've used the approach at work, but interestingly, I've never thought to apply it to my life. Ellie told me that keeping the stages in the forefront of my mind is really important, because this reinforces the idea that real change happens gradually. I need to be consistent and disciplined when implementing the strategies – that way, I can properly embed them into my thoughts and behaviours, and make them a natural way of life. It was good to get a reminder of each stage:

- *Unconsciously incompetent:* This is where you don't know that you don't know something. Before now, I didn't know that I was living at Effect or that living at Cause was even a thing.

- *Consciously incompetent:* At this stage, you know that you don't know something, but you're still not sure what to do and you don't have the skills you need. I'm at that stage right now with this bloody Cause and Effect business – I now know that I need to live more at Cause, but I still need to gain more skills and nail how to do that.

- *Consciously competent:* At this point, you have acquired the knowledge and skills, but you still have to consciously think about doing it. This reminds me of when I learned to drive, actually. I remember thinking, There's just so many things I have to do all at the same time – check mirrors, indicate, look ahead, check behind, figure out when to change gear...change gear! For ages I couldn't even drive with the radio on because it was too distracting. This was me being consciously competent.

- *Unconsciously competent:* This is the stage where the knowledge, skill or behaviour comes naturally to you, without you having to consciously think about it. My driving got to this stage after a few months – eventually I was able to drive along with the music blaring, having a conversation with my mates and eating a snack! And then I'd start to do that thing where I'd drive somewhere and not remember how I got there – my driving skills had become that unconsciously competent that I could go into a daydream and still operate the vehicle at the same time! I look forward to the time I can naturally live at Cause (while eating a snack!). ☺

In other news – I went out for lunch today with Michelle. I've hardly seen her since her business had a massive growth spurt and she had to quickly expand her team to keep up with it. I was worried she'd get overwhelmed by it all, but she seems to be nailing it. Who am I kidding? She was always going to nail it, she's so amazing. I honestly don't know how she does it all – runs a highly successful media agency, sits on a couple of boards, has a marriage that's so functional it makes me sick, three over-achieving kids and she regularly competes in triathlons – she's bloody superwoman. And here I am struggling to get through the day with just a small team in someone else's business and a husband – I can't even find any spare time to fit in a laser hair removal session (much to Steve's dismay). People think I have it all, but I'm completely failing at life in comparison to her.

August 29th

Talking to key people

Faaaaar out, tonight was challenging. In our last session, Ellie suggested I should speak to my nearest and dearest before embarking on our program, to make sure they understand what I'm doing and they're on board with supporting me through it. She stressed to me that, statistically, you're 80 to 90 percent more likely to achieve what you want if you've got someone specifically keeping you accountable. I told her that's why I was working with her! While this was true, Ellie said that the more accountability and support I have the better, because it will ensure I continue to prioritise this stuff and bring all the people and things that are important to me along for the ride. She reminded me of how I said I like quick results, and said that extra accountability and support would most definitely accelerate the process. Dammit! How could I argue with that? She also said that on the flip side, not bringing my loved ones along on the journey with me could seriously affect my results, because they won't understand what's happening and won't be prepared for the changes in me and my behaviour. In this case, they may very well subconsciously sabotage the process (maybe by making me feel guilty for taking more time to work on myself or encouraging me to go back to my old thought and behaviour patterns), because they fear that if I change then my relationship with them might change, which makes them feel insecure and unsettled.

Talking about myself and my emotions though, is pretty much my least favourite thing to do. I do get why it's important, but I also think there's something to be said for doing it on my own. At least that way it doesn't matter what happens – there's no-one for me to let down except myself. Plus, I don't want anyone else knowing that there's something wrong with me. Imagine if that got back to work.

I know Ellie keeps saying that working with a coach or getting help doesn't mean that there's something wrong with you, and doesn't mean you're broken or need to be fixed, but it's still embarrassing to admit that you can't do it on your own. I mean, everyone sees me as this strong independent woman who won't stop until she gets what she wants, and I like that. If I shatter that illusion, what have I got? Something Ellie said on this did make a lot of sense though – she compared life coaching to coaching an athlete. If you think about it, they rely on coaches and experts in order to get to the top of their game. They have a support team who help them to learn and develop, and who create strategies and programs that enable them to be the best they can be. As she said, athletes don't get coaches because there's something wrong with them, they get coaches to enhance their performance and get better results. No athlete on earth would even think about competing without having such a team around them. She's so right. So why can't we do the same in our lives?

After she put forward such a good case for just biting the bullet and talking to people, I did as she advised and arranged to have dinner with Steve so I could bring him up to speed. I can't believe how terrified I was to start the conversation. I've been with the bloke for over six years – he's held my hair back while I've spewed, for goodness sake, and had to put me to bed on more than one occasion. He's seen me at my worst and he's still with me, but for some reason talking to him about how I really feel scares the shit out of me. I don't want him to think I'm crazy or an unstable emotional wreck.

Anyway, I sat there like a mute for the first half an hour, giving myself secret pep-talks in my mind to try to pluck up the courage to open my mouth. Eventually I just blurted out, 'I'm seeing someone.' Fuck! See what I mean? I'm fucking useless at this shit! Of course Steve thought I meant another guy and was so shocked he dropped his knife and fork on the floor. So then I had no choice but to talk quickly to try to dig myself out of the incredibly large hole I'd put myself in. Once I got over the hurdle of getting out the first few words though, it started to flow a bit more easily. He sat and listened, and actually I didn't once feel like he was judging me – which was the main thing I was afraid of. I told him I've been struggling for a while with my lack of energy, my general health and wellness, and constantly feeling flat, overwhelmed and lost. And I told him all about Ellie and how she helps people like me reclaim their health and improve the quality of their lives, and that I'd decided to work with her … and that she is in fact the person I'm seeing! He took it all amazingly well – at first he told me off for keeping this all to myself for so long, and said he felt terrible because he hadn't realised it had got so bad, but then he simply asked, 'What do you need me to do?' Pretty amazing, right? He's always so bloody calm and practical. It was kind of difficult to answer that though, since this is all new to me, but I figured the main things were:

1. Be patient with me

2. Create an environment where we both feel comfortable to say what we think and feel

3. Help keep me accountable to any weekly action tasks when I need it

4. Make sure I keep this work at the top of my priorities and don't let excuses get in the way

He, of course, agreed, and we actually ended up having some amazing sex on the couch after that. I think getting that off my chest and knowing that he's there for me made me feel closer to him and more comfortable with him, so for the first time in ages I just went with it when he made a move on me, and really got into the moment. I was freaking present baby … and damn it felt good! It's nice to feel like there's some connection back between us – it definitely makes me feel less anxious. I just wish I'd had that bloody laser now!!

Ellie's instructions were actually to speak with all the key people in my life who have the potential to help or hinder me on this 'journey' (I'm sure I'll be able to say that word soon without feeling wanky). Steve was obviously the main one, so I've just started with him for now. To be honest, although I did do it with Steve, it was still incredibly hard and I didn't enjoy the process, so I just don't feel ready to open up to anyone else yet – even the thought of it makes me anxious, so I've made an executive decision to definitely take that one slow and steady. I'm sure once I'm a bit more into it I'll have more confidence to speak to the others anyway?

August 30th

I've just finished going through my calendar and putting in times to work on myself – it's so weird that I have to schedule reminders to think about myself. It's all part of Ellie's strategy to create 'non-negotiables' – things that must happen in my day or week, no matter what. I really had to think about what these would be, because once I create a non-negotiable I have to commit to it 100 per cent and do whatever it takes to get it done. I thought this was supposed to reduce my stress, but that's a lot of pressure for someone who hates to fail!

Non-negotiables

So, to get me started (and bag a few quick results ☺), Ellie suggested I just pick three things that I know will make a difference to the way I feel if I do them regularly. She reminded me again that slow and steady wins the race, so advised I choose small things to make it easier to start building the discipline. So here goes:

1. *Time to work on myself and action my stuff from Ellie* – I've given myself an hour slot at the beginning and at the end of the week, so I can set myself up and reflect on how I've gone.

2. *Quality time with Steve* – I've scheduled in one date night per week (which also means I have to leave work on time at least one of the days). I'm a bit nervous about this one in case something comes up at work, but Ellie suggested that once I've decided on the day, I let the whole team know I'll be leaving early too, so again I have extra accountability and I'm more likely to do it. She told me to think carefully about this though, and not commit to it unless I was 100 per cent sure I could do it. I know it will really make a difference if I do, so I'm going with it – eek!

3. *Catch up with at least one of my friends every week* – I've put this in at the weekend and said it can either be in person or on the phone, cos even though I really want to do it, I know if I make it easier it's more likely to get done.

Ellie said we'll develop these as we go along, and that at each stage of the process I'll identify new or different non-negotiables, especially as I get more and more clear on what's important to me and what I want. But for now it's just about building the habit. I'm feeling pretty good about my first ones. I actually spent some time this evening Googling things Steve and I can do on our first date night, and I'm quite excited.

Oh shit, I just looked at the clock and it's almost 11 pm! Oh my gosh – I can't believe how quickly time flies when you're looking at things on the internet. Probably shouldn't have allowed myself to get distracted by Facebook and Instagram – it's like a vortex once you get started, though, and you don't even realise it's happening … urgh, I don't even want to think about how much of my life I've lost to social media. I don't know why I do it either; it used to be a nice escape for me, but now it just keeps making me livid – photo after photo of girls taking selfies with their perfect tits and flat stomachs … I just don't know how these bitches do it. I guess this must be what it's like to have an addiction – you know it's not good for you but you keep doing it anyway. I can't believe it's 11 pm. I was completely exhausted earlier this evening and now I don't feel tired at all – my brain is buzzing.

August 31st

I. Am. Knackered. I slept so badly last night. I just couldn't switch my mind off and go to sleep. Steve, as always, dropped off within 30 seconds, so I had to lie there and listen to his ANNOYING mouth breathing – which made me so angry and even more awake. I feel bad, because he really doesn't make that much noise, but when you're a crappy sleeper like me every little thing is amplified about a million times, so I can't help but shove him and insist he rolls over every five minutes.

Needless to say, I can't be bothered to write much in here today – so I thought I'd just stick in a worksheet I did with Ellie as part of my prep work.

Uppy Scale

This was super interesting. It's a scale that has been designed to help determine where you're at with your overall wellbeing. It's made up of 20 statements and you have to go through and say, on a scale of 1 to 5, how much you agree or disagree with each statement (1 = not at all; 5 = completely). After I'd answered all the questions, Ellie gave me a score out of 100. She explained how the work we're doing is not quantifiable, so this helps to provide us with a measure to track my progress and identify which areas need the most work. Makes sense. Apparently we'll revisit the scale later in the program to see how I'm going.

Anyway, here are my results:

Where's Your Uppy At?

1.	My overall level of health is excellent	2
2.	I have sustained levels of energy on a daily basis that allow me to easily meet my daily responsibilities	2
3.	I rarely feel stressed	1
4.	My ability to concentrate for extended periods of time is excellent	2
5.	I prioritise myself and my personal needs	1
6.	I have enough time to do what I want to do	1
7.	I spend enough quality time with my friends and loved ones	2
8.	I am satisfied with my sex life	1
9.	I am happy and satisfied in my career	3
10.	I am happy and satisfied with my financial situation	4
11.	I eat well at least 80 per cent of the time	2
12.	I regularly engage in physical exercise for at least 150 minutes per week	1
13.	I fall asleep easily and sleep soundly	1
14.	I find it easy to switch off	2
15.	I regularly participate in fun and enjoyable activities	2
16.	I am happy with my body	2
17.	I feel secure in who I am and what I want	2
18.	I don't care what other people think about me	2
19.	My general level of fulfilment is excellent	2
20.	I know what I want for my future and I feel confident that I will achieve it	2
TOTAL/100		**37**

As you can see, I clearly need to do A LOT of work in the areas involving my personal self-care and how I feel about myself and my life – so pretty much all the areas. I was gutted when I got my score – apart from it being the worst result I've ever had in my life, it really brought home to me how much I've neglected myself and how much that has affected me. It was so easy for me to ignore it by keeping myself busy and focusing on my career, but clearly that isn't working anymore. I'm just so thankful that I managed to realise it before I really hit rock bottom, and got cancer or something, or Steve left me.

Okay, let's live at Cause in this situation, shall we? I'm taking responsibility for where I'm at right now and for my Uppy score being 37/100. I accept that it was the choices I made that got me here, so now I'm choosing to do what I need to do to get myself out of it. Check me out – I'm all over this shit. I don't really believe a word of it mind you, but at least I'm recognising the possibility to think differently? Anyway, I need to go – I want to get to bed before Steve so I can try to fall asleep before he starts breathing next to me. Oh God, I'm such a bitch.

September 3rd

Guess who totally knocked her non-negotiables out of the park?! Hell yeah I did. Steve and I had our date night on Friday and I found this cool event for us to go to where you could listen to live jazz music while playing board games. Yeah, I know that sounds super nerdy, but I bloody love a board game! I left work at 5:30 pm (WTF?!) and we headed out for an early dinner and then on to this place. We had such a lovely evening. In all honesty it did take me a little while to relax cos I'd had to leave a few things unfinished at work in order to leave early, which I HATE doing, but I let Steve in on what I was thinking about and he helped me to be present by saying 'goose' to me a few times. It was a good prompt actually, because it not only brought me back to the moment, but also allowed me to identify what had taken my brain away – clearly I was lost in the past and the future all at the same time. I was worried that I hadn't got everything done, while simultaneously worrying that my team would think I'm incompetent if I wasn't completely prepared for our team meeting on Monday. Of course, neither of these things I could control or change at that time – all I could do was enjoy my night with Steve and then work to the best of my ability when it was time to do so.

I also caught up with Sally yesterday and went for a walk. I hadn't seen her in months, and she'd randomly texted me in the week, so I thought I'd take the non-negotiable by the horns and organise a meet-up. It was nice to do something different for a change too – usually we just go out for dinner or drinks, but this felt heaps more relaxed and I always love an opportunity to get out into nature … I was also very happy that I didn't have to find an outfit to wear or put on a bra! And clearly I've been taking the time to work on myself, because I've written the fuck out of this journal! I'm really enjoying it though, so figure I may as well go with it. Ellie was right that slow and steady wins the race – she also said that:

Actions of motivation come before feelings of motivation.

So if I just do one little thing it'll motivate me to keep going and do more. If I wait until I feel like doing it, however, I could wait forever. She was so right – just by doing those three little non-negotiables this week, I'm feeling super-pumped and excited to do more next week.

September 4th

Right, I want to talk about this concept of work/life balance today, because the way Ellie explained it (when I was beating myself up for not having enough of it) made a whole lot more sense than the other bullshit version being banded around everywhere – which makes us feel like we can only be in balance if we have equal time at work and equal time at home.

Balance

Ellie said we all have different values and goals, so we all have different priorities and sets of criteria we must fulfil in order to feel good in our lives. So one person might highly value growth and their career, but another might put adventure and exploration higher up their list. That may then mean that the career person spends more time at work than the adventure person, but does that mean their work/life balance is more screwed? According to Ellie, not at all. Because they're each acting according to their values (the things that are fundamentally important to them), they are in balance.

I'm not sure if I'm explaining this very well. Basically, she was saying that in order to be in true balance, our internal and external worlds must be aligned – so our behaviours and actions must be aligned with our values and goals. As long as we're always acting in a way that serves those core needs and desires, we are in balance. And if that means that we spend a bit more time at work than someone else, that's A-OK … just as long as we're not neglecting our other values and goals, of course, and we're allowing everything to work together like a lovely eco-system. That version makes so much more sense, and relieves so much pressure from my mind – I'm always beating myself up about the fact that my time is not split more evenly between work and home, but maybe that's not ultimately what will make me happy.

We're going to work on my values in the next session, so I guess we'll find out if that's the case or not. I've got my next session with Ellie tomorrow actually, so I thought I'd go back through the prep stuff in here before then, just to make sure I fully understand it and I give myself the best chance possible at getting the best results. I've decided I'll do a little summary about each area we cover so I can organise it in my brain and have something quick and easy to look back at – plus I love a list!

Okay, so I've broken the summary down into three subcategories: things I need to journal, things I need to action and things I need to remember:

Journal

☐ 1. **Learn and remember the principle of Cause versus Effect.**

Ask yourself the following questions to move yourself from Effect to Cause:

- What am I blaming or what excuse am I giving for the way I feel right now or the situation I'm in?
- What can I do to take responsibility for the way I feel/situation I'm in?
- What action can I take to get myself into the mood/situation I want to be in?

☐ 2. **Live in the present by letting go of the past and the future.**

Notice and observe the details about people and situations with curiosity. Ask questions rather than judge:

- What's the reason that happened?
- How can I learn from this and move on?
- What can I do differently next time to prevent the same thing from happening?

Document what you notice and how you feel in your journal so you can reflect and identify patterns and learnings, and proactively create strategies to move yourself to Cause.

☐ 3. **Ask yourself the following questions at the end of each week:**

- What have been my top three wins for the week?
- What have I done or responded to differently?
- What have been my top three challenges?
- What will I do differently to overcome these challenges?

Action

☐ 4. **Fill out the Current versus Ideal worksheet.**

Keep this in your journal so you can check back in as you go and track how your challenges are changing.

☐ 5. **Have open and honest conversations with the key people in your life to let them know what you're doing and how they can help and support you.** Examples of this may include:

- Be patient with me.
- Create an environment where we both feel comfortable to say what we think and feel.
- Help keep me accountable to any weekly action tasks when I need it.
- Make sure I keep this work at the top of my priorities and don't let excuses get in the way.

☐ 6. **Identify your first easy non-negotiables (things that will make you feel good when you get them done) and schedule in non-negotiable time to do them.**

☐ 7. **Fill out the Uppy Scale, rating how much you agree with each statement on a scale of 1 to 5 (1 = not at all; 5 = completely). Identify:**

- which areas require the most attention
- how you would like them to improve
- what you can do to make that happen.

Remember

☐ 8. **Remember the four stages of learning, and that with everything you learn you will have to be consciously competent with it for quite a while before it becomes an unconscious natural behaviour.**

☐ 9. **Nothing is wrong with you, you're not broken and you don't need to be fixed; you're just learning a different way to do things, and enhancing yourself and the way you operate.**

☐ 10. **True balance is when your internal and external worlds align – so your actions and behaviours match your values and goals.**

☐ 11. **Actions of motivation come before feelings of motivation. So just do one little thing to get you going, and then do one more.**

WHO'S IN THERE?

September 6th

So. Core values. What's important to me right down in the depths of my soul. That was the topic for my session with Ellie this week. WOW. I can't believe I didn't know all this shit before now … and how much freaking sense it makes! Why don't we get taught about this in school, or uni, or work?

Ellie spent a bit of time at the start explaining values to me, because she said they are the most important thing for me to uncover and understand – basically they are the foundation for everything I do in life. They form my life blueprint or roadmap – they tell me what I need to do and have in my life in order to feel happy and fulfilled, and they help to guide me whenever I need to make a decision or choose a path to follow. She actually said if I could live my entire life according to my values, and only do things in the present moment that serve those values and my long-term goals, I would be happier and more fulfilled than I ever thought possible. So if it's that simple, why isn't everyone doing it?

Ellie said the trouble comes when we let too many things get in the way of allowing it to be that simple. She calls these things 'mind fuckery'. I love that term! Apparently mind fuckery is everything that influences the way you think, feel and behave, in a way that causes you to question or change who you really are and what you really want. It comes from many places, like your own thoughts and self-talk, past experiences, worries about the future, concerns for loved ones, comments and behaviours of others, and what you see and hear in the media. And it then shows up in many ways – like judgements, comparisons, criticisms, expectations, impossible standards, miscommunications, misrepresentations and assumptions. So you then take on behaviours and states like perfectionism, procrastination, all-or-nothing thinking, insecurities, low confidence, anxiety, depression, anger, over-working, use of alcohol or drugs, over or under eating and unstable relationships, in a bid to deal with all this noise and conflicting information that the mind fuckery is bombarding you with. And you try to change yourself in order to be who the mind fuckery makes you think you should be, which inevitably takes you even further away from who you really are – and makes you even more unhealthy, unfulfilled and miserable.

Once you know, though, what's important to you and what you really want, and you have the confidence to stay true to that, you're able to filter the noise and chuck out anything that's not aligned with it – which means you can indeed live the happy and fulfilled life you want. Hmmmm, sounds a bit more complicated now. Ellie told me not to worry about all of this at the moment, because we'll come to it later. She just wanted to introduce me to the ideas so I can understand the importance of my values and how much they can affect the quality of my life.

Just with what I've learned so far, it makes so much sense to me now, why I've ended up where I am. I've basically had no idea about what's actually important to me or what I really want, and I've been completely taken over by the mind fuckery. So I've just gone along with what I thought I 'should' do and who I thought I 'should' be, but that hasn't always rung true with what matters to me right down in the depths of my soul. So I see now that I've been constantly striving for a lot of the wrong things. It's no wonder I often feel frustrated and a bit lost – because I never feel truly fulfilled or satisfied. But now I see that's because usually it's not actually fulfilling my real needs and desires, so I always feel like I need more or I could do more.

You know, I've always put this down to my perfectionistic and driven personality, but I'm starting to see now that some of the things I thought I wanted will actually never satisfy me, because I'm living according to someone else's ideal. Who that someone is I have no idea – I mean no-one's ever told me who I 'should' be and what I 'should' do, but I guess I've just built this idea up in my head from all the mind fuckery around me. But when Ellie asked me to describe this ideal that I want so badly, I struggled to put it into words. I said I want to be successful, happy, healthy and have enough money. She asked me to be more specific:

- How will you know when you're successful?

- What does healthy look like to you?

- How do you define happy?

- What needs to happen and be present in your life in order for you to be happy?

- How much money is 'enough'?

What?! I don't bloody know. I guess I'll just know when I have it, won't I? So then she asks: How will you know when you have it?

ARRRRRGH! She asks such simple questions but they're so fucking difficult to answer! I've literally never thought about this stuff before. Why haven't I thought about this before? Have I been on the wrong path this whole time and worked my arse into the ground for nothing? Actually, I'm not sure I want to know the answer to that question. I mean, even if I do uncover through this process that, in reality, I want to be doing something different, it's too late to change now anyway. I've invested so much into this career; I can't just throw all that away. And to be honest, I don't actually think I could do anything else – I'm not qualified to do anything else, and I'll be fucked if I'm going back to the bottom and working my way up again. I'm too old for that shit.

Ellie could see that not being able to give any decent answers was starting to frustrate me, so before I spiralled into a black hole of despair she asked me to pull out a big piece of paper and a pen. She asked if I've ever mind-mapped before – I haven't. Lord only knows why I haven't. It seems like the perfect tool for me to organise my busy mind and jumbled thinking, and given that I'm such a visual person it means I can lay it all out in a way that my brain LOVES and finds easy to understand. I'm going to mind-map EVERYTHING from this day forward – not sure what to have for dinner? No worries, I'll mind-map it. Confused about what outfit to wear for a presentation? Let's mind-map it, baby!

So you basically just get a blank page and write the subject in the middle, and then write down all the things that come into your brain relating to that central subject around it, with a line connecting it back, so it ends up looking like a little spider. If something comes up that relates specifically to one of the 'legs' you attach it to that and make a 'sub-leg', rather than attaching it to the central subject – so, say, if the central subject is 'Health', a leg may be 'Exercise' and then a sub-leg may be 'Bootcamp'. I can't be arsed to do an example in here, so I'm just sticking in the ones I did with Ellie. For the first one, I had to mind-map some biggies:

- All the things I'm passionate about

- Everything that brings me joy

- Everything that must be present in my life in order for me to feel good

The whole process was quite interesting, actually. At first, I couldn't think of much. As I stared down at my pathetically clean piece of paper, I asked Ellie whether it was normal to have only four things in answer to all those questions.

Ellie asked me to stop for a moment, put down my pen and close my eyes. She reassured me that there were no right or wrong answers, and I didn't need to filter anything before writing it down – the way to do this task successfully was to just brain dump everything that came up when I asked myself those questions, and then after we could go through and organise it. She told me we were going to sit and take a few deep breaths, and then when she asked me to open my eyes I was to pick up the pen and start writing immediately without thinking – just let it flow out of me.

Taking that little moment was helpful – as soon as I took the pressure away from having to get everything right, and calmed my brain down with those few breaths, it was like it unlocked the gateway that had been standing in my way before. The words poured out of me, and took a lot of my stress and anxiety with them. I'd totally forgotten about a lot of things that I hadn't done in ages, like snorkelling and doing those weird little puzzles where you have to follow the arrows and write the answers, kind of like a crossword … oooh, I think they're called arrow word puzzles. Yes, that's it; I couldn't remember their name earlier! Even just thinking about these things makes me feel happy – but they're such simple little things. Not really what you'd expect of someone who's supposed to be an inspiring leader.

Anyway, here's my very first mind map.

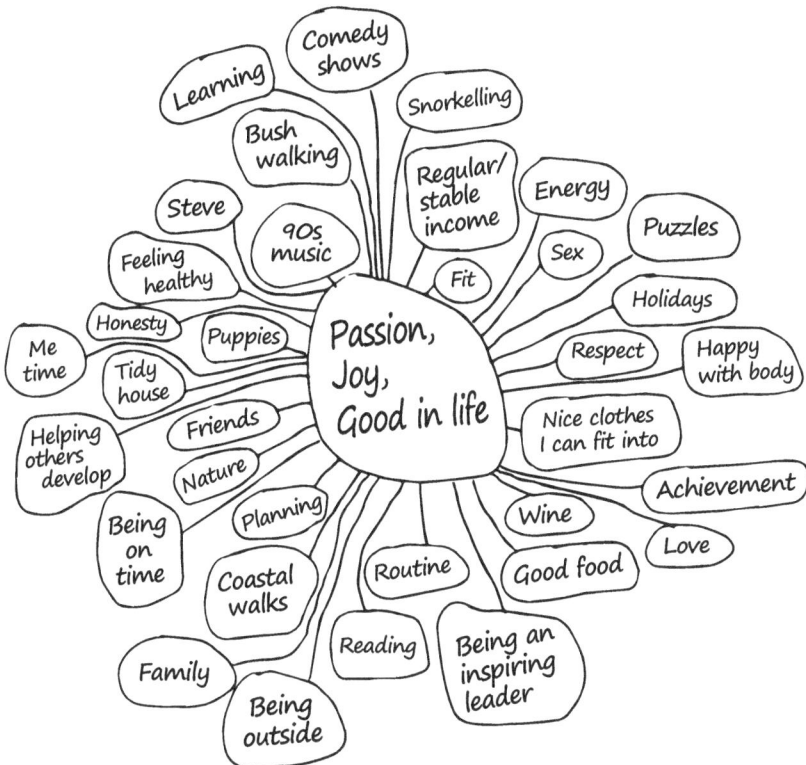

The first thing I noticed, having laid everything out in this way, is that being healthy is clearly important to me – as you can see, there are quite a few words relating to it. But if that's the case, why the hell am I not looking after myself better? If I really do value my health, surely I would make that my top priority – wouldn't I?

Ellie explained that this in itself tells us a lot – if I highly value something but I'm neglecting it, that will cause me to feel lost and out of sorts. I won't necessarily be able to put my finger on why I feel that way, though, if I don't understand what these fundamental needs are. So I'll have that feeling like something's missing but not know how to fill the void. That's exactly how I feel! Of course I know that I'll feel better if I look after myself better, but after talking it through with Ellie I'm starting to realise that it's about so much more than just a flatter stomach and thinner thighs – although that would be a bloody good start. Looking after myself means I'm more confident, motivated, optimistic, content, secure, fulfilled, happy – and probably many other things that I'm not even aware of right now. And that's not just because I feel physically better, but also because I know I'm prioritising myself and what's important to me, and I'm giving myself the best possible chance in life. Gosh, when I look at it like this, I'm feeling much more motivated to squeeze my fat arse into my active wear and move!

So next we looked at the mind map and started to organise it (yay) and identify themes in everything I'd written. My scribbles from the session were barely legible, so I've made it into a pretty little table for you journal.

Health	Relationships	Fun	Growth	Organisation
Fit	Sex	Comedy shows	Achievement	Regular/stable income
Energy	Respect	Snorkelling	Being an inspiring leader	Routine
Sex	Love	Puzzles	Reading	Planning
Happy with body	Family	Holidays	Helping others develop	Being on time
Nice clothes can fit into	Friends	Wine	Learning	Tidy home
Being outside	Helping others develop	Good food		
Coastal walks	Honesty	Reading		
Me time	Steve	Being outside		
Feeling healthy		Coastal walks		
Bush walking		Nature		
		Puppies		
		Me time		
		90s music		
		Bush walking		

As I mentioned, things relating to being healthy featured a fair bit, so that was my first theme. Then we had stuff around taking time out and having fun, learning and developing (of course), having structure and organisation (boring!) and good relationships with my friends and loved ones. We talked quite a bit about these and Ellie asked me some more simple, yet challenging, questions to help dig deeper into what these themes really represent, and how important they are to me and my overall happiness and fulfilment. She asked things like:

- What does being healthy/learning/having fun/structure/good relationships mean to you?

- What does that give you?

- What is the impact of that?

- And what does that give you?

Hard as it was, I followed this line of questioning for all of my themes. Ellie suggested I write down a couple of the streams of answers actually, so I could remember how to do it – then, in the future, I can do it by myself when I need to work through and get deeper into something. So here goes…

What does being healthy mean to me?
It means I have energy throughout the day, I don't have any unnecessary injuries or illnesses, I'm happy with my body and I'm calm.

What does that give me?
It makes me feel good, it makes everything feel easier and I worry less.

And what is the impact of that?
I feel more motivated, optimistic and free.

And what does that give me?
Confidence.

And what is the impact of that?
I feel more secure and content.

And what does that give me?
Happiness.

What does a good relationship look like to me?
Honesty, good communication, mutual respect, being there for each other and no bullshit.

What does that give me?
I feel like I belong, I feel comfortable and relaxed, and I feel supported.

What is the impact of that?
I'm more confident and content.

And what does that give me?
I feel more secure.

And what is the impact of that?
I'm happier.

Ellie asked me to elaborate a bit more on this relationship one actually, because she said she wanted to check if it is indeed relationships that are important to me or if it's something deeper. She asked if all the relationships I currently have in my life make me feel secure and happy. My initial response was yes, but then when I thought for a moment, I realised that more often than not when I'm with a lot of my friends and loved ones I actually feel pretty insecure. She asked me to think about the relationship in which I feel most secure (of course that was Steve) and identify what it is about that relationship that gives me more security and therefore happiness. So I had a think about it and realised it's that he's always there for me and for some reason he seems to love me no matter what.

I did admit to Ellie, however, that I don't always feel completely secure with Steve – I told her about my little freak out around the pregnancy scare and when he was working late. So she next asked me to think of a time when I did feel completely secure with Steve and identify what was present then, which wasn't present when I had my freak out. I thought about when I had that chat with him not long ago about doing all this with Ellie – I remember feeling really connected to him after we'd had a good talk and I felt like he actually understood where I was at…I also remember the sex we had after. ☺ When I had my freak out I felt the opposite – like there was a massive distance between us, and we were both walking different paths. Ellie asked me what was missing at that point. I guess it was the connection. So then she asked whether it's possible for me to have a good relationship without feeling connected. I again thought about my friendships, and realised that the times when I feel insecure are usually the times when I'm feeling particularly shit about myself and I'm worrying about what they're all thinking about me. So the connection is definitely missing, and that's when I start to question the quality of our relationships.

'So do you think,' Ellie went on to ask, 'that the thing that matters to you most could be connection? And in order for you to have a good relationship – with others and with yourself – you must have that feeling of connection, with them and indeed yourself?'

Huh, that was some deep shit. It took me a little while to get my head round it, but eventually I realised that she was right. I have lots of relationships in my life, but I wouldn't consider them all to be 'good' relationships. And when I sit and think about it, it definitely is the feeling of connection that's the missing link. What was most interesting about that, though, was I realised that more often than not, the reason I'm not connected to them is because I'm not connected to myself – I'm lost in my head with all my thoughts and worries, which means I create an invisible force field around myself that the connection just bounces right off of. Ellie wrapped this discussion up by simply asking. So if you were connected to yourself (meaning you had let go of the mind fuckery and you were staying true to who you are and what's important to you) and therefore you were connected to your friends and loved ones (by being your true self, communicating openly and being there for each other), would that make you feel secure and therefore happy? HELL YEAH IT WOULD! So then, connection is your value. Annnnnnnd, breathe. Gosh, these lines of questioning can be pretty exhausting at times, but holy hell they uncover some good shit!

So anyway, as I said, we went through this same line of questioning for all the other themes, and interestingly they all eventually arrived at the same point – they ultimately make me feel secure and happy. Ellie said that in order for us to feel happy we must feel secure, because our brain's number one mission in life is to ensure we're safe (apparently she'll explain more about this soon), so since we arrived at that point with all the themes, with a couple of slight tweaks here and there, it means we can pretty comfortably say that these themes are indeed my core values. So here they are:

- Health
- Connection
- Fun

- Growth

- Organisation

Obviously fun and growth were no-brainers, in terms of why they're important to me. When I'm moving forward and developing myself I feel so much more motivated and confident, and better about life. But I also need to do things that allow me to relax and have fun to balance all that out – which I have most definitely not been doing for quite a long time. Organisation was an interesting one – although I was reluctant to admit it, because it makes me sound like a complete bore, it was obvious that structure and routine make me feel incredibly secure, and actually when I have that it allows me to go off and be more adventurous and have more fun, because I know I have something stable to come back to. What a freaking amazing process – after 39 years of being on this planet, I feel like I'm finally starting to know who I am.

Anyway, I digress. You may be thinking that by this point I'd nailed my core values, but you'd be wrong! Ellie didn't let me stop there. Next we set about trying to articulate what each value means to me in a nice succinct sentence or two (or three). She said it's critical that I understand intimately what's specifically important to me, so I can more easily filter out the mind fuckery in the moment and not get sucked back into this skewed version of the ideal I've been chasing. So I followed the same line of questioning to really drill down into each value. The most interesting thing actually was this idea that I need to feel secure in order to feel happy and fulfilled. I realised that I only truly feel secure when I'm being my true self. I think I probably don't feel content most of the time because I'm always trying to please other people and be who I think they want me to be, rather than just being me. Which means I'm constantly second-guessing myself and worrying, so I feel completely insecure because I'm terrified that I'll get found out as a fraud at any moment. Which also means I don't look after my other values as much either – I work harder and longer to make up for or hide what I'm lacking, so I don't get time to exercise, eat well, work on myself, connect with my loved ones, do anything fun, or learn and develop (because I'm just chasing my tail and not really moving forward). So I guess if all my values lead to security, it's almost like that's the ultimate value. And the key to serving that value properly and consistently is to just be me. Ha, is to be Uppy!

Anyway, here are the sentences we've got so far.

Health
Nourishing my mind and body. Prioritising myself and my personal needs.

Connection
Being connected to what really matters to me and what I really want, and staying true to that. Always being my true self, without restrictions. Nurturing my relationships to ensure I stay connected and present with the people who matter to me.

Fun
Seeking and creating opportunities to take a step back and have a good time. Looking for the light side in everything and allowing my inner child to come out to play.

Growth
Always moving forward and seeking the learnings in everything.

Organisation
Having structure and routines, where necessary, to give me the freedom and confidence to step outside my comfort zone and move forward, safe in the knowledge that I have a solid base I can always return to.

I can see now why it's so important to take the time to describe what each value means to me – now I've been more specific I think I'll have a much greater chance of actually meeting these values/needs. It's just like when I set standards and expectations at work – I make sure they're really clearly defined so everyone knows exactly what parameters they're working to and there's no ambiguity, so the right shit gets done and we achieve what we want more quickly and efficiently.

Before we moved on to the final part of the process, Ellie took me through one last exercise to check that we were indeed on the money with these values and we hadn't missed something. She said now we had a clear understanding of exactly what each one was, we could look at how they've played a part in my life to date. Ellie asked me to put a piece of paper horizontally and draw a line through the middle of it that represented a timeline from birth to now. On the top of the line I then wrote three significant events from my life that were good, and underneath I wrote three that were bad. Then I had to write down what specifically it was about those events that made them so good or bad, and how they served or neglected my values. Here's how it all looked:

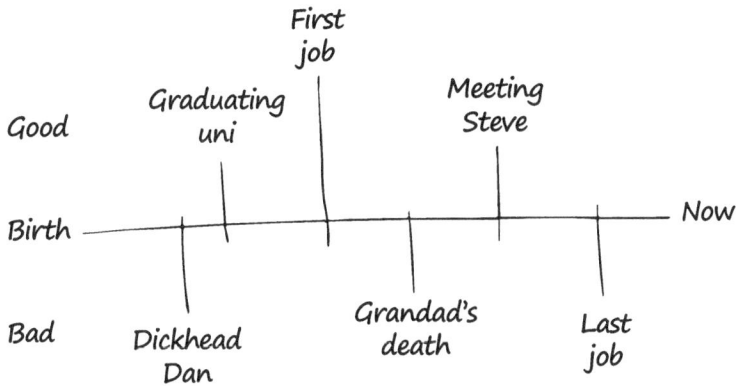

Of course, my relationship with Dickhead Dan had to be below the line, along with my grandad's death and my previous job. They were all really shitty times in my life. Here's what I wrote about each of them.

Event	What made it good/bad	How served/neglected values
Relationship with Dan	He was very unreliable We only ever went out if it was to go to the pub with his mates We drank too much He was really stubborn and selfish – we only ever did what he wanted	I didn't have any fun or experience new things I lost connection with my friends I was really unhealthy from drinking too much and eating shit when hungover Our lives were all over the place and we had absolutely no structure I lost who I was because I never got to do anything of my own, and as a result lost a lot of confidence
Grandad's death	Watching his health decline (this was hard and a really miserable period) Not being able to help him or make him more comfortable Seeing the rest of my family upset	Clearly it was a very sad time, so of course there was no fun and it was difficult to see the light side I felt disconnected from myself and my family because I was trying to be strong for them, so I was putting on a front and not showing how I was really feeling All my routines went out the window I didn't go out or do any exercise for a few months; I just felt like I wanted to hide away, so I put on weight and became quite unhealthy – and disconnected from my friends

Event	What made it good/bad	How served/neglected values
Last job	I felt undervalued and unsupported	There was no opportunity to grow and develop
	I outgrew my role and had no prospects to progress	My health was fucked because I just worked all the time – I had low energy and put on weight
	I had no work/life balance	I became disconnected from my friends and loved ones because I was always at work and too tired to go out
	My manager was a dick	
		I lost some confidence because I felt crap, and like I wasn't appreciated or fulfilling my potential

And here's what I said about the good stuff:

Event	What made it good/bad	How served/neglected values
Graduating uni	I achieved something I'd worked really hard for	I grew exponentially through learning and experiencing a lot of new things (academically and socially!)
	I had a lot of fun and met lots of interesting people	I opened up a lot of opportunities for myself
	I learned loads	I built some really strong friendships
		I went out and drank a lot, so was pretty unhealthy and didn't have a whole lot of structure

Event	What made it good/bad	How served/neglected values
My first job out of uni	I had an awesome boss who mentored me and taught me loads I got promoted twice within the first 18 months I was part of a fun and dynamic team, and made some amazing friends	I grew shit loads and built on my practical business skills, which I didn't really learn through uni I felt completely supported by my boss and colleagues, and was encouraged to be myself and flourish I made some great connections and had a lot of fun Almost everything I did was centred around work (whether it was actual work or going out with work), so I lost connection with some of my other friends and was a bit unhealthy because I drank and ate out a lot
Meeting Steve	He actually does what he says he'll do He generally makes me feel special and like I really matter He sticks around even when I go crazy! He's up for doing different things	Although I moan, I do feel completely supported and am able to be myself with him He encourages me to do what I love and try different things We have a good network of mutual friends We have a laugh together (when I'm not being mental)

What a great little exercise that was. It's really helped me to confirm that I am on the money with the values I've defined. Although I didn't serve a couple of the values a few times in the good stuff, with too much working and socialising, I think the fact that I was serving all my other values so well managed to outweigh that. And like Ellie said, it's not really possible to serve everything equally all the time, but as long as the overall eco-system of values is relatively balanced, then that's perfect.

It seems like none of my values were being served while I was with Dan – it makes sense now why I was so bloody miserable. Of course, it wasn't all bad – at the start, we did have a lot of fun and we did have an amazing connection – but as time went on and he became more unhappy and self-absorbed, we lost those things and so it then began to affect me and I lost all sense of what mattered (of my values), so I became completely insecure and miserable. I see why now.

It's nice to articulate why my relationship with Steve is good too. Sometimes I do feel like he's maybe too steady and reliable, and maybe I'd like him to be a bit more exciting and spontaneous – but after doing this process I can see that he actually serves, and allows me to serve, the stuff that matters at a deeper level, and that's way more important than the day-to-day, surface-level crap. So long term, we're both more likely to be happier and more fulfilled, which seems to be a challenge for people nowadays. I was reading an article in the news-paper the other day about how high the divorce rates have become. I have to wonder if it wouldn't be so bad if more people just knew about this shit, and understood themselves and their partners better.

Right, that'll do for today. I can't actually feel my hand any more after writing all that! I'll write some more stuff tomorrow about the rest of the values process. I'm off to bed now – I think I must be at the seven-day countdown before my period because I'm feeling super fatigued and irritable. Now is definitely not the time for me to fulfil my value and try to connect with Steve – I think I'm more likely to bite his head off and become part of that divorce statistic … so it's probably best if I just go to sleep.

September 7th

Don't have long today as we're off out for Gemma's leaving drinks after work. So I'll just quickly write about the last bit of the values stuff I did with Ellie and bugger off so I have time to top up my war paint before heading out. So the final step, now I was sure I had the right values, was to get even more specific – Ellie told me to ask myself *What needs to happen in order for me to serve this value*, and then write a list of the top three things for each. She said that my general values will not change much (if at all) throughout my life, but as I continue on my journey the way I define them and the ways in which I serve them will likely change and evolve. So to get me started here's what I've put:

Health
1. Stick to my times each week to work on myself
2. Do some physical activity, ideally outside, at least three times per week
3. Eat whole, unprocessed food at least 80 percent of the time

Connection
1. Put my values and goals somewhere I can always see them so they're always at the forefront of my mind
2. Stick to my times each week to work on myself
3. Focus only on the people who bring something to my life and let me be myself, and schedule in time each month to connect with them

Fun
1. Have at least one full day per week where I do nothing related to work
2. Do one new thing with Steve every month
3. Hang out with the friends I can be myself with at least twice per month

Growth
1. Keep writing in my journal
2. Stick to my times each week to work on myself
3. Put my values and goals somewhere I can always see them so they're always at the forefront of my mind

Organisation

1. Make sure all my non-negotiables are scheduled
2. Put my plans for achieving my values and goals somewhere easily accessible so I can regularly check in with them
3. Schedule key dates related to my goals and track my progress towards achieving them

I'm happy I can combine some of the things to fulfil more than one value at the same time – I was nervous that doing this was going to add loads more to my already massive to-do list. The list kind of did seem a bit overwhelming when I first looked at it, but as Ellie pointed out, they're all just small things that I can actually slot into my schedule easily. And I can see what a difference they'll make to my life and the way I feel when I do them … so I guess I'll give them a good go.

Ellie keeps reassuring me that if I do something little each week and build upon it consistently, I'm much more likely to get the results I want for the long term, because it's more manageable and easier to make a natural part of my life without really realising. It's still such a weird way of operating for me, thanks to my obsession with going all or nothing at things, but like I've said, that hasn't really worked for me so far, so I'm willing to at least give it a try.

So let me try to sum all this up. Basically, if I can make sure that I allow myself to be the real me no matter what, I stay connected to what's important to me, I surround myself with (and make time for) good people who are aligned with who I am and what I want, I seek and embrace opportunities to learn, I keep an element of structure and routine in my day-to-day life, and I have fun throughout – life should be pretty damn good. Easy-freaking-peasy!

Ellie said that now I have my core values worked out, I have a solid foundation for the blueprint of my life. I can use them to guide me in everything I do. More specifically, they will help me to:

• *Make better decisions and choices:* I can focus on the things that serve my values best in the long term, and delegate or get rid of the things that don't.

- *Prioritise better:* I know what my non-negotiables need to be, and the things that must get done in order for me to feel good and allow me to live the life I want. So I can start with these and everything else is a bonus.

- *Identify quickly how to make myself feel better:* If I'm feeling out of sorts, stressed or de-motivated, I can check in with my values and easily see what I'm neglecting and what I can do in order to change that.

September 8th

Gemma's leaving drinks were fine last night – I left before I had the opportunity to do something stupid, but I definitely drank too much wine. It did end up with a bit of cheeky sex with Steve when I got home though, so it was totally worth it. I hopped on top too – if only I had that same motivation and confidence to get naked when I was sober! God, I hope I can fill Gemma's position quickly. And with someone who's not just another entitled child who thinks they'll be running the entire company within a couple of years of starting. Oh man, I sound like a whinging old woman, don't I? Is that what I've become? It's difficult not to be when you're faced with this bullshit every day of your life – sometimes I feel more like a kindergarten teacher than a manager. Don't get me wrong; it's super-rewarding to grow my team and help them achieve their goals, but at the same time it's also a massive pain in my arse. I'm essentially responsible for these people's lives – that's a lot of pressure. I decided to discuss this briefly with Ellie, actually, because it does play on my mind quite a lot – possibly more than I'd realised.

She said this was the perfect time to introduce a concept that she believes will be really helpful for me:

Focus only on the things you can control and let go of the things you can't.

Let me tell you, as someone who likes to think they can control everything, this is quite an intimidating concept. How the hell am I supposed to know what I can control and what I can't? She proceeded to inform me that:

The only thing you can ever truly control is yourself.

I freaked out a bit at this – if that's true, I really don't have much control over anything at all. So how can I make things happen and be successful if everything and everyone essentially has a mind of its own and I have no real influence over it? Am I working my tits off for nothing, if ultimately most things are out of my control?? Then Ellie added this:

You can't control what happens around you, but you can always control the way you respond to it.

WTF? What does that even mean?! She reminded me about the whole Cause versus Effect thing – if I can accept that I am responsible for everything that happens to me (i.e. live at Cause) I can take control, because I'll have a clear and logical perspective of the situation, and will know that I can always take action towards what I really want. By believing I can control other people and situations, on the other hand, I'm staying at Effect, because I'm relying on external things to give me what I want.

Okay, so let me break this down a bit so I can make sure I understand:

- I must focus only on the things I can control and let go of the things I can't.

- I can only ever truly control myself.

- To do this, I must live at Cause and take full responsibility for what happens to me.

- In doing so, I can control the way I respond to people and situations.

- So then I can make informed and clear decisions about what action I can take to move forward.

- Ultimately, this means I can create the world I want around me.

- Therefore giving me the ultimate control.

I kinda like the sound of that. It's going to be tricky, though – I've always felt like I can influence others and control situations. Of course, having talked it out with Ellie, I'm not so sure that I can. In reality, I'm probably frustrated with what's going on around me more often than I'm satisfied and content. I'm usually moaning about someone or something because it's not the way I would like it, so actually, I probably don't have a whole lot of control. If I did, everything would indeed be how I want it to be and everyone would respond and behave how I want them to. My entire team would always like and respect me, and do everything to my standards. Those pricks on the board would trust in my ability. Steve would know what I needed at any given time. And my friends would always value and appreciate having me in their lives (even if I'm not always physically present in them).

So if this isn't the way it is and I'm constantly frustrated, is this a sign that I'm trying to control these relationships? Would I take a lot of pressure off myself if I just focused on me? I suppose I do often blame others and their behaviours for the feelings and thoughts I have, which I suppose is me living in Effect, right? So Ellie asked how I could live at Cause in this situation. Hmmmmmm. Maybe I just have to accept that we all have different perspectives and expectations, so maybe I stop trying to push mine onto them, which might help me to stop trying to control them. Then I can just focus on me being the best leader/wife/friend I can be, and allow them to be who they truly are and flourish in their own way?

Wow, I couldn't believe those words had come out of my mouth. Of course, Ellie had helped to get me to that point with more of her famous questions, but it's funny how easily you can get perspective when you just take a step back and look at things in a practical and logical way, rather than operating out of your wild emotional brain.

Oh dear, this entry totally went off on a tangent – I only planned to write a quick sentence or two about how I was feeling a bit hungover, but I'm happy I've gone through that again. I think that'll be super helpful in relieving some of the pressure and helping me to take more control of myself and my life. Okay, back to being hungover. See ya.

September 11th

Whoops, I forgot to write in here the last few days. No particular reason – I was just busy and couldn't be arsed! So I'll continue with wrapping up the values stuff now.

After going through that whole process in my session and feeling comfortable that I'd uncovered and articulated the right values for me, I printed them out and stuck them on the fridge. As well as being a consistent reminder, I figured if they're on the fridge they might help keep me accountable to not eating the fuck out of everything in the evening too. I had a chat with Steve a couple of nights ago to explain a bit about what I've been doing. I suggested it might be helpful for him to work out his values as well. His response was interesting; he said that he supports me in doing what I need to do, but he's okay with his life and he doesn't need to figure anything out or change anything. I get that, and it's nice that he feels content, but I do think it would be good to see if our values are actually aligned, and I don't think it would hurt for him to get a bit more direction in his life. I worry that he'll get to a certain point and then think, *What the fuck is all this about?* And run off with a younger woman or buy a sports car and have a full blown mid-life crisis. I think he avoids thinking about a lot of things and I worry that sooner or later it's going to catch up with him and bite him on the arse … and mine.

Anyway, the interesting bit was, after a couple of days of my values being on the fridge, he started to ask me questions about how I'd figured them out and how knowing them would benefit me. I realised that perhaps the best way for me to get into his brain about all this stuff is not to go on and on (as I love to do), but through subtle suggestion and allowing him to see what I'm doing and how it's changing things for me. I guess he needs to feel like it's his idea and he's calling the shots on what he does. That's fine – I'll let him think that, but behind the scenes I'll be pulling the strings … mwah ha ha haaaaaaa!

So, having done almost a week of being aware of my values and doing things to serve them, I have to say I am feeling a bit calmer. Don't get me wrong; I was still manically busy and had many moments where I just wanted to curl up in a ball under my desk and forget the world existed, but I think having those little things to think about and do throughout the week somehow balanced out the madness a little bit and helped to remind me that a lot of the shit I worry about really isn't worth it. I didn't manage to do everything, and sometimes I just completely forgot, but I definitely got a few of the little changes in there. So if slow and steady wins the race, I guess I'm winning, right?!

We're talking about goals in my session tomorrow. I do loads of this at work so I should nail this bit. Let me summarise all the values stuff before I go on though, so I don't forget the important bits.

Journal

□ I. **Track how you're doing:**
  - What have been your top three wins for the week?
  - What have you specifically done to serve your values this week?
  - What have been your top three challenges?
  - Next week, what will you stop, start and keep doing in order to serve your values better/more?
    - Stop:
    - Start:
    - Keep:

Action

☐ 2. **Create a mind map for the following:**
- All the things you're passionate about.
- Everything that brings you joy.
- Everything that must be present in your life in order to feel good.

☐ 3. **Go through and identify the top five key themes of the mind map.**

☐ 4. **Ask yourself the following questions about each theme to dig deeper:**
- What does [theme] mean to me?
- What does that give me?
- What is the impact of that?
- And what does that give me?

☐ 5. **Define what core value each theme represents (e.g. health, fun, growth) and write a couple of sentences for each to define what it specifically means to you.**

☐ 6. **Draw your life timeline and identify three events that were good in your life and three that were bad. Next:**
- Document what it specifically was about those events that made them so good/bad.
- Identify how these events served and/or neglected your values.
- Decide if this confirms that your values are correct – were your values served during the good times and neglected during the bad? Or did something else come up that you hadn't thought of?
- If something else came up, follow steps 3 and 4 again to dig deeper, and define that value and what it means to you.

☐ 7. **For each value, identify three things you can do to serve it.**

☐ 8. **Write up your values and their meanings and stick this where you can see it regularly.**

☐ 9. **Schedule in your calendar all activities identified in step 7 that you need to do in order to serve your values.**

Remember

☐ 10. Focus only on the things you can control and let go of the things you can't. The only thing you can ever truly control is yourself. You can't control what happens around you, but you can always control the way you respond to it.

☐ 11. Slow and steady wins the race – make little changes often, and build on them once you've made them a natural part of your life.

☐ 12. Values are the foundation for your life and everything you do. Stay true to these at all times and life will be everything you want it to be.

WHAT DO YOU WANT?

September 13th

My session yesterday was all about goals. Ellie explained that goals are important because we need to have an idea of a destination if we've got any chance of actually getting there. She compared it to going on a road trip – she told me to imagine getting in my car and saying to my GPS, 'Take me somewhere up north near a beach with a nice hotel and interesting things to do.' Then she asked me how likely it was that I'd end up exactly where I wanted to be? Slim to none, right? But imagine if you said to your GPS, take me to Coconut Boutique Hotel in Port Douglas, stopping in Cairns for a day to go snorkelling on the reef and allowing a day to explore the rainforest in Cape Tribulation. With that level of detail, your GPS knows exactly what it needs to do, and it will even find the best route for you, so you get there as quickly and efficiently as possible.

Ellie said it's exactly the same for us and our lives – she told me to think of my brain as my internal GPS system. The more specific the instructions are that I give it, the more likely it is to take me to exactly where I want to be. She pointed out that my values are also an integral part of these instructions – they're the difference between going the beautiful scenic route accompanied by your best mates and a great playlist to rock out to, and taking the boring motorway alone with backed up traffic, a broken stereo and malfunctioning air condition-ing. Values make the journey a lot more comfortable and enjoyable. She explained the role of the brain in all this a bit later on, so I'll come back to that in a bit, but for now let me crack on with writing about what we did to find out my real goals and what I really want in my life. Very bloody interesting.

The first part of the process scared the shit out of me, actually. Ellie asked me to get a piece of paper and mind-map everything I want to have present in my life, and everything I would like to have achieved by the time I'm fifty! It scared me because I realised that fifty actually isn't that far away, and there are still so many things I want to do. I feel like I should be further on than I am now – I should be in a better position at work, I should be earning more money, I should be healthier and have my shit more together. It really brought all that home when I started to think about everything I have to do before I hit the big 5-0.

But then, as I was heading for full meltdown, Ellie simply said to me:

You're exactly where you need to be.

And then the conversation went something like this:

Me: No, I'm not! Like I said, I need to be in a better position at work, have more money and be skinnier!

Ellie: According to who?

Me: Well, me, of course!

Ellie: And what will all of that give you?

Me: I'll be successful, be able to live in a bigger house and do more things – I can buy a boat like I've always wanted – and fit back into all the fabulous skinny clothes I still have on the left side of my wardrobe!

It was around then that Ellie asked me to get out my list of values and tell her how being in a better position at work, having more money and being skinnier will serve them.

Me: Well, if I'm in a better position at work, I will have grown; if I have more money, I can afford to have more fun; and if I'm skinnier, I'll obviously be healthier.

Ellie: What needs to happen in order for you to get all those things?

Me: I need to work hard and prove I can handle the higher position, so I get the promotion and obviously the salary increase, and I need to find a diet and exercise plan I can stick to that'll help me to lose these annoying 10kgs that I just can't seem to shift.

Ellie: And how will doing that serve your values?

Me: Like I said, I'll have to grow to get the position, and … hmmmmmmm. I guess if I'm working my tits off I'll probably not have a whole lot of time to focus on other things, like this personal stuff. And look after myself with regular exercise and eating well, or hang out with the people I love, take time to pause, have fun and just be. I may have more money but I probably wouldn't have the time (or energy) to enjoy it.

Ellie: And how will that impact you?

Me: I'll continue to be under a lot of pressure and stress, continue to feel like shit and continue to be disconnected from who I really am and what's really important to me.

Ellie: And how will that be a problem for you?

Me: I'll probably become more insular and even more disconnected from the real me, and the things and people who matter to me. Meaning I'll be unhealthy, miserable and unfulfilled.

Ellie: What does that remind you of?

Me: Right now! I'm in this hole because I've been striving for all those things and doing all the same things for years.

Ellie: And where has that got you?

Me: Tired, overweight, stressed and pissed off. But then, it has led me to seeking help, I guess, so now I have the chance to sort myself out once and for all?

Ellie: So would you say you're exactly where you need to be then?

Me: Ha! Yes I would!!

DAMN HER AND HER LOGICAL BLOODY QUESTIONS! I didn't even realise what was happening or where she was leading me to, but somehow she got me to show myself what I needed to see and hear. It's such a good technique, because I know if she just told me this stuff it wouldn't have such an impact – it'd be a bit like when you were young and your mum gave you advice or told you to do something, and you just said 'yeah, yeah', because you weren't really paying full attention and you didn't really value what she was saying. So you didn't apply any of it, and stayed stuck in the issue and didn't move forward. No, this way is much better, because it makes me feel like I've come up with the solution myself. And somehow that makes me feel more connected to it and more motivated to do something with it.

Anyhoo, that little side-track allowed me to calm the eff down and clear my head to complete the mind map. She advised me to imagine myself there at that time – and write as if I already have what I want and I've achieved all of the things. Here's what I came up with.

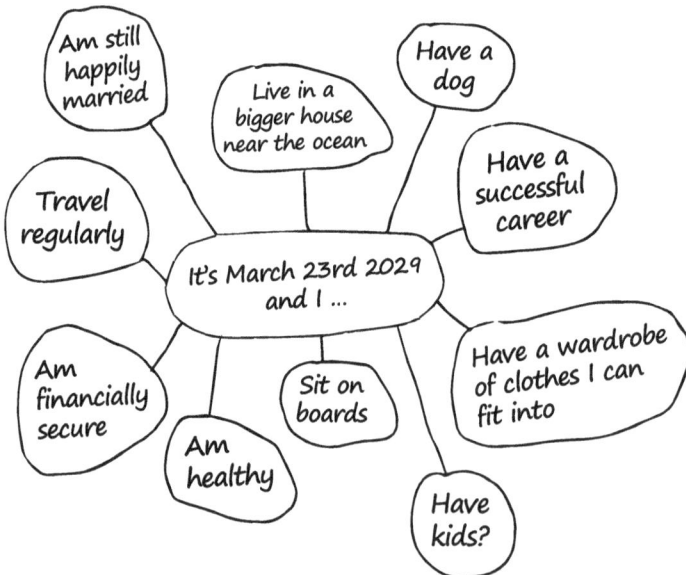

So that was the brain dump, and next it was time to get specific and make the goals SMART. I do use this system when setting goals at work, but I kind of do it without thinking now, so I thought I'd write what it means here to remind myself. My goals need to be:

- *Specific:* Detail all the different elements required to achieve the goal.

- *Measurable:* Find a way to quantify the goal so progress can be tracked and a definite outcome can be achieved.

- *Achievable:* Aim high, but ensure the goal can be achieved given the time, resources, skills and so on you have available.

- *Relevant:* Make sure the goal is relevant and meaningful to you and what you really want.

- *Time-based:* Give a specific date and time frame in which to achieve the goal.

As you can see, my first attempt at mind-mapping where I want to be when I'm fifty didn't have any of these things, so Ellie asked me some more questions to tease more details out of me and ensure that my goals are indeed SMART. Questions like:

- How many?

- With whom?

- Where?

- By when?

- What does that look like?

- What else is present?

It's so funny that at work I can be the detail queen, but when it comes to life I'm all about being vague. It really does make everything more real, though, when you get specific. And, funnily enough, it seems a hell of a lot more achievable. So here are my SMARTer goals.

Working towards our goals together
Having fun & laughing
Veggie patch
Garden
4 bedrooms
Good connection to shops & city
Pug called Winston
Spending quality time together
Am still happily married
Central coast
Live in a bigger house near the ocean
Have a dog
CEO/COO
At least 2 overseas trips per year
Have a successful career
Weekend break every 1-2 months
Travel regularly
It's March 23rd 2029 and I ...
Investment property portfolio
Stocks & share portfolio
Am financially secure
Sit on boards
Have a wardrobe of clothes I can fit into
Size 10
Superannuation/ pension plan
Savings
Am healthy
Have kids?
10 kgs lighter than I am now
Consistent energy
65-67 kgs
No serious illness
Philanthropic companies
???
2-3

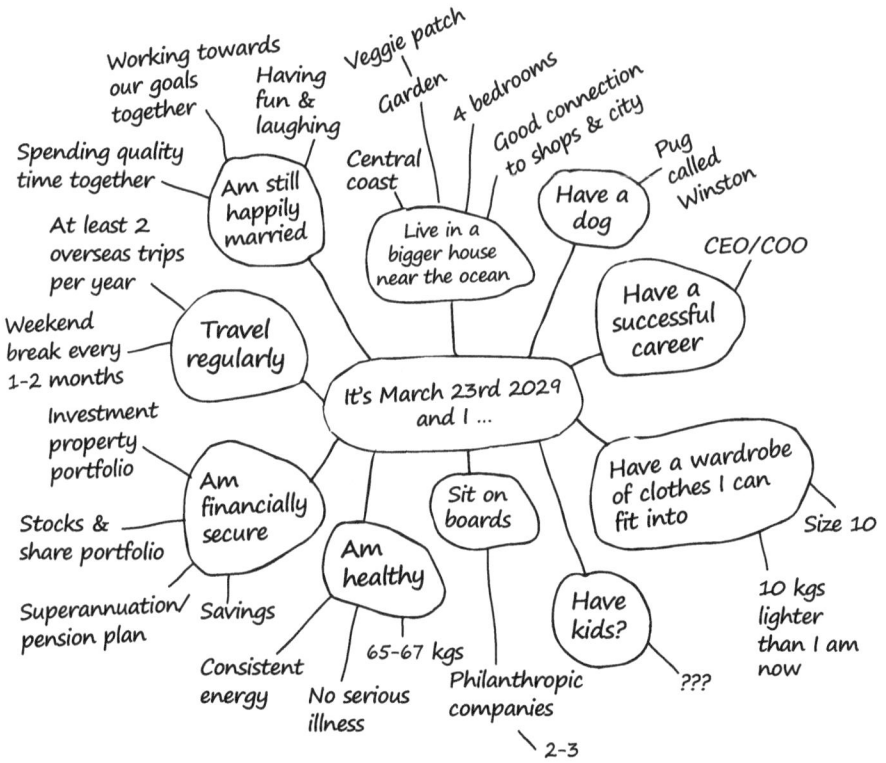

I need to work on a few details this week (as part of my 'actions' for the week), but I'm pretty happy with this as an initial list, because it gives me something really tangible to work with. Now I know, for example, that I really do want a four-bedroom house on the Central Coast with a garden and easy connections to shops and the city, I can do some research to figure out a price range for this kind of house. That way, I have an actual amount of money to work towards – rather than just striving to earn 'enough' money, which is totally ambiguous. And now I've worked out that I'd like to be sitting on boards for philanthropic companies by the time I'm fifty, I can start to look into which companies fit my ideal criteria and start to research what I'd need to do in order to get such a position.

Oh my gosh, I actually might be able to do all of this. I've always looked at my life the other way around, and made decisions based on what I think I'm capable of and what my situation is at that time, but by flipping it around and asking, 'What do I ultimately want, and what do I need to do in order to have that?', I have complete control over my life and everything changes from 'what if' to 'when'. I guess this way of operating puts me totally at Cause, right? It reminds me of that line from *Pretty Woman*: 'I say who, I say when, I say how much'. Julia Roberts was the queen of living at Cause!!!

My other important action for the next week is to sit down with Steve and talk all this through – since I want him to feature in my future, I guess it makes sense to make sure we both want the same future. I'm pretty sure we do want the same stuff, but we've never sat down and talked about it properly, and certainly not with this level of detail. Given his reluctance to plan and commit to things, though, I feel like it might be a bit of a challenging conversation. Ellie, of course, had something to help me with this. She said that in NLP they have these things called 'pre-suppositions' – a number of statements that form the central principles of NLP and provide a set of ethical principles for life (a bit like their version of the ten commandments I guess). NLP, by the way, stands for neuro-linguistic programming. I'd never heard of it before, but Ellie said she uses it a lot in her work, and even in her life. Apparently it looks at our mind, language and behavioural patterns, and uses that to understand how we operate within the world, and then change what's not working for us so we can live the lives we want. Honestly, I don't really care what she uses to help me, as long as I get results. Anyway, the two pre-suppositions she mentioned that would be helpful for me here were:

Respect everyone's version of the world.

and

Everyone's doing the best with the resources they have.

I can definitely be guilty of assuming everyone thinks and operates like me, so that first quote will remind me to put myself in the other person's shoes and respect that they may be different and see things differently to me, and that's okay. So rather than getting irritated or frustrated when they don't do what I would do, or what I want them to do, I can be more empathetic and even take the opportunity to look at things from a different perspective.

The second quote is a reminder that we all come from different situations, have had different experiences and possess different knowledge and skills. So the information we use to think, operate and make decisions with is different for us all, and therefore may produce different outcomes. Ellie said it's important to remember, though, that we will always use this information to make the best decision or choice we can at that time – even if that may seem weird, destructive or wrong to others. So, again, rather than getting annoyed or angry, I can look at things from their point of view and try to understand what resources they're working with, and subsequently what information they have, in order to make their decisions. I can even offer them some new resources or information to enable them to make different decisions, but I must always appreciate that this will only guide them. Ultimately, everyone is in charge of making their own choices – everyone is in control only of themselves.

I can see how this will help me with Steve. I guess he just looks at the world differently to me. So I can either choose to get frustrated by that, or I can appreciate his perspective and offer him more resources to enable him to make different decisions that will help us align and work more as a team. Okay, so this is where I struggled a little. I could understand this in principle, but in practice I wasn't quite sure what 'resources' I would be able to offer Steve to bring him on to my page.

Ellie asked me to think about what new things I now know, having started this process, that motivate me to work through these strategies she's teaching me. She reminded me that before we started working together, I'd placed little importance on the need to work on my personal life, or even thought about it, so she asked me what had changed now to make me want to do so. After pondering this a little, I realised it's that I'm now so much more aware of what really matters to me and what I really want, and I can see that by focusing on these things I'll have a much happier and more fulfilled life – and I really want that, so I'm motivated to do whatever I need to do in order to have it. So I guess through working with Ellie I now have more resources regarding this and therefore can make better decisions about my life. Ellie suggested that perhaps I could help Steve get connected to or remember what really matters to him too. I told her he wasn't keen on doing his values, but she said that didn't matter – I could simply have a chat about it at the start, and just get him to talk about what makes him happy and some of the things he wants to feature in his future. That would be enough to 'get him in the mood' – and once he's thinking about his ideal scenario, I can ask him how important having all that is to him. Presumably he'll say it's pretty important, so then I can ask him something like, 'If I can show you a way that will enable us both to have what we want, individually and together, would you be open to that?' Of course he'll say yes (unless he's a complete maniac) so then I can proceed with taking us through these strategies together, and fill up his resource library a little more. GENIUS plan. So I basically coach him into doing what I want – ha! And Ellie said I couldn't control other people! She said the main points for me to remember are:

- Allow him to create his own vision.

- Ask questions about the details of his vision so it becomes more real and he gets excited about it – for example, what does that look like? What else is there? How do you feel when you have that?

- Let him know that you have the resources he needs to make that happen.

- Ask for his permission to show him.

This process will lead him to engage with me because he wants to, and not because he feels he has to, meaning we'll both get more out of it. Ellie gave me a good simple framework to guide the process once I'd got him to that point. It allows us to see our separate and combined goals, so we can create a plan that considers all of it, kind of like this:

Deb's goals	Our goals	Steve's goals

To be honest, I actually think he's at a point where he's curious enough about the values stuff on the fridge anyway, so he'll be willing to find out a bit more about all of this.

I might apply those NLP pre-supposition thingies to work as well, and see if that changes things, particularly with Rob. Maybe I can give him some more resources that will guide him in the direction of choosing not to be a condescending dick head?!

Okay, I'm out. More goals stuff tomorrow … or maybe not. I'm at an event in the evening so it might be too late by the time I get back. I'll see how I go.

September 15th

Sorry journal, it's actually been two days since I last wrote in here. That awards night ended up being a really late one, and then I just couldn't be bothered to do anything last night cos I was so tired.

Anyway, I'm back. So let me continue writing about my goals. I plan to have that chat with Steve tomorrow when we both have more time, so for now I'll just focus on mine. The next part of the process, once I'd defined all my longer-term/ultimate goals, was to bring the time frame back to one year from now. Ellie asked me to do the same kind of brain dump as before, so I chose a specific date and wrote down all the things I want to be present and to have happened in my life by that time, writing as if I was there and had already achieved it. This time, however, I already had a reference point to work with – I had to specifically think about what I could do within the next year to take me closer to my ultimate goals. Here's the mind map I came up with.

Then it was time to get specific again. I'd already been a bit SMARTer with these goals from the outset, having been through the process before (and knowing Ellie would just make me do it again if I wasn't!), so I then had to ask myself for each goal, *what needs to happen in order to achieve that?* So here you go:

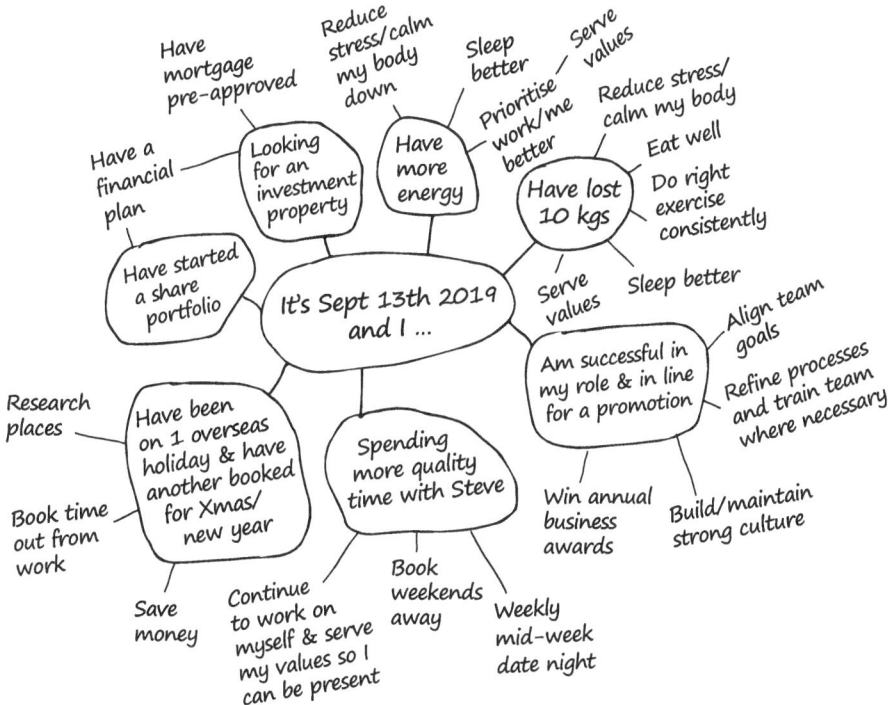

I have to be honest, breaking it all down like this is really relieving a lot of pressure – I feel like a weight is being lifted from my shoulders. I've always felt like there's just so much to do and so little time, but now I'm connected to what's important to me and what I really ultimately want, I can see how I'll be able to focus my efforts towards that and filter out all the other unnecessary crap that drains me of my time and energy. Don't get me wrong – I still think it's going to be bloody hard to put that into practice, but at least now I have a blueprint to guide me. So I don't have to figure out what to do, I just have to figure out how to do it. At every stage along the way, Ellie is getting me to check in with my values to ensure that my goals align with those – because if they don't, chances are it's not exactly what I want and it won't bring me true happiness and fulfilment. Remember earlier when I was freaking out about being fifty and I said I wanted a boat? Turns out that wasn't aligned with my values at all – I would have to take money away from my investments or work harder to make more money in order to pay for it, which would totally screw up all my other values. So once I thought about it, I realised the boat was just a symbol of success I'd conjured up in my mind from all the mind fuckery, and in reality it would end up making me miserable. So needless to say that didn't make the mind-map!

Looking at it all in relation to my values really helped me. I was worried I was wrong about a couple of the goals, because they mean I need to give more to my work and so it might take a bit of time away from the fun stuff and opportunities to connect with my loved ones. But when we looked at my overall grand plan, I could see that ultimately this was allowing me to serve my values long-term and it's a necessary step to take me towards the main prize. And, as Ellie pointed out, I can still have fun things and connection in my life, but perhaps I find different ways to fulfil these values during my busy periods, that don't require me to be so physically present.

We brainstormed some ways I could do this. I can rock out and sing to my favourite tunes while I get ready for work, which is always fun, and I can call my mates on the way home – two simple ways to still regularly incorporate fun and connection with loved ones into my life, so those values don't get completely neglected while I put a bit more focus on some of the other stuff. I guess there really is a solution for everything, hey? Hmmmm, I can see it's going to get increasingly difficult to come up with excuses when operating from this mindset.

Here's where it got even more interesting, though. Ellie said in order for me to successfully achieve and have all the things I want, we need to change my game plan around goals. She started to explain what she meant, by asking me how long I've been trying to lose 10kgs. Huh, at this point it feels like forever, but I guess realistically probably the last two to three years. Initially it was only 5kgs, but in the last 12 months I'm embarrassed to say it's increased quite considerably. Ellie asked me to think about the reasons why I haven't achieved my desired goal yet. The first obvious answer was, of course, work – I've been so busy I just haven't had time to prioritise looking after myself. I haven't had time to exercise consistently, I haven't had time to prepare proper meals, when I've had to work late I've eaten bad food … she stopped me there and asked:

'What goal have you been focusing on in order to lose 10kgs?'

Well, to lose 10kgs of course, was my response. I wasn't sure if it was a trick question.

She said, 'So let me make sure I understand correctly – you've been trying to lose 10kgs by focusing on losing 10kgs?'

Uh, yeah?

'And how's that worked out for you?'

I looked at her with a confused and slightly agitated look on my face. *Are you taking the piss?*

'Let me ask you another question: what do you need to do in order to lose 10kgs?'

Eat better, move more, calm my body down…

'So you need to do some things differently then?'

Uh, yeeeeeeah?

'So what would happen if you shifted your focus to nailing those things – the things that get you to the outcome, rather than simply focusing on the outcome itself?'

Huh, I guess they'd get me to the outcome?

Ellie's line of questioning seemed really dumb, but it did lead me to see that it's my behaviours that make or break my ability to achieve a goal, and not the actual goal itself. Up until now, I've been blaming work for my inability to lose weight, but actually it was my behaviours (thc bad eating, inconsistent exercise, over-working and so on) that have. So if that's the case, if we switch the game plan from setting goals purely focused on outcomes to setting goals that change the behaviours that affect the outcomes, the chances of me achieving the goals will be greatly increased. I can see that – if I set goals around eating well, moving more, sleeping better, managing my workload and time for myself more effectively etc, etc, I'll definitely be more likely to lose the 10kgs than if I just keep focusing on simply losing the 10kgs – which clearly hasn't worked so far. That seems so obvious. It feels WAY more achievable when the goal is broken down like that. I think that's been another problem – 10kgs has always just seemed like such a massive feat, like this big scary thing far off in the distance that doesn't feel real. So when I think about it I just get overwhelmed and it paralyses me from taking proper action. But doing it this way means I'll be able to collect quick and consistent wins along the way, which will definitely motivate me to keep going.

So we got to work on setting behaviour-based goals for the short term that would indeed take me towards the outcome-based goals I'd defined for the long term. She gave me a good worksheet to help me define and break down these behaviours, including managing any-thing that might get in the way of me doing them before it has the chance. I filled it out for all my yearly goals, and put the key dates in my diary with periodic automatic reminders to ensure I don't forget along the way. I've put the sheets focused on each of my goals up on my new pin board dedicated purely to me and my personal stuff in the study, so I've always got a constant visual reminder too.

She also gave me a good template for a weekly planner so I can define the most important stuff for each week and have it all there in one document.

For each key date Ellie also asked me to choose a way to celebrate, so I have extra motivation to achieve it. She said it's important to have nice things or experiences as a reward for achieving a goal or nailing a behaviour because it's like a 'power up' towards achieving the next one. In fact, she said it's a good idea to even do something small when I achieve the simpler/smaller tasks (like rock out to a particular song, for example), so that I allow my brain to acknowledge that I did well. She explained that:

Our subconscious brain is like a child

When we want a kid to adopt a new behaviour, we firstly have to give it the parameters it needs to keep to, and then give it recognition and/or reward when it achieves them, so it reinforces the behaviours and associates a good feeling with the action. That way, the kid is motivated to do it again. Apparently our subconscious brains are the same. So if we give ourselves a virtual high five and do something that produces a good feeling when we achieve something, our subconscious says, 'Oooh, I liked that. How can I get more of that?', so it will motivate you to keep chasing that good feeling and therefore – get more of that shit done!

Mic drop.

September 16th

Before I write more about my goals session today, I have to get some stuff out of my head. Last night I had to have an emergency catch up with Michelle cos she was having a meltdown, and I just can't believe all the things she said. She admitted that she and Phil haven't been happy for a long time and she's finally reached the point where she can't take it anymore. I was shocked. I always thought they had the most amazing marriage – I was always quite jealous of it, actually. Apparently Phil has been getting more and more distant with her, and doesn't seem to give a shit about her and the kids. She said he's always working, and even when he is at home he's always on his phone or laptop, and is always saying how busy he is and how many important things he has to get done. She said most of the time it's like she's talking to a brick wall and she can never get his attention for more than a few minutes. And they haven't had sex in almost a year…WTF?! Poor Michelle. Doesn't Phil realise how many things she has to do? He only has to worry about work, but she has to worry about her business PLUS three kids and a husband, and everything that comes with that. I'm sure Michelle would kill for the opportunity to only have to worry about work. She'd confronted him the night before and asked if he was having an affair. Good on her. He insisted he wasn't and was pretty upset that she'd even think that. He said he's just got a lot going on at work, and he's taken on more projects to make sure they can cover all the school fees without having to struggle as much as they did the year before.

I mean, it all sounds feasible – I can totally relate to being so busy your body is there but your mind is not. I said this to Michelle, and told her about the time Steve had a go at me in the café and refused to spend the day with me unless I got my head into the present moment. I suggested she could try a code word like we did, to make him realise when he's not being present with her and the kids. She didn't even want to entertain my ideas, though. She said it's been going on for so long, she's just over it. She was even talking about how they could arrange the kids and split their time between her and Phil. I just can't believe it. How could I have gotten it so wrong about them? I mean, I thought I was a good actress but Michelle definitely gets the Oscar for putting on the best front I've ever seen. She was such a mess last night though. I asked her why she hadn't come to talk to me before now and why she'd struggled on alone. She just gave me a knowing look and said, 'That's what we do, babe.' Ha, true that. She was devastated that she was even considering ending her marriage, especially when she still loves him so much and nothing specific has happened. But she said she just needs more. And although it'll be difficult initially to sort everything out and deal with it all on her own, she'd rather do that than live with an empty shell of a husband.

Fuuuuuuuuuck, alarm bells were going off all over the place in my head. That's exactly how Steve described me that day at the café when he got angry at me for not being present. Was this a glimpse into the future of my marriage? Was Steve going to reach the end of his tether with me and throw it all in? I wish I could get hold of Phil and shake him. He totally needs to do something like I'm doing. He's such a nice guy, and I don't want to believe that he's having an affair. Honestly, I do believe he probably is just lost in his work and busyness, but clearly he can't see what that's doing to his life. Is it really worth losing his wife and kids for? I wasn't sure whether to tell Michelle about what I'm doing with Ellie or not. I still don't feel comfortable with people knowing, but I do wonder if it would help for Phil to know that there is another way. I couldn't find an appropriate time to bring it up anyway, so I just left it for now. We ended the night with her going away to have a serious think about whether the situation really is irreparable, and we agreed to check in again next week. I can't stop thinking about it all. I feel so bad for her. I still can't believe how I got it so wrong about them.

The whole thing shook me up so much I put off having my chat with Steve about our shared goals. I know – I'm a wimp – but I just couldn't face hearing any of the things Michelle had been saying about Phil coming out of Steve's mouth. Next weekend, I promise.

Anyway, I feel a bit better now I've spoken about that, so let me write a little bit more about the goals stuff before I sign off. So the other thing Ellie has asked me to do to ensure my success is to make friends with my to-do list. It probably goes without saying that I'm a to-do list queen, but I do seem to have a bit of a love/hate relationship with it. It definitely does keep me on track but at the same time it has the ability to make me feel constantly overwhelmed, because it never bloody ends. I can get to the end of the day, having ticked loads of things off, but still there's always so much more to do, so it makes me feel like I haven't actually done as well as I thought I had, and I feel deflated. And then there's those days where I just end up putting out fires all day and don't even get to my to-do list. They're the worst. I always go home feeling like I haven't achieved anything on those days. And then of course I start to feel like an underachiever and question my ability to do anything well. To help with all this, Ellie asked me to repeat the following statement after her:

I will never reach the end of my to-do list ... and that's okay.

Even the thought of this sent shivers down my spine. How the hell can I be okay with not getting everything done? She asked me to get out my current to-do list and categorise the tasks as follows:

- *A = Absolutely.* These are the tasks that absolutely must get done, or something bad will happen.

- *B = Be helpful.* These tasks are important, and it would be very helpful if they got done, but it wouldn't be the end of the world if they didn't.

- *C = Could be good.* The tasks that would be nice to get done, but don't have a massive impact on the ultimate outcomes.

- *D = Delegate or delete.* These tasks have little to no impact on the ultimate outcome and can be done by someone else or not done at all.

WOW. What a really freaking interesting exercise. Turns out there's actually a lot on my to-do list that I can get rid of, and there's really only a small percentage of tasks that will have a big impact on the ultimate outcomes, and give me a good return on my efforts.

She advised that I think about it in terms of the 80/20 rule – that is, identify what are the top 20 per cent of my tasks that will give me 80 per cent return on my efforts, and just focus on those. If there's time left over after I've done the '20' tasks, then I can move on to the '80' ones, but I must make it non-negotiable that I don't even think of the '80s' until the '20s' – or A/B tasks – are complete. Apparently, most of us spend most of our time working on the '80s' or C/D tasks because they tend to be easier, but they generally only give us a 20 per cent return on our efforts – which is why we're all so overworked and stressed. We're focusing our time and effort on the insignificant stuff – we're working hard, not smart.

As a result of all this, one of my actions for this week is to only do the A and B tasks on my weekly to-do list, and see what happens. I am slightly terrified that my new boss will kick my arse for not getting everything done, but if what Ellie says is right, I should be able to deliver better on my overall targets, so that should make him happier than if I simply ticked everything off…right? Fuck it, what's the worst that can happen? He'll think I'm completely incompetent and question my existence on this planet? Oh, so only my greatest fear – no bloody worries then.

Ah shit, I need to run – Steve suggested we have an extra date night together on Sundays, focused purely on chilling out. He knows I usually get anxious on Sunday evenings as I start to think about the week ahead, so he thought it would be a good idea to distract me from that so I don't cut my weekend short with the worry, and I can go into the week with a clear head. I think he's probably just pissed off with having to deal with the tension while he's trying to eat his fun size chocolate bar and watch a movie, but I guess this'll work for me too so I've agreed to do it. Okay he's actually calling me now so I better go. Night.

September 17th

Our first Sunday chill night was so lovely. We had a good old snuggle on the couch and watched a couple of stupid movies. I, of course, did think about my upcoming week a few times, but being with Steve like that helped me to keep a lid on the anxiety of it all and I did manage to stay fairly relaxed. And actually I had a pretty good sleep too, so I started the week feeling slightly less shitty – result!

I can't believe it's almost my session with Ellie again already, and I'm only just finishing writing about what we covered last week! She did say it would be quite a lot of info and new stuff at the start – but I can see how once I've put in this initial groundwork it'll save me a ridiculous amount of time in the long run. Plus I do have a tendency to get side-tracked when I'm writing. I maybe don't need to write everything we discuss down, but I don't want to forget anything! Maybe one day I can write a book on it? Ha, yeah right – and have everyone know what a nutcase I am – not a freaking chance. Okay, so the last thing we did on goals was visualisation.

Now I have heard about this before but to be honest I've always thought it was a load of crap. How can I make something happen just by thinking about it? I've heard people talk about 'manifesting' and 'putting it out into the universe' but, seriously, it all sounds like a fabulous waste of time to me. Surely at some point you actually have to do something? You can't just sit and wait for it all to come to you? Turns out, I was absolutely right. Ellie said visualisation is like a shopping list – you make note of what you want so you know what to look for, but then you actually have to take yourself to the shop and put yourself in the position where you're more likely to actually see, and therefore get, the stuff you want. If you just stayed at home you'd have no chance of getting anything you want – you have to take action. I said to Ellie, I think I need to try it and experience it firsthand before I fully believe, which she totally agreed with, but she then went on to give me a bit of 'science' around how and why it works, which made me much more open to it.

First she talked about the NLP model of communication. So apparently every single second we absorb over two million bits of information through our senses (what we see, hear, feel, smell and touch). But of those two million bits, we only consciously process 134 of them, which means every second there are 1,999,866 bits of information that we're never consciously aware of. So what that essentially means, is that:

Reality is bullshit

Reality is only our perception of the world and not the way it actually is, because everyone processes a different set of 134 bits – so we never truly see anything the same as anyone else. WTF?! This was blowing my mind by this point.

Ellie went on to explain that the brain does one of three things with every single one of the two million bits of information it receives:

1. It will **delete** it, so we never even consciously know it existed.

2. It will **generalise** it or categorise it, and put it into a pigeonhole related to what we already know. (For example, there may be a flat metal structure with four other long cylindrical metal structures coming off the bottom of it, which you can sit on – so that information goes into the pigeonhole of 'chair'.)

3. It will **distort** it, and make it fit into one of the pigeonholes related to what we already know. (So there may be another structure that is coming out of the ground and looks like a lump of wood, which has a flat bit on the top that you could also sit on – so this could be distorted and put into the 'chair' pigeonhole too, even though it's actually a cut off tree trunk.)

The way the brain decides which of these three things to do is based on our values, beliefs, memories, experiences, attitudes and thoughts. So if we can give the brain information that relates to what we want, it will use this to filter all the bits it lets into our consciousness, so that they're in line with this information. This means our brains start to allow us to consciously see things in the external world that relate to what we want in our internal world. According to Ellie, what we want and the opportunities to get that are already all around us; we just have to give our brains the right information to ensure we see them. Like she said earlier, our brains are our internal GPS systems, so this is the process our brains use to ensure they take us in the right direction and we reach the right destination. She gave a great example to help me make sense of it all.

She asked me if I had ever bought a new car and whether all of a sudden I had then started to see that same car everywhere I went. I actually had experienced this, and Ellie said it was really common. Of course, this isn't because all of a sudden there are more of these cars on the road; it's just that we've given our brains the image of this car, so it's using that information to filter all the bits we absorb and allow those relating to that car into our consciousness, so that we do indeed see that in our external world. The part of us that does all this work is called our reticular activating system, or RAS, which is a bundle of nerves at our brainstem that does all of this filtering. So if we just put what we want into our RAS (ha ha … put it in your RAS!!) consistently, we're more likely to see it within our external world, and therefore we're more likely to get or achieve what we want.

Ellie stressed to me that our brains always want our inner and outer worlds to be aligned, so they will always look for ways to make this happen. So if we can get our inner world the way we want it – by being connected to our values and goals, and releasing limiting beliefs that are holding us back (she told me she'll explain these later) – our external world will follow suit … and we'll totally be in freaking balance and have what we want!

With all that in mind, this is why visualisation can be so powerful – because it's a way of consistently giving our brains all the specific information it needs to seek out what we want in the world around us. Apparently, our brains don't know the difference between real and perceived – so if I tell it that I have a four-bedroom house on the Central Coast and I sit on the board for philanthropic companies, it believes that to be the truth, and will filter information and seek opportunities that are in line with that. So, essentially, my thoughts will create my reality. Holy freaking shit! That sounds freaking awesome! So how do I make that happen?? Here's one way we tried that I quite like (I think this is pretty close to the process Ellie took me through):

1. Sit down and get yourself comfortable with your feet firmly on the ground.

2. Close your eyes and take five long deep, slow breaths, right into the pit of your belly.

3. Focus on each breath.

4. Now start to think about what you want.

5. Imagine the scene with as much detail as possible. Imagine that you're floating up above the scene looking down on it and watching yourself in it. Notice the sights, sounds, smells and how it makes you feel in your body. Notice where in your body that feeling is and what it specifically feels like.

6. Now float yourself down into the scene and look at everything through your own eyes, as if you're there.

7. Again notice all of the detail around you like you're right there and it's happening – see what you would see, hear what you would hear and feel what you would feel.

8. Now imagine you've got a dial and you're turning up everything in the picture – turn up the colours, saturation, brightness and contrast.

9. Now turn up the volume and sharpness of the sounds.

10. And now turn up the dial on the feelings you feel in your body so they're as intense as they could possibly be.

11. Sit within this new heightened scene while taking five more big, deep belly breaths and noticing all of the detail around you and all of the feelings in you.

12. Turn up those feelings one more time, take a massive deep breath in and a big sigh out, and then when you're ready slowly open your eyes.

This whole process takes less than five minutes, and actually I found that it made me feel calm too – I guess because of all the breathing? Maybe that's a bit what meditation is supposed to be like? So apparently I should do this daily and make it non-negotiable, so that I'm constantly feeding my brain with the information I want it to have, and it will believe that this is reality and seek to make that so. I've only done it once so far – I just kept bloody forgetting. I think I might have to start setting alarms or something for all these little tasks and rituals, because it's just not ingrained into my natural way of living yet – and it won't be if I keep forgetting!

Talking of memory – I was reading an article last week (during one of my famous procrastinations) that said there's a natural herb, I think it's called Ginkgo biloba, that helps improve memory. Mine's been shocking lately, so I thought I'd give it a go. I swear to God this isn't bullshit – I bought the tablets six days ago and I've forgotten to take them every single day!! How funny is that?! I must be the only person in the world stupid enough to buy memory pills and then forget to take them!

Sorry, another slight side-track. To conclude, I think I will go ahead and set alarms – it's really annoying when I fail at my daily actions just because of my shitty memory. Anyway, I think that's enough on goals – I thought I was all over this shit going in to that session, but I've learned so much throughout this process. Not just about efficient goal setting, but some amazing strategies to help me actually achieve them and ensure they're actually what I want to achieve!! So let me include my summary here before I go into my next session. (I think we're talking about lifestyle – so plenty for me to work on there!)

Journal

☐ 1. **Track how you're doing:**
- What have been your top three wins for the week?
- What have been your top three challenges?
- What are three ways you've served your values this week?
- Next week, what will you stop, start and keep doing in order to serve your values better/more?
  - Stop:
  - Start:
  - Keep:

Action

☐ 2. **Create a mind map for your long-term/ultimate goals:**
- Pick a specific date to achieve these goals by.
- Write as if you're there and you've already achieved what you want.
- Don't edit it – just put whatever comes into your brain; you can filter and organise later.

☐ 3. **Go back through the goals and add more detail, ensuring you make them SMART:**
  - Specific
  - Measurable
  - Achievable
  - Relevant
  - Time-based.

☐ 4. **Create a mind map for your one-year goals:**
  - Ask yourself, what needs to happen within the next year in order for me to start moving towards my ultimate goals?
  - Again, pick a specific date and write as if you're there and you've already achieved the things.
  - Make the goals SMART.

☐ 5. **Fill out the behaviour goals worksheet and define the behaviours needed to achieve your yearly goals.**

☐ 6. **Fill out the Personal Planner for each week, before the week starts, and identify the top three behaviours you're focusing on for that week and write them in the top section:**
  - Identify the 20 per cent of tasks that give you 80 per cent return.
  - Prioritise your tasks into A, B, C and D.
  - Put the top 10 tasks for the week (work and personal) in the 'To-do' section.
  - Write the things you need to do every day in the 'Daily tasks' section.
  - Write your steps back for the week (you'll learn about this in the lifestyle section).
  - Choose a mantra that will keep you on track and motivated for the week; e.g. 'Focus only on what I can control', 'I've got this'.

☐ 7. **Print all your ultimate goals out and have them somewhere you can see them, along with your values. You may like to make this a visual thing by sticking pictures or objects on to a board that represents your goals (commonly known as a 'Vision Board').**

☐ 8. Organise to sit down with your partner and talk about your individual and combined goals. Follow the above processes for your combined goals.

☐ 9. Schedule in five minutes every morning to go through the visualisation process.

Remember

☐ 10. You're exactly where you need to be.

☐ 11. Although this process takes a bit of time, commit to putting the work in now, because it will save you an abundance of time in the future.

HOW THE HEALTH ARE YOU?

September 20th

OMG! I'm still kind of buzzing from my session yesterday with Ellie. Everything makes so much sense to me now! Why I constantly feel like shit. Why I struggle to get out of bed in the morning and don't function properly until I've had a coffee. Why I get bloated so often for no obvious reason. Why some weeks I can go days without going to the toilet (sorry, I know this is gross), and others I can't stop. Why I have my stupid muffin top and can't get rid of it. Why I get moments of anxiety where my heart races and I feel panicky. Why I become a complete bitch before my period, and sometimes get it late. Why I often can't think clearly and my moods are up and down.

God! When I write everything down like this it makes me wonder how I've kept going at the pace I have for so long. It's no wonder everything's been feeling so much harder and a constant struggle. I had no idea that my busy lifestyle could cause all of these physical things in my body. And I certainly had no idea that the source of all this is my brain.

Needless to say, the session yesterday was excellent. We started talking about my physical lifestyle – as Ellie rightly said, without my health I have nothing, so it's critical we get plans in place to optimise that, and we of course now know that it's one of my core values too.

So I need to create habits and routines that allow my body to function as it's supposed to, and give me the energy to live my life properly and do what I want to do. I definitely want a piece of that – at this stage I think I've pretty much forgotten what it feels like to have energy. I genuinely can't remember the last time I felt full of beans, and light. That's the best way I can think to describe the feeling I want to get back – I want to feel light again. And for once I'm not even talking about that in relation to my weight. Right now, I just feel heavy – like there's some sort of force pushing down on me all the time. I feel restricted and like I constantly have to push just to get through the day. I don't want to push any more. I want to feel light and free. Free to focus on the stuff that really matters to me, and free to be me again. Although I'm not even sure I know who 'me' is anymore – I've buried her so far down underneath all this shit I wonder if she'll ever be able to come back out again. It makes me kind of sad to think about it, actually. For so many years, I've been so focused on growing my career and being the best at that, that I've completely lost the real me. I've become a tired, miserable and unfulfilled shadow of my former self. Steve was right; I am an empty shell – I'm like one of those chocolate bunnies you get at Easter, and if you break me open there's nothing inside. How did I not realise this was happening?

Anyway, as Ellie said, I can't change what's happened so it's useless to dwell on it, but I can most definitely learn from it and do things now to ensure I keep moving forward from this point on. I really like that mindset – rather than focusing on everything that's gone wrong in the past, focus on the learnings I can take from it and use those to make positive changes. I've always been a dweller – I love to play re-runs over and over in my head about what didn't go well in a situation and what I said or did wrong, but I always get stuck on repeat there and never move on to look at what I can take from it. Imagine if I did do that, and then applied it to ensure a similar situation has a different outcome next time – I'd have so much more space in my brain and so much more energy, because I wouldn't be stuck worrying about the same shit day after day, and losing countless hours of sleep thinking about things I can't change or control. Huh, imagine that.

I suppose this is part of me always feeling like I could do more. I'm never satisfied. One of my previous bosses used to tell me this a lot – she'd tell me to stop and take in my successes, and celebrate how well I'd done. I never really got this to be honest; it always seemed a bit self-indulgent to me. But now Ellie has said the exact same thing, so maybe my boss did know what she was talking about after all. I guess it's the perfectionist in me – I like to pick things apart and look at how I could have done better, or more. I rarely feel like I nail something 100 per cent. I know often I feel like this because I haven't had enough time to do something as well as I would like, but I've just got so many things to bloody do I can't afford to dedicate all my time to just one thing.

This came up near the beginning of my session with Ellie, actually, and she challenged me on it. She said it connected in nicely with the work we'd already done, particularly around the values and living at cause, and that it was a great chance to work through a real life example. By asking some more questions (again with the questions!) she basically uncovered that perhaps my busyness is a way of me protecting myself from failure. I freaking HATE failure, by the way – have I already mentioned that?! Having so many things on the go all the time and not being able to fully focus on just one thing gives me a convenient excuse if something's not 100 per cent perfect, or 'the best'. By blaming my busyness for any sub-standard effort, I'm no longer personally responsible for the result, so I don't have to consider it a personal failure – because as far as I'm concerned, the circumstances were beyond my control. Apparently, however, the circumstances and busyness are well within my control and that is the way I've *chosen* it to be – I've been living at Effect. I was a bit pissed off when Ellie said that – I don't feel like I do have control over my time. The deadlines and expectations from above dictate a lot of what happens, and I can't control that – I just have to keep delivering, whatever it takes.

Ellie could see I was agitated by this so she reminded me of her concept about how we can't control what happens around us in our physical environment but we can always control the way we respond to it. So what she was saying was, although I can't necessarily do anything about what's handed to me, I can choose how I deal with it – either by creating stress and pressure, or by remaining calm and present, and working through it in a logical way to the best of my ability. She said this is easier now I know what my core values are, because they allow me to prioritise and ensure my focus and responses remain aligned with the stuff that's important to me. She worked through an example with me to illustrate what she was talking about.

She asked me to think about a situation where I have a deadline to meet and I feel like I don't have enough time to do everything (*Shouldn't be hard*, I thought, *since that's basically the scenario for every day of my life*). She pointed out that while I can't control or change the deadline, I can control the way I respond, and I can decide which way to respond based on my core values. We then worked through two different scenarios, based on how I could react to the same situation.

Scenario one: Create stress and pressure

- *Health* – this will not be served because I'll be adding more stress to my body, unnecessarily zapping myself of energy and throwing all my personal needs out the window.

- *Organisation* – initially I thought I could still serve this cos I always have a plan and strategy to follow at work, but to be honest in this state I tend to become more disordered (especially in my thinking) and my focus switches to purely getting it done, rather than sticking to a structure, which means I wouldn't be serving this value at all. And, of course, any sort of structure or organisation with my personal life would go to shit too.

- *Fun* – I won't have time to seek new opportunities or do anything outside of work because I'll be completely focused on trying to get everything done. In this state I assume it will be very difficult to see the lighter side of things too because I'll be lost in my thoughts and worries.

- *Growth* – I suspect I won't be looking out for learnings or moving forward a whole lot; I'll be stuck in survival mode and just trying to make it through.

- *Connection* – I'll be so consumed with my work I won't make time or headspace for the things and people that matter to me, and I won't be able to be fully present because I'll be lost in my thoughts and worries, which will likely push me even further into stress and overwhelm, and get me completely stuck in this cycle of mind fuckery.

Scenario two: Remain calm and present

- *Health* – my body will be more calm, so I'll be able to stay more energised and focused, which will probably mean I'll get shit done more quickly and efficiently, and still have time to look after some of my own personal needs.

- *Organisation* – I'll be able to maintain the structure in both my work and personal life because I won't be in 'just get it done' mode, which will make me feel a lot more secure (and calm) because I'll know where everything's at. So I'll be able to stay focused on what I need to do and what's important to me, therefore maintaining balance while getting results.

- *Fun* – although I may not physically have time to do fun stuff, with a clearer mind I'll be able to stick to the lighter side of things and not get weighed down with worry, which in turn will make me more energised and motivated.

- *Growth* – I guess I'll be learning by operating differently, and achieving the outcome properly rather than scrambling to just get the bare arse minimums done.

- *Connection* – again, although I may not have physical time, if I'm not consumed by the thoughts and worries I'll have more headspace to keep a line of communication open with the people and things that matter to me. Plus I'll be able to remain more present cos I'll be in practical mode rather than survival mode, so again I'll be able to achieve what I want more quickly and efficiently because I'll be more energised, motivated and confident.

Holy shit – she was absolutely right about how important these bloody values are. Now I can actually see how I can use them in my everyday life to keep me on track and move me forward. I can have clarity in the moment about what serves me best for the long term, which will help to pull me out of the mind fuckery hole I could potentially go down in the short term. And this then means my health and energy are better because I'm not constantly worrying and taking on too much, and putting my body into a constant state of stress (I'll explain more about that in a bit). LIGHTBULB.

Clearly I'm going to have to be consciously competent with all this for quite a while, because it does take some thinking to work through it, but I definitely think it'll be worth putting the work in, exhausting as it may be. I really think it will help me to get the perspective I need to take control of my life and the way I feel once and for all. I still can't believe I haven't known about all this before.

Okay, I'm out. I wanted to write about Steve tonight too cos he's been getting on my nerves, but my brain is too fried after recalling all those things. Ah well, it was good to go over that stuff again. It's funny because now I'm aware of it, I can see that actually a lot of my colleagues must be thinking in the same way, because they're also extremely competitive and rarely satisfied. Who knew? I thought it was only me who thought all this crazy shit. Maybe I am indeed not that unique after all! Night.

September 21st

Okay, just a quick one on Steve before I write about all this physical stuff. I might stick a few things in actually that Ellie gave me on it, because there was quite a lot of info to take in and I don't want to get it wrong. So interesting, though.

Right. Steve. I feel like he has no idea about what's really going on with me. Don't get me wrong, he listens when I talk, but he never seems to be able to give me the right response – he either tries to prob-lem solve everything or just says nothing at all. IT'S SO ANNOYING. And he never starts a conversation and asks how I'm going, even though it must be blindingly obvious when I'm not okay and I need him. He knows I'm no good at talking about my shit, so why can't he help me and make it easier for me? I don't see why I should have to ask him for support anyway – he should know and be proactive about it. I spend my whole life leading others; I don't want to have to do that at home too. It makes me feel like he doesn't value my issues or what's going on with me, like he thinks I'm being oversensitive and I just need to suck it up and get on with it. Well, guess what Steve? I've tried to suck it up for a very long time and that's why I'm in this mess. His lack of appropriate support is actually making me feel quite lonely. All day, every day, I have to have the answers, I have to make the decisions and I have to be the driving force. I have to put on my war paint and make the world think I know what I'm doing and I'm all over it. I can't let anyone see what's really going on, and that gets really bloody lonely at times. So when I don't even feel like Steve's got my back, it makes me feel like I'm well and truly doing it all on my own. I can, of course, do it on my own, that's how I've always rolled, but maybe I'm just over having to do that.

Anyway, I feel a bit better now I've got that out of my brain. I don't know what the answer is. Maybe I'll see if Ellie has any advice next week.

Now, let me tell you all about this physical health/lifestyle stuff. One of the first things Ellie stressed to me in the session was that health is not just diet and exercise. In fact, she reckons they are only a small piece of the health puzzle. I immediately thought, *Awesome – so if I don't go to the gym and eat salad every day, it doesn't actually matter that much. Result.* Apparently, though, the other important components, as well as the physical stuff, are emotional, mental and spiritual. Oh Christ, spiritual. I didn't think Ellie was in to all that tree-hugger shit. That's why I decided to work with her. And that's why I didn't want to work with anyone before now – I hate all that touchy-feely bollocks that life coaches often go on about. Just tell me what to do and I'll do it. I remember when Michelle took me to that workshop where they were talking about finding our inner Goddess, or some shit like that. What a fabulous waste of time that was. I do not have a Goddess inside me, nor do I want to try and find one. I just want to be able to get through the day without relying on caffeine, wear all the clothes from the skinny side of my wardrobe and stop worrying about every little thing. Call me crazy, but I just don't see how a fictional Goddess can get me all of that.

Anyway, before I could go on a rant about this, Ellie put my mind at ease. She shared her experiences from when she hit burnout and had to find her way back to health and happiness. It's so helpful to know that she's been through it too. It turns out she'd had many similar experiences – in fact, she said the time she was taken along to an inner Goddess workshop was a pivotal moment for her. Before that, she'd tried all sorts of different therapies, healings, treatments and even medications, and while some of them had made her feel a bit better, she still wasn't recovering as quickly as she felt she should be. So after she'd found herself in a room full of women screaming at the ceiling and jumping up and down trying to summon their Goddesses, she finally realised it was time to stop spending endless amounts of time and money on all these random solutions, and really get to the bottom of what was going on, and why she'd got to that point in the first place. And that's when she really started to get back on track.

So the key to her turnaround, she said, was when she started to focus on changing her mindset, because she had come to learn that it was indeed this that was driving her body and causing her physical health to decline. She realised that actually true health and wellness is when all four elements of ourselves are aligned – physical, emotional, mental and spiritual. She said the core of the spiritual is really our energy. It's the thing that allows us to get a deeper sense of connection with ourselves and the world, and is the home of our intuition and higher sense of knowing. Mental is concerned with things like our thoughts, beliefs, values and goals, and emotional predominantly refers to our feelings. And, of course, physical is physical. Ellie said the spiritual is kind of like the glue that runs through everything and allows all of these elements to remain aligned. It instils balance by bringing our inner and outer worlds together, and allows us to move from simply thinking and doing, to being. Huh, when she puts it like that, I guess it doesn't sound quite so wanky. She said it will continue to make more sense as we move through the program and peel off more layers.

Anyway, she explained how she had also experienced all the same health issues as me (although hers were supersized compared to mine) – so, again, it seems I'm not unique in all this. The whole 'mind driving your body' thing is totally new to me. I've heard about the 'mind–body connection' in some of those health magazines I read, but I've never fully understood what they're going on about. Usually they just talk about it when they're doing a piece on yoga or meditation, and I'm really not into that so I haven't paid much attention. And I have to be honest – I don't really understand how my mind can create my muffin top. Surely it's the chocolate and wine that does that? But, hey, if I can do something to my mind that allows me to keep eating chocolate and drinking wine and not have a muffin top, I am on board with that. Ellie explained that while the things I eat and drink do have a direct impact on my weight, they are still only behaviours, which are in fact a product of my mind and brain. Apparently, our brains actually have the ability to change, even at my age! In fact, even until the day we die. I thought your brain stopped developing when you became an adult, so I'd figured all hope was lost for me.

Turns out there's a thing called neuroplasticity, which is this ability for the brain to change, re-organise itself and form new neural connections. It does this based on our environment, behaviour, emotions and thoughts, and it all happens through repetition. So what this means is, if we repeatedly do or think something over and over, our brain will physically change to then make that thing a natural part of who we are. During this process, the neural connections that are fired repeatedly to enable the thought or behaviour to happen then fuse together to form new neural pathways – hence the physical change and the birth of the new natural trait. This was blowing my mind (pun intended!) Although I still couldn't understand how I could actually physically change my brain just by doing something consistently.

Ellie gave me some examples to help me get it. She said it's the same scenario as when we exercise – if we just go to the gym once or twice, we're never going to get toned abs and a tight arse. In order to achieve that, we have to go many times and repeat the same exercises, and eventually we start to see the physical changes and achieve the desired results. And if we then stop doing these exercises, eventually the definition will go and the muffin top will return – so if we don't use it, we lose it. This is the same for the brain too – if we give our focus to a new thought or behaviour and think/do it many times, eventually this will be the one we naturally go to, and the old one will start to fade away, because we haven't been using it, so the neural connections will not be as strong.

So basically what this means is, if I identify which thoughts and behaviours will serve my values and goals best, and allow me to be me without restrictions, and I keep my focus on these, my old unhelpful thoughts and behaviours will die out and the new ones will become my natural way of life. She reckons when I operate in this way my body has the ability to function at its peak, meaning it doesn't hold on to fat unnecessarily, meaning the negative impact of eating a bit of chocolate and drinking some wine every now and then is greatly reduced. And as well as these physical benefits, my mindset and drive around eating 'bad' food will be different too, so rather than me feeling like I *need* it, I'll be able to just enjoy it when I want it and not be compelled to eat the fuck out of it. If she can make that happen, she's a freaking genius and I'll name my first born after her (if I have one of course)!!

Apparently, we'll revisit this later when we start to look more deeply into the specific thoughts and behaviours that are holding me back, but for now Ellie wanted to go into more detail about my physical body and its relationship with my mind. She said it's not only my external behaviours that are driven by my mind, but also the internal ones inside my body on a physiological level. She asked me to name some of the things my body was doing at that exact moment without me having to tell it to do so. I had to take a minute to think because I'd never considered this before, but then I came up with things like breathing, moving, blinking. These were all correct, but Ellie took it even deeper than that – our bodies keep our hearts pumping and the blood circulating, they extract tiny micronutrients from our food and transport these to precise parts of the body, and they send in an army of white blood cells to specific areas when we need to fight infections … as well as many, many other important functions that we're never consciously aware of. She wanted me to appreciate just how clever our bodies are, and understand how powerful our subconscious minds are because they make this happen 24/7 without us consciously having to do anything. Woah. Another thing I can't believe I've not thought about before.

She told me that the main priority of our subconscious brain is to maintain our survival, so it will do whatever it needs to do in order to keep us safe, alive and reproducing new life to ensure the future of our species. So when my subconscious brain senses a threat to my survival, it will drive my physical body, thoughts and behaviours in the best way it knows how to protect me. This gets a bit technical and I don't want to get any of it wrong, so I think it's best if I just stick in the info sheet Ellie gave me.

THE STRESS RESPONSE

Although the world has evolved at an incredible pace, and continues to do so, fundamentally our bodies and brains have not. They have not adapted to deal with all the constant stimulation and pressure we're put under, and as a result they think we are regularly in danger. Since the body's main priority is to ensure our survival, it naturally tries to protect us and keep us safe in these situations of stress and constant busyness. Unfortunately, the body does not understand the difference between *real* and *perceived* danger, so even though we may only be stressing about the amount of emails in our inbox, the body thinks it must respond to this stress/danger by preparing us to be able to fight or run away, setting off a chain reaction of biochemical events to ensure our safety. This process is commonly called *fight or flight mode*. Ironically, however, since we are rarely actually fighting or running away, this response is not being utilised appropriately by our bodies, so it's having massive consequences on our long-term health and happiness. The strategies to overcome this response are actually quite simple, but in order to make them a consistent part of our lives, we must first understand their importance.

So let's take a look at what specifically happens inside our bodies when we're stressed. Here's a simple diagram to illustrate the process:

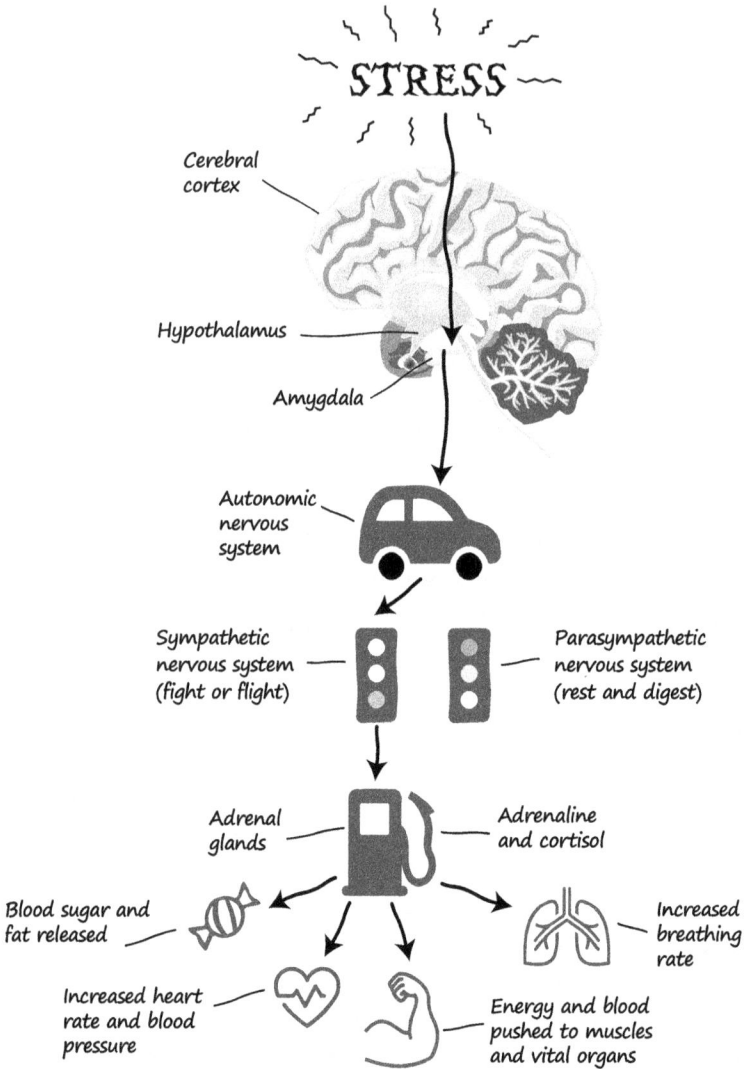

STRESS

Cerebral cortex

Hypothalamus

Amygdala

Autonomic nervous system

Sympathetic nervous system (fight or flight)

Parasympathetic nervous system (rest and digest)

Adrenal glands

Adrenaline and cortisol

Blood sugar and fat released

Increased breathing rate

Increased heart rate and blood pressure

Energy and blood pushed to muscles and vital organs

As soon as the brain senses stress, the amygdala (responsible for emotions, survival instincts and memory) sends a distress signal to the hypothalamus – the command centre of the brain. The hypothalamus controls functions such as releasing hormones, regulating emotional responses, controlling appetite, regulating body temperature, managing sexual behaviour and maintaining daily physiological cycles (the circadian rhythm). It's also responsible for communicating with the rest of the body via the autonomic nervous system (ANS), which controls and regulates unconscious bodily functions such as heart rate, breathing, blood pressure and digestion.

The ANS is the prime system responsible for the stress response and comprises the sympathetic nervous system (SNS) and the parasympathetic nervous system (PNS). The SNS is also known as the 'fight or flight' system, because this is in play when we're stressed. If you think of the ANS as a car, or the driving force of our bodily functions, the SNS would be the accelerator. As you can imagine, if you were to constantly keep your foot on the accelerator of a car, it would eventually run out of fuel and break down – it's the same for our bodies. Ideally, we should regularly apply the brake throughout our daily lives so we can ensure effective fuel consumption and optimal functioning of our bodies. The PNS is our brake. It's also known as our 'rest and digest' system. You may notice when you're completely relaxed, perhaps when you're having a massage, chilling out on the couch with your loved one or in bed on a Sunday morning knowing you don't have to get up for work, that your stomach starts to gurgle? That's because you've applied the brake and allowed your PNS to come out to play, so your digestion is able to do its job and function business as usual. Your body is literally thanking you for giving it a break!

Now let's talk about what happens when this stress response, and your sympathetic nervous system, is triggered.

As mentioned, when stress occurs, the amygdala sends a distress signal to the hypothalamus, which then activates the SNS by sending signals through the ANS to the adrenal glands (two small glands located above the kidneys, responsible for producing a variety of hormones). The main hormones required at times of stress are adrenaline and cortisol, so the adrenal glands pump these out into the bloodstream to enable the body to quickly react and be able to fight or run away from the stress/danger in question. These hormones also trigger the body to release blood sugar (glucose) from its stores into the blood stream for energy, and increase the heart rate and blood pressure to enable the blood and glucose to be pushed around the body, and into the muscles and vital organs required to ensure your survival. The breathing rate is increased to enable more oxygen to reach the brain, while at the same time cortisol enhances the brain's use of glucose, and so it becomes more alert with sharper senses, and is able to react more quickly to the stress/danger in question.

Of course, this reaction is perfect if you are indeed in danger and need to utilise these physical processes; however, when you're merely sat at your desk stressing about all the things you need to do, or in your car trying to negotiate the traffic on the way home from work, you're left with surplus adrenaline and cortisol in your body. In essence, your internal body is all dressed up with nowhere to go. As you can imagine, this causes all sorts of issues with your health and wellbeing, many of which are often accepted as normal or 'just the way it is', but over time can develop into something much more serious – such as adrenal fatigue, depression, obesity, diabetes and heart disease. Let's look into the specific issues in more detail.

As we now know, when the stress response is triggered the body's main priority is to keep you safe, so in order to help you do that as quickly and efficiently as possible it will also slow or even shut down any functions of the body that are not essential in enabling you to fight or run away. The two major systems concerned here are the digestive and reproductive systems, and within these systems, the thyroid and insulin are also vitally important.

Digestion

During times of stress, blood and energy will be diverted from the digestive tract and sent to the areas that require it more, such as your arms, legs and brain. As a result, you may experience physical symptoms like erratic bowel movements (diarrhoea, constipation or both) and unexplained bloating. The integrity of the gut wall can also be compromised, meaning you may develop issues such as irritable bowel syndrome, leaky gut or new food allergies. This stress response can also affect the microbiota of your gut. Your gut microbiota contains tens of trillions of bacteria, each of which play an important role in the development and functioning of your body, both physically and mentally, from regulating your weight to controlling your anxiety and activating your immune system. So a lack, or over-population, of certain types can seriously affect your health, and lead to issues such as obesity, mental health and even cancer.

Inflammation

If the body is unable to excrete waste efficiently, it becomes toxic and inflamed. Inflammation is a defence mechanism of the body and part of the protection process, in which it is attempting to remove harmful stimuli. This, of course, is an extremely beneficial process if you do indeed have an infection or wound that needs repairing, but when inflammation occurs consistently in response to external stimuli like stress, it can lead to many health issues, including:

- problems regulating weight
- poor sleep
- damaged gut
- heart disease
- pulmonary disease
- higher risk of cancer
- damage to joints (rheumatoid arthritis) and bones (osteoporosis)
- skin issues like psoriasis
- gum disease
- depression.

The other main players in the detoxification process are the liver and the lymphatic system, both of which are also affected by stress.

Liver

The liver is our largest internal organ. Its primary functions are:

- filtering toxins and foreign substances from the blood stream, breaking them down and excreting them
- producing bile to break down fats
- regulating sex hormones and eliminating excess hormones
- converting carbohydrates, proteins and fats into energy
- maintaining fluid and electrolyte balance
- storing glycogen (sugars) to be used as fuel.

The liver works 24/7, so if it becomes overloaded and overworked by having to process excess toxicity, it is unable to cleanse your body and ensure you have appropriate energy and overall health. Classic issues of a poorly functioning liver include:

- fatigue (inconsistent energy, sluggish and 'heavy' feeling)
- erratic moods (depression, anger, irritability, brain fog, difficulty making decisions)
- digestive issues (bloating, constipation, indigestion)
- hormone imbalance (heavy, painful and/or irregular periods)
- sugar cravings
- fluid retention
- skin breakouts.

Lymphatic system

This is the largest circulatory system of the body, and the primary detoxifier even before the liver. It's also the main route for transporting the immune system around the body and delivering energy to all of our cells. It is particularly susceptible to stress. Think of this system as the highway of the body – when you're stressed, congestion occurs and these essential vehicles can't get through.

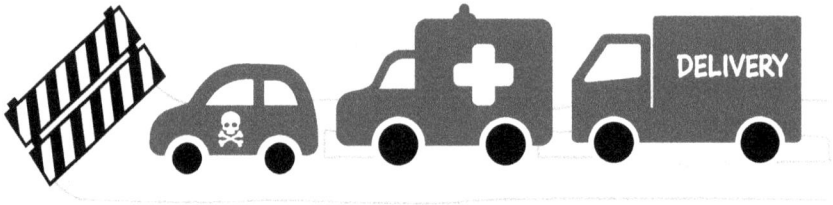

When this back-up occurs consistently, common issues include:

- low energy or fatigue
- weight gain and stubborn fat
- water retention
- brain fog
- digestive issues
- bloating
- cellulite
- muscle stiffness.

Reproductive system

As mentioned previously, when in fight or flight mode the body doesn't deem the reproductive system as essential to its immediate survival. In fact, as far as it's concerned, if danger is present, it most definitely does not want to bring a baby into the world, because it assumes its survival will also be at threat. So the stress hormones block secretion of the main fertility hormone, gonadotropin-releasing hormone (GnRH), which is responsible for releasing the sex hormones. The results include:

- low libido, for both men and women
- low sperm count for men
- failure to ovulate for women.

And, of course, there are also the added issues mentioned earlier with regard to poor regulation and elimination of sex hormones due to an overworked liver, meaning that the liver can't deal with these hormones so it just spits them back out into the bloodstream. As a result, you end up with excess hormones in your system, which can cause painful and irregular periods, PMS and even cause or heighten issues such as Polycystic Ovarian Syndrome (PCOS).

Thyroid and insulin

The thyroid is responsible for releasing hormones that govern metabolism, and is controlled by the pituitary gland. It determines how your body uses energy by regulating vital bodily functions such as:

- heart rate
- breathing
- nervous systems
- body temperature
- cholesterol levels
- body weight
- menstrual cycles
- muscle strength.

The functioning of the thyroid can be affected by issues such as poor liver function, too much oestrogen in the body, infections, iron deficiency, low levels of selenium and iodine, and elevated levels of cortisol. Most of these have been mentioned already with regard to the stress response, so it shows how sensitive the thyroid is to stress and how easily it can be affected by it.

Erratic blood sugar also causes thyroid dysfunction. If blood sugars are consistently high (as a result of this stress response and, of course, a poor diet), the pancreas secretes insulin so that the excess glucose in the blood can be moved into the cells to produce energy. After a while, however, the cells will eventually stop responding to these high and constant levels of insulin (like a defiant teenager who stops listening when they're being told off), so the pancreas will secrete even more to try to get the glucose into the cells (the parent shouts even louder to get the teenager to listen), but eventually insulin resistance occurs (the teenager stomps off and slams the door), and the cells no longer respond normally to insulin. These insulin surges, and the body's inability to deal with them appropriately, causes destruction to the thyroid.

When blood sugars are below normal, the body thinks it's in danger, so it sets off the same stress response already covered here, one of which is to trigger the adrenal glands to release cortisol. When cortisol is repeatedly released in this manner, it suppresses the function of the pituitary gland (which as we know is the controller of the thyroid), so the thyroid becomes dysfunctional.

Both of these scenarios with the blood sugars also have other negative impli-cations, such as tired adrenal glands, inefficient gut functioning, hormonal imbalances, poor detoxification and disrupted metabolism. The effects of these issues to the overall functioning of the body have already been cov-ered, but needless to say they all have a negative impact on the thyroid also.

As with a lot of these stress responses, the thyroid and blood sugars can find themselves in a bit of a 'chicken and egg' situation. While irregular blood sugar levels do indeed affect the thyroid, a dysfunctional thyroid can also affect blood sugar levels. It basically slows everything down – the rate at which the cells uptake the glucose, the response rate of the insulin to increased blood sugar, the clearance of insulin from the blood, glucose absorption and there-fore functionality in the gut, and the response rate of the adrenals.

So, in conclusion, the thyroid is vital for optimal functioning of many of the key systems and processes in the body, and due to its intimate relationship with these systems and its susceptibility to the stress response, it has the potential to cause many health issues when dysfunctional.

So how do all these processes affect your lifestyle and your ability to live the life you want?

Sleep

If your brain thinks you're in danger, it certainly doesn't want to allow you to sleep, because it wants you to be alert and available to fight or run away, so it often prevents you from having a restful and full night's sleep. The stress response can also disrupt your circadian rhythm (your internal clock that cycles your sleepiness and alertness throughout the full 24 hours of your day), so you may find your energy becomes erratic and you're sleepy during the day, and awake or wired at night.

Sleep is the body's opportunity to restore, regenerate and rebuild. The immune system goes to work, the pituitary gland releases growth hormones for mus-cles and tissue repair, and the brain organises all the information from that day allowing optimal memory and cognitive functioning when you're awake. If you're not allowing all of this to happen, your performance, both consciously and unconsciously, will be seriously disrupted. Lack of quality sleep also dis-rupts the hormones ghrelin and leptin, which turn your appetite on and off, and tell the brain what to do with the fat (whether to use it for energy or store it). Clearly if this process is confused, you're going to experience unnecessary hunger, not know when you're full and store fat when it should be burned. Of course, poor sleep then has other knock-on effects like:

- low mood and irritability
- impaired judgement and inability to make good decisions
- greater tendency to eat poorly and avoid exercise
- higher stress because everything is harder – and, therefore, all the responses mentioned occur!

Mood

When you're in the midst of the stress response, the function of your pre-frontal cortex is impaired, which is the home of your higher-level thinking, so you tend to be more reactive and emotional, rather than reflective and logical. In this state, getting a real perspective on a situation and making rational decisions is very difficult, so often this leads to issues such as:

- poor motivation
- irritability
- feeling overwhelmed
- anxiety
- sadness
- depression.

Inevitably, behavioural issues that are detrimental to a healthy lifestyle often follow, including:

- over- or under-eating
- excessive alcohol consumption
- use of drugs
- smoking
- reduced activity and exercise
- isolating self
- procrastination
- self-sabotaging behaviours.

Stress and high amounts of cortisol also disrupt certain neurotransmitters in the brain that are linked to memory and mood. Serotonin and dopamine (sometimes referred to as the 'happy hormones') are the main victims here. When these hormones are low they also effect sleep, energy, appetite and sex drive.

Body weight

Weight control can become the bane of most people's lives (or at least feel like it). When embroiled in the stress response regulating weight can be very difficult. Of course, behavioural traits that come as a response of stress, such as poor eating, lack of exercise and sleep, impaired decision-making and self-sabotage can be major contributors to this; however, all of the physiological processes mentioned in this fact sheet also have a big impact.

Here's a summary on how they specifically affect your weight:

- *Cortisol:* As well as flooding the body with energy, cortisol's role is also to store it so that you have enough fuel to get you through the danger period. Its favourite place to store this energy, which becomes fat, is around the mid-section. This is sometimes referred to as 'Cortisol belly'.

- *Fat hormones:* As discussed in the sleep section, when ghrelin and leptin are disrupted, the body gets confused when it comes to communicating when you're hungry, when you're full, and whether to burn fat or store it. So, often the body becomes extremely inefficient at burning fat because it thinks it needs to hold onto it to protect you and refuses to release it to be utilised as energy.

- *Liver:* When the liver is not functioning properly, it can lead to weight gain because it's unable to break down fats or convert carbohydrates, proteins and fats into energy. It also affects detoxification and mood.

- *Lymphatic system:* Since this system is responsible for delivering energy and nutrients to all areas of your body, poor functioning results in an under-nourished body right down to a cellular level. And as it's also the major detoxifier of the body, poor functioning can lead to a toxic body – which puts more pressure on the liver and increases inflammation.

- *Thyroid:* The primary concern of the thyroid is the metabolism, and the metabolism controls how your body uses energy, so this will have a massive effect on weight if its functioning is impaired. An overactive thyroid (hyperthyroidism) causes weight loss and an underactive thyroid (hypothyroidism) is responsible for stubborn weight retention or weight gain.

- *Reproductive system:* Hormone imbalance, particularly excess oestrogen, in the body can promote weight gain, especially around the mid-section, because it causes more fatty tissue growth, increases sugar cravings, slows the thyroid, causes fluid retention and affects appetite and sleep.

Summary

So, as you can see, consistent and long-term stress can cause many issues in the body and lead to serious illness, as well as influence your thoughts and behaviours, keeping you stuck in the 'stress loop' and ultimately affecting your general level of happiness and fulfilment. Unfortunately, many of these physical symptoms are often addressed with external means, like medication and drastic diets, but the source of the issue (stress and busyness) is largely overlooked. If stress is not managed and the body is not taught to allow the parasympathetic nervous system to come out to play more often, these external 'remedies' will only serve as a bandaid and the underlying problems will persist, and quite possibly show up in a different (or worse) form.

So I urge you, if you believe you are suffering from any of the issues mentioned, to seek expert advice. I recommend trying a more holistic approach with an integrative doctor or naturopath, because they will be able to help you get to the root of the physical problems and treat the cause rather than the symptoms, through natural supplementation and specific dietary and lifestyle advice. And, of course, seek help with the mental side of things, so you can learn techniques to calm your body and brain, and unlock the triggers and elements of your mind that are causing you to respond to situations in a stressful manner. Such elements commonly include perfectionism, the desire to please everyone, fear of failure, fear of not being good enough, fear of not being liked, fear of vulnerability and fear of rejection or abandonment (can you see a theme?!). Ironically, these elements may actually be the very things that prevent you from seeking help and support, but please remember that if nothing changes, nothing changes – so by stepping out into the discomfort in the short-term, you'll be able to create unbelievable comfort (that is, the body and life that you want) in the long term.

I mean, seriously, is this shit mind-blowing or what? Who knew so much could go wrong just as a result of a busy and pressured lifestyle? Like I said, though, it explains A LOT. Clearly my adrenal glands have been working overtime – ha, ironically as a result of me working over-time, and not only physically but mentally too. With my incessant thinking, worrying and stressing I've been constantly telling my brain that I'm in danger, and so now my adrenal glands are knackered, my digestive system has taken unpaid leave, my reproductive system has put up the barricades and my entire body is just one big ball of inflammation. All this time I thought that all the problems with my body and the way I feel were down to physical stuff like my diet, exercise and working hours, but now I see that's just the surface level. I've been trying to make myself better by constantly changing all this external crap, but that hasn't allowed me to get to the source of the issue, and so I've just been going round in circles. I see now that if I want to really get on top of this and create proper change, I need to work from the inside out – not the outside in.

I'm even beginning to wonder about this medication I'm on from the doctor, and if they've diagnosed me correctly. Is it actually just stress that's given me a larger than average 'girth' and made my PCOS symptoms go crazy?? All the things mentioned in Ellie's info sheet would certainly suggest that. Or maybe it started that way and now I really do have an illness? But I haven't been doing anything to try and calm my body down, I've just been smashing those pills the doctor gave me, so I wonder if I'm just putting a bandaid on my situation like the information said? But how the fuck do you calm your body down and put your foot on the brake when there's so much to freaking do?! Along with the tips from my previous sessions, Ellie did give me some other strategies to help with this. I'll talk about them later, but I have to say, they just seem so simple I'm not convinced they'll actually work, and be able to undo all this damage I've clearly done to myself.

Anyhoo, I'm off out for dinner with Steve tonight so I better shut up – I need to give myself enough time to change outfits at least three times (which seems to be standard procedure now). Chat soon.

September 22nd

Right, where was I? Ah yes, the physical stuff. First Ellie wanted to talk to me about adding another expert to my support team. She said that she can help me to calm the body and get to the source of why I'm experiencing these things, and help me to make changes to improve them and prevent them from happening again, but we also need to address the actual physiology and give it a helping hand to restore itself as quickly as possible. As her info sheet suggests, she recommended that I see a naturopath or integrative doctor, who will be able to look at me from a more holistic point of view, and diagnose any sub-clinical conditions that may be going on, which won't necessarily have been picked up by the standard blood tests. According to Ellie, with a combination of the right diagnosis, natural supplementation, and the mindset and behavioural changes we'll be making, I'll be able to accelerate my results and feel better quicker. Let's bloody do that then, I said – we know how much of a fan I am of quick results! I must remember to make an appointment with the naturopath actually – Ellie gave me the number of someone to try, so I may as well start there.

So next we took a look at my weekly tracker. This was a worksheet Ellie had given to me the week before and asked me to complete every day between our sessions. I have to admit, I forgot to fill it in for most of the week, so I just did my best to remember what I'd done before I spoke with her. I'll stick it in here, but basically the purpose was to get an idea of what I'm currently doing in terms of my lifestyle, and how that's making me feel. I've filled in things like this before, but I've never had to rate how it's affecting my daily levels of energy, stress and mood. That bit was super-interesting. Sadly last week was a bit all over the place as I had quite a few meetings, the awards night and then that emergency catch up with Michelle (which turned into a bit of a boozy and bad eating one), so I was a bit embarrassed to show the tracker to Ellie.

Day	Eating	Activity	Sleep (hours)	Working (hours)	Stress I = Super chilled IO = Out of control	Mood I = Rock bottom IO = On top of world	Energy I = Buggered IO = Buzzing	Physical symptoms
Monday	Bircher muesli, apple, chicken salad, wrap with peanut butter, salmon and veggies, yoghurt	None	7.5 ☺	10	5	6	6	
Tuesday	Bircher muesli, banana, tuna salad, wrap with peanut butter, apple, ham wrap	None	6.5	10.5	6	6	6	
Wednesday	No breakfast, croissant, 3 small sandwiches, muffin, ham wrap, chocolate bar	None	6	11.5	8	4	4	Really bloated in the afternoon, couldn't sleep
Thursday	No breakfast, banana bread, ham salad, apple, 5 lollies, pre-packed chicken salad from supermarket (which was disgusting), fun size choc bar	None	6.5	10	8	4	3	Felt really irritable all day, and really bloated again in afternoon

Day	Eating	Activity	Sleep (hours)	Working (hours)	Stress 1 = Super chilled 10 = Out of control	Mood 1 = Rock bottom 10 = On top of world	Energy 1 = Buggered 10 = Buzzing	Physical symptoms
Friday	Apple, yoghurt, chicken salad wrap, banana, lots of canapes and a few glasses of wine ☺	None (although I did dance a little bit at the end of the night – does that count?!)	7	16 – if you count the awards night	7	6	4	Found it really difficult to wake up this morning, needed an extra coffee to get through the day
Saturday	Buckwheat pancakes at café, banana smoothie, ham wrap, lots of Thai food and wine, gelato	Bit of a walk along the coast after breakfast	8	2.5 – I had a couple of bits I needed to get finished for next week	5	7	4	A little bit dusty from the wine last night and quite bloated all day
Sunday	Bacon sandwich, mixed berry smoothie, peanut butter wrap, 4 fun size chocolate bars, pizza, yogurt	None	10 – well I was in bed for that long but probably only slept about 6	0 ☺	5	5	4	Still bloody bloated, and definitely hungover today

Even just a quick look at it shows where I'm going wrong. The start of the week wasn't bad – although, to be honest, I was trying extra hard to be good cos I knew Ellie would be looking at this. And, okay, when I say 'the start of the week', I mean just Monday and some of Tuesday. ☺ Wednesday was back-to-back meetings, hence my low energy and high stress, and then after the awards night and my night with Michelle it really started to go downhill. Oh well, at least it's a bit more realistic than it would have been if I'd managed to stay good all week. Ellie pointed me towards some info sheets online about general healthy eating, which were super-helpful. We then created an easy weekly plan for me to try. Basically she said, for now, let's just try to get me eating real whole food consistently, then we can make tweaks if we need to once I'm in that habit, or if the naturopath recommends something specific. So I just need to remember to make my meals up of fresh veggies, good protein, good fats and low-GI carbs. Right-o, so WTF are good fats and low-GI carbs, then? I thought all fats were bad, and when trying to lose weight carbs are the devil? Ellie pointed me back to the info sheet that explains everything, so I won't bother writing about it here too. But basically it talks all about the importance of a varied diet and why certain carbs and fats are actually helpful, and indeed essential, for our overall wellbeing and achieving our ideal weight. She also asked me to make a shift with my mindset. She said that at this moment in time our biggest priority is to get me healthy – to get me out of this stress response, and restore normal functioning throughout all areas of my physical body. Until we do that, weight loss is going to continue to be difficult. As my body begins to calm down and get back to operating business as usual, though, my weight will naturally start to drop because my body doesn't need to cling onto it anymore to use for survival, and the fat can be processed efficiently. I know that sounds excellent in theory, but for someone who's been on a diet for as long as I can remember, this could prove to be the most difficult thing Ellie's asked me to do. I'll give it a go, though. I guess as long as weight loss does happen, that's the main thing. And it's painfully clear now why I've failed so epically with my diets and exercise plans, so why the hell would I continue to starve myself or eat tuna out of a can like a savage beast if I don't have to?

So here's my plan for this week. I like that it includes some of the same meals throughout the week, so I actually don't have to cook as much and can just re-heat it when I want it. Also Ellie said, if I find this is all too much at the moment I can have the meal deliveries as a fall-back, but we'll just make sure we choose a company that is most aligned to what I want to achieve (i.e. healthy eating and not weight loss). Anyway, I'd like to give this a crack, so I'm going to the supermarket with Steve tomorrow to buy a heap of stuff. Bless him – he's said he'll help me cook it all too, to try and make it easier for me (which is handy because I'd already put that on my behaviour goals list!). I did mention it wouldn't actually do him any harm to be a bit healthier as well, so he's going to follow this with me for a bit – although he made it very clear that under no circumstances is he willing to give up his after-dinner fun size chocolate bar treat! It's so cute how happy such simple things make him.

Day	Breakfast	Lunch	Dinner
Monday	45g oats made with milk/water, 2 tablespoons shredded coconut and 150g mixed berries	Colourful salad made with whatever salad/ vegetables you like, 100g lean meat or fish, handful of mixed seeds and ½ cup quinoa	Thai green curry (chicken or prawn) with cauliflower rice
Tuesday	½ small avocado, tomato and egg or smoked salmon and spinach on 2 slices rye or gluten free bread	Chilli con carne with ½ cup brown rice	Soup – any flavour you like, ideally with lots of vegetables

Day	Breakfast	Lunch	Dinner
Wednesday	Green smoothie – I cup spinach, I small cucumber, ½ banana, I cup blueberries, ½ small avocado, 200ml almond milk or coconut water	Thai green curry with ½ cup brown rice	Stir-fry with whatever vegetables you like, 120g lean meat or fish and handful cashew nuts – use tamari, fresh garlic, chilli, ginger and lime juice for sauce
Thursday	½ small avocado, tomato and egg or smoked salmon and spinach on 2 slices rye or gluten free bread	Colourful salad	Soup
Friday	45g oats made with milk/water, 2 tablespoons shredded coconut and 150g mixed berries	Chilli con carne with ½ cup brown rice	Stir-fry
Saturday	Green smoothie	½ small avocado, tomato and egg or smoked salmon and spinach on 2 slices rye or gluten free bread	Dinner out
Sunday	Breakfast out	Soup	Steak with vegetables and roasted pumpkin

Snacks (if required): Handful raw nuts, I piece of fruit, vegetable sticks with ½ cup hummus, I tablespoon nut butter

My next big question was about exercise, and I asked Ellie if I should join another bootcamp or maybe look for a personal trainer. She reminded me of the old story of the tortoise and the hare, and said that the notion of slow and steady wins the race is critical as far as exercise is concerned at the moment. She explained that exercise is actually perceived as a stress by the body, so when we do it at a high intensity or for a long period of time, cortisol is released just as it is in the stress response. Usually in a normal functioning body, this doesn't pose a problem because the body can deal with the cortisol appropriately, but when it's already under constant stress and releasing too much cortisol, hard exercise is likely to be adding fuel to the fire and making matters worse. So, for now, my focus needs to be on calming the body and consistently communicating to it that it's not in danger and it doesn't need to be in fight or flight mode.

To ease me into it Ellie has recommended I just go for walks this week. We agreed that my bare arse minimum would be three walks, and if I can manage more, that's a bonus. I'm 95 per cent sure that if I just walk for my exercise I'll become morbidly obese, but I've promised to commit to this so I'll just keep an eye on my weight and if it starts to go up I'll have a word with her. She did mention the dreaded 'Y' word as well … yoga. I told her about my previous experience and said I'd vowed never to go again, but then she did put forward a pretty good case for giving it another crack. She said that yoga is a great way to calm the body, because it promotes deep breathing practices and being present in the moment – two things essential for restoring normality in my body. She recommended I try a different form of practice called yin, or restorative yoga, that's much slower paced and very much focused on relaxation and letting go. She said it's perfect for getting the parasympathetic nervous system to come out to play – in other words, applying that brake to my life and getting myself out of this constant survival and go, go, go mode. Apparently you hold the poses for longer and they're all supported with either the floor or equipment, so hopefully if I do try it, I shouldn't embarrass myself by falling over while sat down or something – although I'm sure I'll find a way. She said to just focus on the walks for now, but she wanted to give me a heads up about the yoga so I can mentally prepare myself, and urged me to have a look around for some of these restorative classes. I'm sure Michelle will be able to point me in the right direction.

Right, so I've said my three walks will be on Tuesday, Friday and Sunday. Ellie wanted me to schedule them then and there so I could give myself a greater chance of getting them done. She said:

What gets scheduled gets done

I swear she has a saying for everything!! More bloody non-negotiables! I am looking forward to it, though – I really do need to get moving again, and I need the accountability to make me do it. I think that's the good thing about having this support actually, it's a constant reminder to do the things that I know I should do but just don't prioritise. And it's nice to have someone to celebrate my little successes with too. It kind of makes me wonder if I would have ended up in such a shitty place if I'd had a personal support network along the way. Although God only knows where you'd find one of those. As Michelle rightly said, we women always just struggle through on our own.

Anyway, that's enough for today. These entries seem to be getting rather long. I feel a bit like a kid with a new toy though – I'm learning so many things and it's all so interesting, I just can't help but go on and on about it!

September 23rd

Did my walk today – yeah, baby! Steve came along too, so I managed to kill two non-negotiables with one stone. ☺ Talking of non-negotiables, I set a few more during my lifestyle session. These are what I was talking about earlier – the strategies that will allow me to put my foot on the brake and communicate throughout the day to my body that I'm not in danger, and in the process calm everything down and even energise myself. Ellie described these things as 'steps back'. At first I thought she was mental for even suggesting that I 'step back' while I'm at work – has she not listened to anything I've been saying? I don't have time to pee most days, so how the hell can I find time to 'step back'. She promptly asked me to recite my values. 'Health, connection, fun, growth, organisation.' Before she had the chance to open her mouth again, though, I jumped in and said, 'Okay, okay! I get it. Stepping back serves me and my values more than pushing forward. Now tell me how the hell to do it!' We had a little giggle at my stroppy teenager moment. At least we know it's getting through to me, though, even if I was trying to resist it.

So Ellie started describing this notion of stepping back by asking me to think of a bow and arrow. She talked about how the purpose of the bow is to shoot the arrow as far forward as you can in order to hit the target. To do that, though, you have to draw the arrow back in the opposite direction to where you want it to go. This gives the arrow the momentum it needs to reach the target as quickly and efficiently as possible. If you don't take it in the opposite direction, you have to keep pushing it forward a little bit at a time and picking it up off the floor in between each go. The arrow might eventually get to the target, but it's going to take a long time and require a lot of effort. This is exactly what we need to do in our lives. Taking these little steps back communicates to the body that all is well and we're not in danger – because if we were, we'd just have to keep on pushing and running – so it powers us up and gives us momentum to move forward effectively. I'm not sure this could make more sense if it tried. I am that second arrow – I've been pushing forward and pushing forward, but still I'm not where I want to be. Ellie said the best way to step back is to do something that aligns well with some or all of my values. That way, it'll make me feel good right at my core, which again wouldn't be possible if I was indeed in danger, so it will give me an even deeper sense of calm. She had a few suggestions that she said work well for most people. I'll write down a quick summary of them here.

Breathe

Apparently most of us don't actually breathe effectively most of the time. Our breaths tend to be quite shallow and largely in our chest. She likened this to those bellows you use to get air into a fire – it's like only pressing them halfway together, which, as you can imagine, only pumps half the amount of air into the fire, so it doesn't burn as brightly. Our bodies are the same. Deep (Ellie also called it diaphragmatic) breathing pumps oxygen in and carbon dioxide out of the body much more effectively, so our inner fire burns more brightly and we enjoy benefits such as a lower heart rate, decreased blood pressure, increased energy, more relaxed muscles and decreased stress. Slow, deep, diaphragmatic breathing is a great way to communicate to the brain that you're not in danger, because if there was indeed a danger present, slowing down would be the last thing on your mind.

We did a few rounds so she could guide me through it. I liked this process, actually, and it eased me into it nicely. Let me see if I can remember the steps:

1. Get comfortable and close your eyes. At first, just watch your current breathing, without changing anything.

   • Observe where you're breathing – is it in your chest, your belly, the front of your body or the back?

   • Observe if you're breathing in and out through your mouth or your nose.

   • Observe if you're breathing quickly or slowly.

2. Next take your awareness to your torso – from the pit of your belly to your chest, and everything in between.

   • As you breathe in, focus on expanding your whole torso to the front, sides and back.

   • As you breathe out, allow it all to contract back in.

3. Now start to count in your head how long it takes for you to breathe in and out – perhaps it's three, four or five counts. The number doesn't matter but ensure the count is the same for the in and out breath.

4. Then start to extend the count. Maybe just by one or two – again, it doesn't matter just as long as the length is the same for the in and out breath.

5. Continue with these slow breaths into your entire torso for as long as you have allowed yourself and, when you're ready, open

your eyes slowly and give yourself a moment to just be, and take it all in before you get up.

I swear I felt my whole body relax within the first minute. I guess slowing down properly is so alien to it, once I did have a go it was like HELL, YEAH! Don't get me wrong – I was still thinking about everything while I was doing it – but it just didn't feel quite so hectic in that moment, which was nice.

As Ellie rightly said, breathing is the easiest, quickest and cheapest way for me to communicate calm to my body. It's always accessible to me and I can do it anywhere, any time. She said it can be my go-to when I feel myself getting stressed, tired or anxious, but also I should have dedicated times throughout the day when I do it proactively, so I can get ahead of the game and accumulate some calm in my 'calm bank'. She also advised me that the toilet can be a great place to do this during the day, cos I'm guaranteed not to get disturbed in there! I like that idea, but I'll just have to make sure no-one sees me go in, so they don't start to wonder why I've been in there so long – I'm sure breathing wouldn't be the first idea in their mind! So I've decided to sit and do 10 breaths every day when I first get up in the morning, at lunch time before I eat and before I go to bed.

Meditation

Here she goes again with her tree-hugger shit, I thought when Ellie first mentioned this one to me. I tried meditation in the past when work got someone in to try to teach us, but it just made me more anxious. It was the same as those stupid five minutes at the end of that yoga session – all the thoughts in the world came into my brain as soon as I closed my eyes, so rather than feeling like I was floating calmly down a gently flowing river, I felt like I was careering down a set of rapids and being dragged under by the force of the angry waves. Not pleasant.

Anyway, again she said that I didn't have to worry about it right now but it was something to think about for the future. She said, as well as being the ultimate calming tool for my body, meditation also has many other important benefits – such as improved emotional health, decreased inflammation, better sleep, decreased blood pressure, greater pain control, enhanced concentration, better focus and memory, and increased cognitive functioning. Apparently studies have shown that it actually decreases your brain wave activity, so it gives the brain a moment to process everything that's going on inside it, as it does when you sleep, meaning it's less busy and cluttered, and able to function more efficiently.

Well, when she puts it like that, maybe it might be worth a go. Ha! I feel like that teenager again – I know doing my homework will make my life easier and set me up better for the future, but I still want to resist doing it because it's hard and I can't be the best at it immediately. Ellie reminded me again of the stages of learning, and that the only way I'll ever make something a natural and unconscious behaviour is to ride out the uncomfortableness of the consciously competent phase, which can be frustrating and take a bit of time – but only in the short term. After I make it through that, I get to reap the benefits for the long term. She said to always keep in mind that:

Uncomfortableness isn't permanent

She said that this is particularly important to remember when it comes to my health and lifestyle, because we ladies typically have a lot of emotion wrapped up with our bodies and what we do to them, so we need to rewire quite a few pathways in our brains to embed the right routines and habits that will give us the health and lifestyle we really want in the long term – that is to say, to live better for longer. I hear what she's saying – so far to date I've always focused my 'health' efforts on trying to be thin, but I'm starting to see that ultimately it's actually making me more unhealthy. As Ellie rightly pointed out, by continually doing these fad diet and exercise programs, and eating 'diet' food (like processed meats, protein bars and nothing but cans of tuna) with absolutely no nutritional value, all I've been doing is confusing the hell out of my body and starving it of proper nutriment. What a dumb-arse. And this could quite possibly result in me dying earlier or at least living out my latter days in poor health with a poor quality of life. I always say I'm afraid of failure, but if I got to that point and I knew I could have done something about it, I think that would be the biggest failure of all. I don't want to rely on food as my emotional crutch any more, and I don't want to be constantly consumed by thoughts of how I look or how much better other people look compared to me. I've had enough. I just need to remember all this when I get impatient about being consciously competent, and remind myself that the long-term game is the one that's worth playing. Ellie suggested I find an image of something that represents that long-term game to me, something that reminds me of how good it feels to feel good, so I can get that feeling every time I look at it and give myself a kick up the arse to do what I need to do to get it. I've gone with this:

I don't know who these people are but when I look at them I get a lovely warm feeling in my heart. I want to be like them when I grow up – active, in love and still young at heart with my little backpack! Yeah, this definitely makes me want to get my shit together so I can enjoy my life for as long as possible. I'm going to put it on the fridge next to my values.

Okay, so I've agreed to commit to doing my three breathing sessions this week, and then next week I'll download a meditation app and think about swapping it in for the morning session. Christ, before long I'm going to have a wardrobe comprised exclusively of stretchy pants and ankle bracelets, and a house full of incense sticks and crystals!

Set boundaries

Ellie asked me to think about my day and identify which things cause me particular stress, anxiety, worries and racing thoughts, and zap me of my energy. Hmmmm, where do I begin? I guess one big one is when I feel like I can't get anything done because I'm constantly being interrupted by my team with questions or problems. I know managing them is a major part of my role, but I feel really inefficient when my days are like this because I don't get the opportunity to focus on a task and get it done as quickly as I know I could if I wasn't disrupted. Ellie asked, of all the things they come to me with, what proportion of them have to be dealt with immediately, because if they're not, bad things will happen? Well, realistically, most of the time nothing bad will happen if it's not done immediately, but it may hold someone up and prevent them from getting on with their work. Ellie then asked what happens if I'm in meetings all day and so not around to help them. Good question. They ask someone else or just wait for me to come back, I suppose.

So then Ellie said, 'What would happen if you had a certain time each day where the team knew they couldn't disturb you? What if you had two hours of power each morning, where you could just get your head down without distraction – would that be helpful?' Hell yes it would, but I'd feel bad for not being there for the team. To help with this, Ellie taught me this concept of pre-framing that she said they use in the coaching world – so basically all you do is let people know what's going on before it happens, and allow an open discussion about it to take place if necessary. So I can speak to the team and say to them that every day, the time between 8.30 am and 10.30 am is my two hours of power to get shit done, so please don't disturb me unless it's an absolute emergency. Apparently, the key to a successful pre-frame is to get everyone involved to agree to the conditions before it happens, and give them the opportunity to raise any concerns or objections. So then once all issues are dealt with, and everyone knows the conditions and they all agree, it's game on. Plus I get a better buy in, because people feel like they're involved in the process and not simply being told. It makes a lot of sense, and sounds fairly simple, so I've agreed to give it a go. It could actually come in quite handy for a lot of things – I wonder if I could pre-frame Steve to wash my car this weekend?!

I guess just the general consistency of constantly doing shit gets me down too. I feel like as soon as my eyes open until the time I go to bed, I'm on. Sometimes I can't even remember what I've done in my day – I know I've been doing stuff all day but it gets difficult to define the individual tasks because they all blend in to one. Ellie asked me what I do for my lunch break. I believe 'Al desko' is the term! Of course I eat at my desk while I work most days, or on the run in between meetings if I'm back to back – as if she even needed to ask. I knew where she was heading, though – giving myself an actual lunch break will allow me to step back, take a break from all the shit, and then get momentum for the afternoon. Sometimes that's just not possible, though – often I might actually be in a meeting over lunch time so of course I can't tell them I need to stop and take a step back; I'd never live that down. Although I think most of them could probably do with it too.

Ellie said, even though we're setting boundaries that need to be kept to, it's important to remember that I'm in control of them so I can shift the posts a little bit if I need to – they're firm but not rigid. So we set a boundary that if I'm in a meeting and need to work through lunch, I can give myself a moment elsewhere in my day – even if that moment is just an extended toilet break to do a few deep breaths. And for the days that I am indeed just in the office and I do have control over what I do, I can remove myself from my desk and give myself the time to eat lunch without distractions. Seems fair.

Ellie also pointed out that another critical moment in my day for taking a break from the shit is between work and home. It's important that I create a clear definition between the end of my working day and my personal time – otherwise, the shit just carries through and it affects the quality of my down time. She's right you know – most of the time when I'm irritable with Steve at night it's because I'm still thinking about work, or carrying the residual stress and pressure from the day. And when I'm like that I tend to eat more bad things or feel like I need a glass of wine to chill out, and generally I just collapse on the couch because I can't be bothered to do anything else. According to Ellie this is a typical scenario for a lot of people, but it can easily be changed with a simple non-negotiable step back before I set foot into the house after work. She said what this step does is signify to my brain that the working day is done, so it can park everything to do with that at the front door and leave it to be picked back up again in the morning … if it needs to. I guess it's kind of like the school bell in a way – as kids, we knew school was over when we heard the bell ring, and so our brains immediately switched into 'play' mode. Oooh yeah, how good would that be? To be able to switch into play mode before I got home – I know Steve would be happy with that. We'd already talked about calling a friend on the way home, so that's a good way to break the day, but Ellie suggested I do something specific just before I walk in the door to trigger the play mode, just like the school bell. I decided to make up a fun little rhyme that I can say as I approach the door:

'Three, two, one … my working day is done.'

He, he; I like that – it kind of makes me feel like a little child too. That's perfect to get me into play mode!

Thinking about it, it also really stresses me out when I can't get to sleep at night – I wasn't sure if that counted. Ellie was quick to reassure me it did, and asked me to describe my night-time routine. That didn't take long. I fall into bed, have a little look through Instagram and Facebook, maybe watch something on Netflix, check my emails one last time and then try not to yell at Steve for breathing. She asked me how I felt this was working for me, in terms of setting me up for a good night's sleep. Ha! Obviously not very well, since I sleep badly pretty much every night. She reminded me of the fundamental part of the stress response – that it happens when our brains are constantly on the go and never switching off. So if I'm looking through social media (which will inevitably spark all sorts of thoughts in my brain as I compare myself to all the people I see on there and how much better their lives are than mine) and getting involved in something on TV or Netflix, I'll be keeping my mind in that stimulated state – so the brain will naturally want to keep me in fight or flight mode and on alert, so I can protect myself from the danger that the brain thinks is present.

Apparently there's also another matter. All these pieces of technology contain a blue light, which kills melatonin – the hormone that's released to make you less alert and help you go to sleep. So, basically, by using my phone and laptop right before bedtime, I'm fucking up any chance I may have for a good night's sleep. I think Steve did try telling me something similar a while ago, actually. I hate it when he's bloody right! So we set a boundary that I wouldn't use technology thirty minutes before bedtime. We decided that would be a perfect time for me to do my breathing anyway, so it would work out well. She said that getting into a regular night-time routine will really help with my sleep, because the body can get into a rhythm (and restore normal functioning of my circadian rhythm), so trying to go to bed and get up at a similar time every day will be ideal. And, on that, she recommends I set a little boundary to not look at my phone as soon as I wake up either, because that will immediately over-stimulate my brain and kick me into fight or flight mode before I've even wiped the sleepy dust from my eyes. Ideally, I'd wait until after breakfast so I can eat my first meal of the day in a calm state, but if that's too terrifying she said I can start by just committing to waiting until I've had my morning wee and done my breathing. Ok, that I can do.

Do what I love

This one is easy because I've already got a big old list of what I love from my initial mind map during the values stuff. Well, it's easy to know what to do but I guess the harder part is actually doing it, right? As Ellie said, if I'm doing something that makes me happy and feel good, my brain will assume that everything's okay and there's no danger present, because if there was I'd have to be fighting it or getting the hell out of there. So making sure I specifically do something that brings me joy on a regular basis, ideally daily, will be a fun way to tease my parasympathetic nervous system out to play and allow my body to calm down.

Initially, I was a bit overwhelmed by the idea of doing something every day, but when we looked back at my mind map we realised that it's really not that hard – we'd already talked about listening to some music while I get ready for work, or I can pop my headphones on during the day and rock out to a tune. I can spend five minutes on an arrow word puzzle for a cheeky morning tea step back. And I can even have a little afternoon break by looking at some videos of puppies on the internet! I know, that all seems so stupid but, actually, even thinking about it makes me feel happy and calmer.

Eat well and eat calm

I have my plan for eating so that bit's sorted, but Ellie said the biggie for me is to ensure I'm in as calm a state as possible when I eat. As her info sheet said, when you're in fight or flight mode, your body shuts your digestion down, so I certainly don't want that to be in play when I'm putting food into it. That's why my lunch breaks are so import-ant. She recommended I do a few deep breaths before I start (which is fine cos I've already set that as one of my non-negotiable breathing times) and I put away my phone and laptop, and give all my attention to my eating. She talked about 'mindful eating', which is basically just another way of saying be present. To do it, I focus on all the details of what I'm doing – what the food looks and smells like, how the tex-tures feel in my mouth, even how many times I have to chew it before it's ready to swallow. Sounds a bit wanky but seems simple enough, although I suspect in practice I'll probably get incredibly distracted. Ellie told me not to worry if that happens, and just to make sure that once I notice I've been distracted to return my attention back to the eating – eventually, I'll be able to go longer and longer without distractions.

Move according to what I need

I've already covered what Ellie told me about exercise being a stress on the body, so I understand it's important that I listen to my body and do what it needs, rather than pushing through and doing what I think I 'should' do. She said that by knowing my values and goals, I have a much better insight into what I fundamentally need and what makes me tick, so this will make it easier to tune into my body and understand what it's telling me. She reminded me of what she said about the subconscious brain and how this keeps our bodies functioning without us even being aware of it. She told me that it stores an incredible amount of information and so it always knows what's going on in every part of our body. Subsequently, one of the major outcomes we're looking to achieve with this whole process is to re-align my mind and body, so the channels of communication will be more open and I will always know what to do in order to serve myself and my body best at any given time. She said this is where the spiritual element comes into play – it's all about 'feeling' and 'knowing', and trusting that my body will tell me what I need to know. Ellie advised me to keep documenting what I'm doing and how it's making me feel, and then I can look for patterns to help me decode the messages and start talking the same language as my body again. So, for now, I'll keep using my weekly tracker so I can make sure I record the right information and I've got a standardised format to help me see the patterns more easily – oooh my organisation value is LOVING this plan! And I've already set my non-negotiable for walks this week as my movement, so let's see what my body says to that!

Okay, so my steps back to get me going will be:

1. A breathing session every morning, lunch time and night.

2. Two hours of power every morning between 8.30 am and 10.30 am.

3. Eat lunch away from my desk when not in meetings.

4. Eat calm – breathe before I start and eat mindfully.

5. No technology thirty minutes before bed.

6. Say my little rhyme before I walk in the house at night: 'Three, two, one … my working day is done'.

7. Have two times in the day where I do something simple that I love (quick puzzle, look at puppies, go for a wander, call a friend, listen to a tune).

8. Document daily what I'm doing and how I feel in my weekly tracker.

Seems a lot, but as Ellie pointed out they're all pretty easy to slot into my day, so the hardest part will just be remembering it all. I've set little reminders in my phone to sort that issue out, so I literally couldn't have made it easier for myself to succeed. I can totally bloody do this … I think.

September 25th

Okay, so it's Tuesday – which means I've had two days of doing all these things since I planned them out at the weekend. Yesterday morning I ended up snoozing for too long so missed my morning breathing session, and I had to work through lunch to meet a deadline, but I did manage to find a '90s smash hits playlist on Spotify and listen to a bit of Ace of Base on the way home, and I did manage to do my evening breathing session instead of trolling on social media. Ah, and my end of the working day rhyme worked a treat – I had to say it a couple of times once I'd actually entered the house too cos I found myself getting consumed by work thoughts again but, each time I said it, it was like I gave myself a mental kick up the butt and came right back to the present moment. It felt a bit like I was part of a hypnotist act. You know when they click their fingers and say 'Three, two, one, you're back in the room', and the subject wakes up – that's what my rhyme did for me. As soon as I said it, I woke up from my stressed state and came back into the room. Although I still sat on the couch and didn't do much for the entire evening, I did feel more engaged and connected with Steve. I think I even found his breathing slightly less annoying last night, and I managed to drop off to sleep slightly quicker, so maybe that was the result of me calming myself down? We'll see if it happens again tonight or if that was just a fluke.

Ah, just as a quick aside – I spoke to Ellie about Steve and how he was annoying me by not knowing how to give me what I need emotionally. I'd thought about it a bit more and realised it is indeed that emotional side of things where he's letting me down – he's great at physically doing things for me, and he will engage to a certain level when I initiate something (which, let's face it, isn't very often), but a lot of the time it feels like he just doesn't get me on that deeper level. As Ellie pointed out, I haven't really got myself on that deeper level until very recently, so perhaps I was being a little hard on Steve and setting my expectations a little too high. She said the way we all operate and have our needs met are very different, and usually we can't figure that out on our own … we need our partner to show and teach us. So this was a perfect opportunity for me to remember those NLP pre-suppositions she'd taught me, and to respect Steve's version of the world and appreciate that he's doing his best with the resources he has. So if I want him to do something differently or see the world differently, I need to offer him some more resources to enable him to do so. In short, I need to teach him how to give me what I need.

Hmmm, maybe I should hold off on that for a moment then, since I'm only just getting to grips on that myself. It still does feel like another thing to add to my to-do list, though – but when I said that, Ellie promptly reminded me of the stages of learning, and said the situation is exactly the same for Steve. At the moment, he's unconsciously incompetent because he doesn't even know he doesn't know how to meet my emotional needs, so by me being open with him and pre-framing some expectations that allow me to remind him what to do when I need to, eventually I can move him to conscious and then unconscious competence – I just need to put in a bit of work initially to reach that ideal place. Although she did also say it's worth pointing out that he'll possibly never reach unconscious competence with some things, so the sooner I make my peace with that the sooner I can ease some of the frustrations I have around this! She said when we get to the communication part of the framework she'll share with me a good process I can go through with Steve that will help us both to understand each other within the relationship at a deeper level, so I'll hold off on saying anything until we've gone through that.

Anyway, where was I? Ah yes, today was a better day. I managed to get my morning breathing session in, although I had to rush about straight after to get out the door in time (which I'm not supposed to do), but I've set my alarm for five minutes earlier tomorrow, so I can do my breathing and still fit my snooze in – I'm just not ready to give that up yet. My two hours of power have been good so far – I've actually got loads done in that time so it sets me up really nicely and motivates me for the rest of the day. The team seem to have responded really well to it, too. I muddled my way through the whole pre-framing thing with them, and no-one had any objections, so we all just agreed and got stuck into it. Rob did forget though, and came into my office at around 10.00 am, but as I looked up at him he just went, 'Oh shit, you're still in your two hours of power – I'll come back in a bit.' How good is that?! I'm not sure if I gave him a death stare or if he was just being considerate – either way it worked. ☺

I also managed to take ten minutes for a lunch break. I went and sat in the kitchen, but I think I'll have to find somewhere else in future – although I didn't have my phone or laptop to distract me, apparently personal space is not a thing in the kitchen so I had people talking to me the whole time and it was stressing me out. The food Steve and I prepared has been pretty good, though – it's nice to not have to think about what I'm going to eat and go through the mental trauma of should I have something good or bad. I'd told Steve about the looking at puppies thing (I thought he'd find that funny), so he texted me a puppy compilation video at 3 pm to help me remember to take a break – he's so cute. It did the job nicely – 3 pm is usually my worst time of day cos I get so freaking tired and have to constantly talk myself out of visiting the lolly jar, but that silly distraction took my mind off the tiredness and need for sugar just long enough to give me a bit of my focus back.

So, all in all, it's been pretty good – I certainly haven't been perfect, but the little bits I have done have made me feel good, so I can see that once I get them all going consistently it'll make a big difference. I finally remembered to call that naturopath Ellie told me about too, so I'm seeing her in a few days. I'm not quite sure what to expect, because I've never seen anyone like that before. I hope she's not a crazy hippy.

Right-o, let's summarise all this lifestyle stuff before I move on to the next section with Ellie.

Journal

☐ 1. **Track how you're doing:**
  - What have been your top three wins for the week?
  - What have been your top three challenges?
  - What are three ways you've served your values this week?
  - Next week, what will you stop, start and keep doing in order to serve your values better/more?
    - Stop:
    - Start:
    - Keep:

Action

☐ 2. **Fill out the weekly tracker daily – do it as you go so you don't forget anything and you can effectively assess how you're feeling.**

☐ 3. **Read through all the information regarding the stress response and identify which elements might be going on for you.**

☐ 4. **See a naturopath or integrative doctor to discuss these things and your situation.**

☐ 5. **Read the eating and nutrition information and use as a guideline to create a weekly meal plan that includes three complete meals per day of real whole food.**

☐ 6. **Schedule time in your diary to do a food shop for the week and prepare the meals on the food plan.**

☐ 7. **Find two or three healthy food options near your work and home that you can grab on the run if you need to.**

☐ 8. **Eat calm.** Do a few deep breaths before you start and remove distractions while eating.

☐ 9. **Check in with how you're feeling and identify what kind of physical activity will work for you at that moment.** If you're tired, start with lower intensity options like walking, swimming and yoga. Schedule non-negotiable time into your diary to do some movement at least three times per week.

☐ 10. **Identify which steps back will work for you, define which ones will become your non-negotiables and schedule them into your diary daily.** Set reminders on your phone if you need to.

☐ 11. **Create a non-negotiable morning and evening routine for a deep breathing session and/or meditation.**

☐ 12. **Continue to fill out the weekly tracker so you can identify patterns of how you're feeling versus what you're doing. Adjust the above accordingly.**

Remember

☐ 13. **Again, slow and steady is very important here.** Make small consistent changes and track how they make you feel, so you can more easily build the habits and tune in to what your body needs at any given time.

☐ 14. **Your brain's main priority is to ensure your survival, so communicate to it regularly that everything is okay by stepping back and staying connected to your values, and your health and stress levels will start to improve.**

☐ 15. **You've got this!**

WHAT'S YOUR STORY?

September 27th

At the beginning of my session with Ellie this week we went over all the lifestyle stuff I'd done throughout the week and had a look at my latest weekly tracker. All in all, she was pretty happy – I was a bit embarrassed because I knew I hadn't been perfect, but she said she didn't expect me to be at this stage. It was clear that I've been making an effort with it, so she just told me to continue with what I've done this week and add on a few more things next week. Slow and steady wins the race, right? I'd still prefer to be nailing it all already, though.

Ellie also reminded me to keep checking in with my values and goals constantly, because they will help to motivate me to do the right things. If I think I'm too busy to step back or I can't be arsed to make something to eat, checking in with what's important to me and what I really want will remind me of the bigger picture and help me to overcome short-term pain for long-term gain. I must remember to put my values and goals somewhere I can see them at work, actually, because that's the time I need to remember the bigger picture the most – it's so easy to get wrapped up in all the stuff, and forget that there is life beyond it. Yeah, good call – I'll put that on my to-do list for tomorrow.

Okay, so next we moved on to beliefs. Ellie calls this the transformation section. She said I'm now at the point where I've built some really solid foundations and started to get some good habits in place to calm my body and ensure I'm consistently serving what really matters to me, so it's time to release some of the strong restraints that are trying to pull me back from doing those things, and from being my true self for the long term. She calls these limiting beliefs, and she set all this up by bringing back the concept she'd introduced me to during the goals and visualisation section: Reality is bullshit. She reminded me of the NLP communication model, and how we only consciously absorb a very small proportion (134 bits out of 2 million) of what's around us, and that proportion is determined by things like our values, attitudes, thoughts, experiences, memories … and beliefs.

So that means the world we see around us is in fact 'our' reality, and not 'the' reality. And we have no way of knowing what 'the' reality actually is, because we all absorb the information differently and so we all perceive the world, and reality, differently … therefore, it's bullshit! Apparently, we start to construct this idea of reality and our version of the world from a young age, based on what happens around us and the subsequent beliefs we form as a result. We observe what our parents and/or main caregivers do, and we accept this as the way it is, we don't even think to question it. So we live our lives according to that, but sometimes, if we're lucky, we get to a point where we realise that this version of the world doesn't work for us anymore. We start to acknowledge that we're unhappy with our health, relationships, finances, achievements and future prospects, and we look for ways to try and 'fix it', but we don't realise that it's actually ourselves and our versions of reality that are causing it. So often we try to fix it with external solutions like diet, exercise, a different job, a new car, a grand adventure, or perhaps a new lover, but all this does is move things around in our reality; it's still not changing it at its core. So by changing our attitudes, thoughts and beliefs, we can change our reality, and therefore change the way we see and respond to the world. Meaning we can create a reality that allows us to truly be ourselves, and serve what's important to us and what we really want.

Wooooooooah, this is some weird shit. Change reality? Change the way we see the world? If Ellie had said this to me back at the beginning I think I would have run for the hills, but as we talked about it,

I realised that I may have experienced a little bit of what she's going on about. I didn't write about it in here at the time because I hadn't realised its significance, but I think I may have started to change my reality a bit already. The other day I opened an email newsletter that usually I would ignore because I receive about a million of them every week, but for some reason this one jumped out at me – and you'll never guess what the main feature was all about: 'Top tips to build your board career'. Why would I open that email out of all the hundreds of emails in my inbox? Was my brain looking for it? I'd done my visualisation a few times and imagined myself on a board, so do you think my brain was subconsciously drawn to it? Is that possible? Or was it just a coincidence? No, wait, now I think about it something else happened too – I was having a chat with Rob (I know, even that's a bit weird) the other day on the way to a meeting, and he mentioned he'd been up to see his sister on the Central Coast at the weekend. I said to him my goal was to buy a house there one day, and he then told me that his sister's husband is in real estate up there, and he can connect me with him if I'd like a chat. I honestly think if I hadn't had that clear vision of what I want in my life, I wouldn't have picked up on what Rob said about the Central Coast, and I definitely wouldn't have shared my goal of wanting to live there … so then I would never have gotten the opportunity to speak to someone who could specifically help me to achieve my goal. Hmmm, these are really subtle little things, but I can see how they have the potential to make a massive difference to my life. Holy fuck, this might actually work!

Anyway, back to what happened in our session. Ellie said that in order for me to change my reality to one that serves me and what I want better, I need to first understand what it currently is. And the best way to do that is to understand more about what life was like for me growing up, because that is the time when the fundamentals of my reality were formed. She asked me the following questions, but she said to try to think about the answers from the perspective of me at that time, rather than now. For example, if my Dad was always working, I might not see that as a problem now because my logical adult brain knows he was doing it to provide for the family, but my child brain back then may have seen it as him not wanting to spend time with me.

I was a bit apprehensive because I don't have much memory at all of my childhood, but Ellie told me not to worry and said we could just start and see what happened. We did a few deep breaths to relax my body and brain, and then off we went into the unknown wilderness of my past. So here are her questions:

1. What was the dynamic between you and your parents?
    *   Did you feel like you got all the love and recognition you wanted and needed as a child?
    *   Did you feel like no matter what you did, it was never quite enough (for one or both of your parents), or did you feel like they were proud of you no matter what you did?
    *   Were both of your parents physically around as much as you wanted and needed them to be?
    *   Did you feel like your parents were emotionally there for you? Did you talk about how you were feeling, or were feelings avoided?
    *   How did your parents show their love? Was it through their emotional support, or more external means like providing and doing things for you?
    *   Who did you feel you needed to be for your parents?

2. What was the dynamic like with your sibling(s)?
    *   Did you feel equal to them in terms of ability, talent and attention from your parents? Or was there an imbalance?
    *   Did you have a loving and respectful relationship with them? Or did you fight a lot?

3. Did any other people play a significant part in your life when growing up?
    *   What was your relationship like with them?
    *   What significance did they have in your life?

4. Are there any significant events that happened during your younger years that stand out in your mind?
    *   What were they?
    *   What impact did they have on you?

5. What was school like?
   - Were you a good student or naughty?
   - Did you think your intelligence was above or below average?
   - What social group did you fit in to? Were you a cool kid, a nerd or somewhere in between?
   - Did you get bullied? Were you a bully?
   - Did you have a core group of friends?
   - Did your friendships change as you went through school?

6. What was your first significant romantic relationship like?
   - What was good about it?
   - What was bad about it?
   - Did you feel loved and like you got everything you needed?
   - What was your behaviour like? Did you behave like yourself, or did you change to fit with your partner and the circumstances?

7. Have any significant events happened in your adolescent or adult life that have had an impact on you?
   - What were they?
   - How did they impact you?

It was difficult to stay in the perspective of my child brain at times, particularly because of my rubbish memory, and I certainly wouldn't have been aware of such intricate details at the time. But I think I managed to get a good insight nonetheless. I'll write a little summary here while it's fresh in my mind:

Growing up I was always doing a million different activities that Mum and Dad would have to shuttle me around to – dancing, swimming, band practice, gymnastics. They were always ridiculously proud of me and everything I did – I swear to God, they would even burst with pride if I did a good fart sometimes! Interestingly, though, although they used to tell me all the time how proud they were of me and how much they loved me, I still felt like there was a bit of distance between us. There was no doubt in my mind that they loved me unconditionally, but looking back now I think I needed more emotional support than they gave me. I remember always hiding in my room or the bathroom if I wanted to cry. Come to think of it, I used to see Mum secretly crying a lot too. She wouldn't always know I was there, but then when she did, she would quickly wipe away the tears and try to be upbeat. And I would never talk to either of them about anything, unless it was good or about something I'd done well. I remember spending quite a lot of time in my bedroom by myself. I feel like I was always quite sad when I was on my own. In fact, when I wasn't doing an activity I think I spent most of my time in my bedroom – I'd just watch hours and hours of TV, and secretly eat chocolate and lollies. I say secretly because I would sneak them up in my bag and then hide all the wrappers, so no-one saw how much I'd eaten. I didn't necessarily think that was a problem back then, though, I don't remember feeling guilty or beating myself up about it, but I guess I must have realised that it wasn't normal – otherwise, why would I have covered it up? Maybe I wanted to be like Mum – I used to see her with a secret packet of chocolate down the side of her chair every night too, even though she was always on a diet.

I remember I used to get angry – like, really angry. If something didn't go my way or I got told off, I would immediately become a beast. I couldn't control myself. I would throw and hit things, and even intentionally break stuff just to be spiteful. Wow, that's fucked up. I remember still being like it in my first major relationship (with dickhead Dan) actually. I would get so angry, I would explode. I think the worst time was when I threw his new phone over the balcony and it smashed all over the driveway. He was so angry with me, but I remember feeling at the time like it was worth it – there was such an enormous release of pressure from inside me when it flew out of my hand and I heard it break into tiny pieces on the hard concrete. I suppose I still do it with Steve in a way – okay, so it's not quite as destructive, but I do get to the point where I feel like I'll lose it, so that's when I run off into the other room and withdraw. I think I know what I'm capable of, so I'd rather take myself away than let Steve see the beast.

Dad was great, I always knew I was his little princess, but he did work a lot. He's a lawyer, so he always had something going on and he worked really random hours. But he would always try to make it to a big swimming competition or dance recital when he could, and he always made sure he spoiled me at birthdays and Christmases. He was constantly trying to be funny when he was with me and David – it was like he vomited Dad jokes. I do wonder now, though, as an adult if he really was always that happy, or if again he was putting on a front for David and me. He'd have a completely different tone when I'd hear him talking to people on the phone, and I never saw him joke around with Mum. And over the years, as we've gotten older, he's definitely changed. It almost feels like life has worn him down. He's on so many different medications and just spends most of his life in front of the TV when he's not working. It's quite sad really.

David and I had an interesting relationship. As his older sister, I expected him to do what I said, and if he didn't, I'd do something to make sure he did. A lot of my rage came out with him actually – I remember getting infuriated with him on a regular basis, and we would have the most horrendous fights. He was much more intelligent than me, I'll give him that, so he would have this way of making me feel like I was completely stupid, and like he was better than me because he was cleverer than me. I hated that. In terms of his relationship with Mum and Dad, I don't remember feeling like they treated him any differently. I suppose I just got more attention because I did more stuff, but when he did do something he got the praise too. It's funny that I don't think I've mentioned David throughout my whole time of writing in here. He's just not a big part of my life anymore. I'm not really sure why. We did get on much better after we stopped living under the same roof, and we actually used to see quite a lot of each other, but I guess life has just happened and neither of us has made an effort to stay connected. It's a shame, really, because once we'd grown up a bit we had quite a laugh together. Come to think of it, I haven't mentioned Mum and Dad either. Wow! That just shows how self-absorbed I've become. I have definitely been slack lately – well, over the past couple of years if I'm honest. I've just been so busy I haven't had the headspace or energy to put on my happy face for them, and I didn't want them to know I was struggling and make them worry. So rather than pretend, I figured it was just easier to avoid. That's my special skill. I guess I should probably do something about that, hey? I'll put it on my to-do list. ☺

Anyway, back to growing up. School was pretty normal. I wouldn't say I was the most popular kid, but I definitely wasn't a nerd. I do remember when my best friend Lizzie dropped me, though, from out of nowhere. One day we were inseparable and the next I could see her sniggering at me with Gemma Vincent in the corner of the playground. They didn't bully me or anything, but in some ways this was worse, because it all felt very sneaky and there was absolutely no explanation for it. I couldn't for the life of me figure out what I'd done to her. And she never did go back to being friends with me. That really upset me, and I guess I was probably quite wary of friendships after that. It would take me a long time to trust people and then I'd be constantly worried that I'd do something wrong, and they'd drop me the same way Lizzie had. That's probably why I ended up being a bit of a friend hopper – I never really belonged to one group, I'd just bounce between them and move on when the time felt right. Hmmm, do you think that's where my commitment issues have come from?!

Okay, so I guess I also have to talk about my first relationship, with dickhead Dan – ha, that probably says it all. It was great in the start and we had a lot of fun. We'd go out all the time and I'd always find something random and exciting for us to do, but slowly things started to change, until it got to the point where the only time I would see him was if I went down and sat with him at the pub. So inevitably that's what I did, because I wanted to be with him, so we ended up being pissed most of the time – which is why I got so fat. He became very unreliable – I'd try to organise something different for us to do, but more often than not he'd either not turn up or he'd have too many beers in him when he arrived and be a complete pain in the arse. He never did anything to make me feel special, or even like someone who vaguely meant something to him. The best I'd get would be a meal out on special occasions, but we'd usually be in and out within an hour and back at the pub for a post-dinner drink. I barely saw Mum and Dad during that time. I didn't see the point – I had nothing to offer them because I was just working in a call centre, and I didn't want them to see how much weight I'd put on. Plus I knew they didn't really like Dan, so I didn't want to give them any opportunity to validate that – not that they would have said anything anyway (keep calm, carry on and don't make a fuss, right Mum and Dad?).

I think I really lost my confidence with Dan, and to be honest I'm not sure that I ever got it back. He made me feel completely under-valued and like I didn't matter. Some days I'd even find myself wondering if he'd care if I just disappeared, or if he'd even notice. Ha, what am I talking about? Of course he'd notice – he wouldn't have had anyone to pay off his ridiculous bar tabs if I wasn't there … although I'm sure he would have found some other gullible fool pretty quickly. I lost contact with most of my mates too. In the beginning we'd all hang out together, but Dan managed to piss each one off, one by one, until they'd all had enough and stopped calling. Man, what an idiot I was. I didn't see any of this at the time. It was like I was trapped in a hole but I didn't even think to look for a way out. Luckily, though, the way out was shown to me when I caught him cheating on me. I let it go at first, because I couldn't bear to think of my life without him (WTF?!) but then when he did it again I knew I had to go. That was the toughest thing I've ever had to do. He broke my heart. I never want to feel that again.

This is pretty much everything I told Ellie I think. It's funny that initially I was worried I wouldn't have much to say, and then after a while I was worried I was going on too much! It really is amazing what happens when you just take the pressure off from having to get it all right – once I got going it just seemed to flow quite easily. In fact, I think that's the most I've ever talked about myself to another human being. It felt okay, actually. Anyway, she assured me that all of it was amazingly helpful in allowing us to understand how I've constructed my perception of the world, so I guess I did do alright after all.

We ended the session there. I'd talked for a really long time (and now I seem to have written for a very long time too!) and Ellie said she wanted to go away and digest it all, and produce a summary of her thoughts for me to be able to read through. I was happy with that – I was pretty exhausted after talking so much about myself, and bringing up stuff I hadn't thought about for a very long time, if at all. The other good news about that is I don't have any extra actions for this week, result! So I can keep focusing on what I've already got and hopefully get better at nailing that.

October 2nd

I saw the naturopath today…she wasn't a crazy hippy! Happy days! She was actually bloody lovely – I instantly felt comfortable with her, which was handy considering I was talking about the texture of my period blood and what my poos look like! I didn't realise these things could tell you so much – I've always been grossed out by stuff like that, but maybe I'll take more of an interest now since they're clearly so important. I told her about the medication I'm on from the doctor too. She wants me to get some fresh blood tests done so she can see where I'm at right now, but at first look she thinks that most of my issues are indeed as a result of stress, so that medication is probably not necessary because it doesn't really get to the root of the problem. She said as far as she's concerned, our first priority will be to calm the body down and support the main systems of the body to get them back to functioning efficiently. Once she's seen my test results, she'll be able to give me a more specific plan of natural supplements and lifestyle changes, although she thinks that I'm probably already doing well with that thanks to my work with Ellie. I guess that's even more motivation for me to focus on getting it all right. I have done better this week, but still have a way to go. I had a little eating episode one morning this week when I was working from home and stressing about getting a report finished, but I did manage to get myself back on track that afternoon, which I think is massive progress – I managed to fight the 'fuck it – the damage is done now' feeling and not go immediately to the lolly jar when I got to the office or order take-away for dinner. That's actually pretty huge for me.

I know I haven't been writing in here every day when I said I would, but at the moment something's got to give, so I figured it was best to really give this lifestyle stuff a good go and concentrate on getting into the habit with that – I know I have the habit of writing in here, so I feel like I can get back to that more easily once the other stuff is coming a bit more naturally to me.

October 4th

Holy fucking moly, my session with Ellie yesterday was amazing. It was like a whole new world was opened up to me, like I'd walked through the wardrobe in the *Chronicles of Narnia*. I genuinely believe my life will never be the same again now. Before I go on too much and get distracted, let me just move right on to the good shit. So Ellie gave me her summary of my beliefs from my epic talking session about me and my life. She pre-warned me that this was just her perception and opinion – it wasn't necessarily the truth – but it was up to me to decide what felt like the truth and what resonated with me. Let's just say, it resonated. She wrote it all down for me so I could read back over and reflect on it all, so here it is!

> You seem to be suffering from what I like to call 'Golden Child Syndrome'. It's where your parents shower you with love and praise so often, you come to expect it for everything you do. You almost become addicted to it. So you start to look for recognition and valida- tion every time you do something, and you become unable to give that to yourself. You start to believe that unless you receive that level of recognition for something, you can't have done a good job or you've failed. So you seek it everywhere you go with everyone you meet, and you hold them to this very high bar that your parents set so many years ago. Golden children have this subconscious need to show people how good they are at whatever they do, in a bid to gain, or keep, this love and recognition they're craving so much. They fear that if they fail to get this, it will mean that they're not good enough and they won't be liked or loved, so they'll be rejected. They tend to turn any lack

of attention onto themselves and question if they've done something wrong or if they haven't done enough, and then they adopt different or more extreme behaviours to try to get noticed.

This behaviour can often make relationships challenging, because they expect a lot of attention and recognition from their partner, so they behave in ways they believe will get this, and often act out when they don't. They start to question if they're even worthy of love, and start to become insecure, which may show up as anxious and suspicious behaviours or avoidance behaviours, where they constantly put barriers up in order to protect themselves.

Most of our behaviour as an adult is influenced by our dynamic with our parents or main caregivers as children. When we're young, these people are literally responsible for our survival – they are the only way we can get food and shelter – so if they abandon us, we will die. This is why we crave their love and appreciation so much, because it makes us feel secure. Remember what I told you during the lifestyle section: the body and brain's main priority in life is your survival, so if it thinks the very people who ensure your survival are withdrawing or rejecting you, it will adopt whatever thoughts and behaviours it deems necessary to win them back.

In contrast, the Forgotten Child is the opposite of the Golden Child. In this scenario, you didn't get what you felt you needed from your parents when you were young. This doesn't mean they didn't love you, or indeed look after you well, but for some reason you didn't get their love and recognition in the way you wanted it. Or perhaps this even occurred in just one incident, but that one time could have been enough to trigger fears that your parents were withdrawing from you or rejecting you. The parents of Forgotten Children may have worked a lot, so would not have been as physically present as the child desired. Or they may have been strict and had high standards, so the child felt like they could never do enough. Or perhaps the parents (or parent) just weren't overtly loving or affectionate, so it wasn't easy for the child to understand how they felt and get consistent validation that they were loved and, of course, safe. Forgotten Children tend to spend their lives trying to get what they feel they missed out on in childhood.

They assume that they're not good enough as they are, and that's the reason their parents withdrew their love, so they search for ways to prove otherwise, and prove that they are in fact worthy of recognition, and indeed love.

So when you peel back all the layers for both scenarios, the core is the same – a fear of not being good enough and a fear of not being loved, and, ultimately, a fear of rejection, abandonment and death. As far as the subconscious brain is concerned, if you're shut out by the people who matter to you, your survival is at risk and death is a real possibility. So as already mentioned, you try to avoid this at all costs by adopting whatever thoughts and behaviours you think will keep them on your side and you safe. This is why change can be so challenging – because it takes you into the unknown, where you feel unsafe. So the resistance you feel is actually your brain trying to protect you and keep you in a safe zone.

For you, Debs, I think your child brain made a link between your achievements in your extracurricular activities and your mum and dad's love. Because you did so much and it was always accompanied with their praise, you decided that, 'If I show Mum and Dad how well I can do things (that I'm the best), they will keep loving me, and therefore they won't abandon me.' You essentially created a condition, or a rule, for their love, and then started to apply it to other relationships and situations in your life.

Forgotten Children, just so you're aware, will do the same, but their condition may look more like, 'If I prove that I can do things, then Mum and Dad will love me, and therefore won't abandon me.' It's similar, but the fundamental difference is the Golden Child is striving to keep the level of love and recognition they need, whereas the Forgotten Child is trying to gain it.

I believe you also applied another condition: 'In order for me to know that I'm loved, I must get physical recognition and validation.' Unless you receive this, your subconscious brain assumes that you've failed to show how well you can do, and therefore you've failed to hold on to the love, and therefore abandonment and death is surely imminent. I know this sounds dramatic, and indeed it is in our logical adult brains, but remember we're looking at this from your child and emotional brain – which is incapable of such logical thought.

So with all this in mind, it's now easy to see why you think and behave as you do. You have a constant need to show how good you are, and you're constantly seeking recognition and validation for it, because you believe that this is the only way to know you're loved, respected, and therefore safe.

Let's look at other evidence that supports this. It seems a lot of things within your upbringing promoted this notion of putting on a front and presenting yourself to the world in a particular way. The first one that jumps out is the way your family dealt with emotions – in that you didn't. You learned that it's not okay to show your emotions and you have to hide how you truly feel, and even who you truly are, in order to maintain harmony and, therefore, love and security. We saw this with your mum when you would catch her crying and she'd pretend to be upbeat, and your dad seemed to reinforce this too, as you said he would always have his funny persona on with you but be different with others. So in your child brain, this would have helped to validate your suspicions that you have to present to the world in a certain way and show it what you think it wants in order to be loved and accepted.

In your child brain, you decided that as long as no emotions are being shown, everything is okay. So when someone did or does show emotion, you assume that something is wrong and you either run to their rescue or you start to question yourself and if you did something to cause the emotion (again triggering your fear of abandonment). As a result, you try to avoid upsetting people at all costs and you regularly replay situations in your brain to try to figure out if you did something wrong. You also often invest too much energy and headspace into worrying about others and making sure they're okay. You probably think that if you're the one who ensures they're okay, this is another way of showing them how good you are, and therefore another way of ensuring they will stick around. This very much comes back to what we've been talking about regarding you trying to control what other people think and do – your desire to do this is so strong because it's your way of trying to ensure they will continue to like and/or love you.

If you don't see physical evidence of this, however, you believe abandonment is just around the corner, so you start to second guess and change yourself (kind of like a chameleon) in a bid to be the person you think they want you to be, so you can indeed gain this evidence and feel secure.

I suspect that your anger issues while growing up were linked to this belief of having to hide emotions. Eventually your emotion pot would become too full, because you had no outlet, and boil over. At that time, the only way your child brain knew how to deal with that was physical outbursts. Obviously, as you've grown up, you've started to understand that this is not acceptable behaviour, so you've adopted alternative behaviours that are less overt but still serve the purpose of releasing that valve. I'm talking about behaviours like over-eating, over-working, excess shopping and procrastination. These are all classic self-sabotaging behaviours, which typically are adopted as an escape. It's important to remember that these behaviours are not the issue; they only show up as a clever disguise for fear. So in order to get on top of them, you need to take off the mask and reveal that fear to the cold light of day. In your case (and actually in most people's cases), that underlying fear is indeed the fear of not being good enough or the fear of not being loved, and therefore the fear of rejection, abandonment and death. Often there are more surface-level fears wrapped up in it too, such as fear of failure, fear of success, fear of being judged, fear of looking stupid and fear of missing out.

As well as being a disguise for these underlying fears and associated emotions, self-sabotaging behaviours also serve as an escape from your mind. With so many thoughts and worries racing around in your brain all day every day, you get to the point where you need a break, and the only way to get this is distraction. These behaviours allow you to flip that off switch, even just for a moment, because you can focus your mind completely onto something else. Think about it: when you're tucking in to your third chocolate bar or pressing submit on that full shopping cart, how many other thoughts and worries are there at those exact moments? All of your energy is in the task at hand. Sure, there may be thoughts present about how you shouldn't be doing it, but at least your thoughts only have one theme rather than a million, so to your mind it's still a little moment of respite. If you were able to stay present in the moment, focus only on what you can control and let go of the things you can't, therefore letting go of unnecessary thoughts, worries and fears, how do you think that would affect your self-sabotaging behaviours? You wouldn't need to procrastinate because you'd be focused on the task, and not getting lost in your worries about not knowing what you're doing or imminent failure. You wouldn't need to eat everything in sight because you wouldn't be consumed with concerns about how you feel or what other people think about you. And you wouldn't push yourself beyond your limits and take on more than you can handle, because those worries about having to prove how good you are would be non-existent. Can you imagine how different life would be if you were simply in the moment? And you were just being you, without being driven by this insatiable need to prove your worth?

I think by now we're starting to get a really good picture of why it is you think and behave in the way you do, but let's look at just a couple more pieces of evidence. You said that in school you had a best friend, Lizzie, and she dropped you out of nowhere and with no explanation, which left you upset and confused about what you could possibly have done to warrant that. This, of course, was your greatest fear coming true – you had been abandoned by someone you loved. And you believed it was your actions that had caused it to happen – that is, you'd failed to show her how good you were, so you'd failed to maintain her love. This, of course, would have made you feel insecure, because your safety was called into question, so you used this experience as a template to avoid putting yourself in a similar scenario in the future, meaning you learned to keep a bit of distance between you and others to essentially keep yourself safe. Back when you were younger, you said you 'friend hopped' rather than committing to one group, and even now you've said that you're often not fully present and open with your friends. This is simply you trying to keep yourself safe.

We saw with 'dickhead Dan' how you changed yourself and your behaviour, and even went against your core values and goals (even though you weren't consciously aware of them at that time) because you so badly wanted to please him and ensure he maintained his love and didn't abandon you. This is all too common, particularly with us ladies – we mould ourselves into who we think we should be or what we think our partner wants, in a bid to avoid rejection and abandonment, but eventually this often leads to us losing our confidence because we've lost all sense of who we really are. And, ironically, the relationship often breaks down after that anyway, because we've become an insecure shadow of our former self – which, of course, is not sexy and becomes too hard work for the guy, so he does the very thing we were trying so hard to avoid and buggers off!

And, of course, this is why you work so incredibly hard – because it's your way of showing everyone how good you are, and therefore how worthy you are of their love and respect. As well as being a modelled behaviour that you learned from your Dad, who you said also worked incredibly hard.

So to summarise then, Debs, your version of the world up to this point has been largely built on this belief that you have to show people how good you are in order to gain and maintain their love, and you have to constantly see physical evidence through recognition and validation to know that you do indeed have this love. At the core of this is a fear of not being good enough, a fear of not being loved, and a fear of rejection and abandonment. So our focus will be to change these beliefs and therefore minimise these fears, so you can change the blueprint for your world and align it with your values and goals, and stay true to what really matters to you and what you really want. Ultimately, you can free yourself from the mind fuckery, unleash your Uppy and be a healthier, happier and more fulfilled Debs ... can I get a hell yeah!

See what I mean? It totally resonated. It's freaking amazing how we can get so much understanding based on just that small amount of information. Don't get me wrong, it was extremely confronting, and at first I wasn't quite sure how to process it all, but after I read through it a couple more times and digested it a bit better I could see how it really does make a hell of a lot of sense. It's crazy how much of an impact the past can have on you, though – even when you think you had an awesome childhood like I did. I can't help but wonder – if I had been taught about all this values stuff earlier in my life, like at school, would these beliefs have continued to have such an impact? I mean, if I had been living my life more connected to who I really am and what really matters to me, and therefore living more in the present moment with less mind fuckery, I probably would have naturally released these beliefs I'd built up earlier, because they naturally wouldn't have served what I was focusing on and what was important. Ellie stressed that while it's important for us to understand the past we don't need to dwell there – the point of this exercise was to just pop back and extract the information, and now we can return to the present with the learnings and use them to move forward. That was a good heads up she gave me – as I've mentioned, I do love to dwell. I guess I'll never know if things would have been different, but as Ellie keeps telling me, I now have the power to make them different from this point on, and that's really all I need to know. Okay, I'm digressing now … let me think what we did next. Ah yeah, that's right, we started to look at how I can change these beliefs (or 'stories' as Ellie likes to call them – because that reinforces the fact that they're not real).

Before we got cracking with that, Ellie reminded me again of the stages of learning, and said it's critical I keep that at the forefront of my mind with this. She pointed out that I've lived my entire life with this blueprint of my world, so it's not something that will change overnight. I need to really apply myself and commit to staying consistent with the strategies, and remaining vigilant for the changes because they will be subtle. I think she realises how impatient I am, so she was really hammering this in to me.

She asked me to refer back to the summary in the final paragraph at the end of her review and define in my own words what the main story is I'm telling myself consistently in my head – so, in other words, what I think my core limiting belief is. She said that there will be many beliefs at play, and I can work on those over time, but for now we just want to focus on the one we believe is at the heart of it all.

That was a bit tricky because it all resonated, but I guess it really does all come down to me thinking I always have to show how good I am, and be who I think people want me to be, in order to be liked/loved/accepted etc. When you think of all the things I think and do, that belief fits into everything. Then Ellie asked me, what would happen if I were just me. 'Urgh, just me,' I said. 'Who would be interested in that?' I mean, seriously, how inspiring is a chubby workaholic who gets her pleasure from arrow word puzzles and puppies? Ha! It's so sad it's actually quite funny! Ellie then asked, 'So what's the problem with that?' I knew where she was going. She wanted me to see that it doesn't matter what makes me, me – just as long as I stay true to it. I get that in principal, but when you look at all the things that make me, me they just don't seem very exciting, and they're certainly not what you would expect of an inspiring leader. So Ellie asked, 'What would you expect of an inspiring leader?' Hmmm, interesting question – I wasn't really sure, to be honest. I mean there was the usual stuff of getting shit done, leading an engaged and passionate team, and being highly respected – but, in terms of personal things, I'd actually never thought about that before. One thing I did know for sure, however, is that their list of personal passions would be a lot more impressive than mine. This prompted Ellie's next question: 'So what would it take for you to feel like your passions are enough?' Ummmmmmm. 'What would it take for you to feel like you are enough?' Fuck. I burst into tears at that point. Talk about hitting the nail on the freaking head. She was right. I just don't feel like I'm enough. I always feel like I have to be more or do more in order for people to respect/like/love me and to fit in. And I do everything I can to try and cover up the real me to ensure that no-one can get to her. That's really fucking sad.

So that was it. My core limiting belief that's been driving everything I think and do is 'I'm not good enough'. The next thing Ellie asked me to do was think of a different story, or belief, that would be more helpful in allowing me to be the real me and serve my values and goals. I thought this was a trick question, because the only thing I could come up with was, 'I am good enough'. Was that too obvious? Apparently not – Ellie said if that resonated with me then that was perfect. She asked me to say it out loud – I couldn't say it without

183

crying. I can't believe how much power this belief has had over me. It didn't matter how many times I repeated it, I just didn't believe in any way that it was true. As soon as I said, 'I am good enough', a little voice would come out of nowhere and say, 'No you're not'. Ellie said that was okay, and perfectly normal. She reminded me again that this would take time to change, due to the length of time I've been living with my old story of not being good enough, so she didn't expect me to believe it right away. She said all we have to do now is convince the subconscious that this new story is how I roll.

I'll tell you all about that tomorrow – it's getting late and I need to do my breathing stuff before bedtime. I think I need some extra calming down time after going over all this again! Plus Steve is away for work tonight, so I'm looking forward to having the whole bed to myself … and silence. Is it right that I'm this excited to not be sleeping with my husband? Sometimes I think how good it would be if we just slept in separate rooms, but I know that'll never happen – it's just not the 'done thing', is it? It would be bloody lovely every now and then though.

October 5th

Before I carry on with the beliefs stuff I did with Ellie, I want to talk a little about my lifestyle activities over the last week – I've been a bit consumed with talking about all the things in my session so forgot to write it up in here. I have been documenting it, but in the notes bit on my phone cos that's easier and more private to carry around. My intention was to then summarise it in here but I got side-tracked. Anyway, first up, let's get the shit stuff out the way – I had one late night in the office where I ate the fuck out of everything, which wasn't good. And I have to admit I've still been doing work on the train on the way home each night too. HOWEVER, I have been sticking to my 'Three, two, one … the working day is done' rhyme before walking into the house every night – and that has been making a massive difference in terms of allowing me to be more calm in the evening and more present with Steve. I told him about the Uppy concept, so he's changed the code word to make me present from 'GOOSE' to 'SHOW ME YOUR UPPY!' It made me giggle when he came up with that – I keep thinking he's saying 'Show me your puppies', which is a whole different scenario, but it definitely does bring my mind back into the moment and remind me to just be me – and a couple of times I did indeed 'show him my puppies', which of course he was very pleased with … and one of the times even led to a nice quickie on the couch!

Apart from that one bingey episode, I've been pretty good with my eating – I've eaten our home-cooked meals most days, and on the days that I haven't (usually because I forgot to take them in) I've grabbed a salad from the café, but made sure to include some good fats and good carbs so it's more complete than the tuna and lettuce option I used to get before. I'm really enjoying the roasted pumpkin or quinoa for the carbs, actually, and the salmon or avocado for the good fats is delicious. Who knew eating well could actually taste good? And I've even found I've been feeling a bit less hungry and lethargic around the 3 pm mark too – which is a welcomed change. Most days I've managed at least one step back – usually with breathing or a cheeky three minutes or so listening to a cheesy tune – and my walking has happened three times. Oh, and I've been really good with my morning and evening routines of breathing and limiting my use of technology. I had to ask Steve to help me with that one because I realised I'd actually become a bit addicted to my phone and was making excuses to look at it – things like, *I just need to see what meetings I've got tomorrow*, or *I just need to check one thing in an email so I don't forget tomorrow*. Of course these things could wait, but I needed Steve to help me do that – so he pulled the 'Show me your Uppy' line out for that too, which again brought me back and made me realise that calming myself down was more important.

So, all in all, I'm pretty happy. It's still a bit patchy, and I haven't managed to do all the things in one day yet, but I am definitely consistently building it up, so I can see that if I just keep going like that then eventually I'll be able to do it all and it'll stick. To be honest, I'm kind of surprised that I've taken to this as well as I have. I think it's probably helped that Ellie's been continually managing my expectations, so I'm always reminded that we're playing the longer-term game and I don't have to get everything perfect right away, which has helped to keep my all or nothing and 'fuck it' thinking under wraps. And also, I think because I was so desperate to get out of the shitty place I was in, I told myself I have to just trust in the process 100 per cent and apply myself, which has made me more committed to just sucking it up and doing what I need to do. Anyway, let's get back to the beliefs stuff:

So before Ellie took me through the strategies for convincing my subconscious mind of my new way of operating, she wanted to teach me a process that she said I could use any time I felt like I was losing control or stressing, and which would help me to make sense of a situation and understand the possible paths I could take. She said that when we're in that 'stressy' zone, we're operating out of our emotional brain, so we become reactive and impulsive, and tend to make poor decisions and enlist unhelpful behaviours to try to get us through. By taking a step back, however, and forcing the logical part of the brain to do some work, we can get a clearer perspective on a situation and have the clarity to take proactive and practical steps forward. By changing where we think (or, as Ellie said, which part of the brain we use), we can change how we think, and therefore what we think. Sounds simple when Ellie says it.

So she asked me to draw a line down the middle of a piece of paper and write my old story on one side, and the new one on the other – she calls this 'the possibilities process'. I had to think about what my life would be like when living by each of the stories and write it down in as much detail as possible, considering all the main areas of my life. She reminded me of the line of questioning she'd taught me before when trying to get to the bottom of my values and goals, and recommended I used a similar technique here to get deeper:

- What's the impact of that?
- How would that be a problem for me?
- What will that give me?

I've power-phrased a bit here, just to get the main gist:

I'm not good enough	I'm good enough just the way I am
Health: I'll continue to work like a maniac and will fully burnout. It may affect my ability to have children, if indeed I decide I want them. It may result in a serious illness and even early death.	*Health:* I would look after and prioritise myself better, because I would feel like I didn't have to work harder to prove myself to people. I'd have more energy and more motivation to do the things that make me happy and work towards what I ultimately want. My body would be ready to do whatever I wanted to do, and I'd live better for longer.
Work: I could damage my reputation by dropping the ball and producing sub-standard work. I won't be an inspiring leader. I would damage my chances of getting promoted and accepted onto boards.	*Work:* I wouldn't feel like I was pushing uphill all the time. I'd be able to stay focused on the important tasks and outcomes and let go of the other shit, which would make me a better leader and help me to produce better results. So I'd be more likely to get a promotion and get accepted on to boards.
Finances: If I don't get to where I want to be with work, or I can't work because I'm sick, I won't have the money I need to live the lifestyle I want. This will not be good for my mental health and will make me even more unhealthy because it'll add a lot more pressure onto me. And also onto my marriage.	*Finances:* A better work position and more energy, motivation and confidence to go for what I want, will mean I can earn what I need to live the lifestyle I want. It will ease any unnecessary pressure on me, meaning my health will be better, and my marriage. I could even retire earlier if I'm smart and working efficiently, which will serve my values and goals better too.

I'm not good enough	I'm good enough just the way I am
Relationships: Extra financial pressure and health issues may cause problems with Steve, because I'll be even less present and more insecure. It could even end in divorce if it got really bad. Then I'd be alone, and too old to get back in the game. I'd probably continue to withdraw from Mum and Dad because I'm embarrassed about the state I'm in, so I'd miss out on valuable time with them, which would cause even more stress and guilt, and reinforce all the other issues I've highlighted.	*Relationships:* No unnecessary financial pressure will make things easier. If I'm heathier and happier, my relationships will be also. Steve and I live a full and happy life together.
Overall wellbeing: I'd be physically and mentally unwell, which would affect my ability to operate at my best in both my professional and personal life. This would affect my finances and inevitably my marriage and relationship with my family, meaning I could lose everything that's important to me, which would send me even further down the hole of physical and mental issues, and end up with me being depressed, alone and fat – or in an early grave.	*Overall wellbeing:* I'll be healthier and happier, with more energy, motivation and satisfaction – in all areas of my life. I'll be doing what I want to be doing, both personally and professionally, and I'll be able to enjoy it for as long as possible. I want this life please. ☺

Wowee! Such a simple task but such MASSIVE impact. I was crying my eyes out again when I did it for my current (or old) story. Life will be so shit if I continue to live with it. It looks kind of over the top when you write it down like this, but it's a very real possibility I could end up that way. I already feel crap, so if I don't make these fundamental changes, it's only going to get worse. I just can't believe how one little story can affect your life so much, but it makes so much sense. It literally drives everything I do. It's hard to imagine a life without constantly trying to prove myself, comparing myself to others, holding myself to unrealistic standards and beating myself up for not achieving this non-existent version of perfection I'm obsessed with. Well, let me correct that – it has been hard to imagine, but this exercise has certainly helped to make the possibility that I can live without all this shit much more real. I feel like Neo in *The Matrix* – I can either take the blue pill and stick with this story and live a sub-optimum life. Or I can take the red pill, run with this new story, and be happier and more fulfilled than I ever thought possible. Um, I'll take a bucketload of the reds please!

If only it were as easy as just swallowing a pill, though. Sadly, I have to work for my new life. Goddammit. Again, though, the solution seems so ridiculously simple – but the key, as always, is in consistency. As Ellie explained to me before, the subconscious is like a child. If I want it to do something new, I need to keep repeating what that thing is and reinforcing it every time it's done. Luckily, however, Ellie has been priming me for this moment all along – so I already know what to do, and I've already been doing it, so it's actually just a case of adding a bit on to my current routine. Happy freaking days! She reminded me about the neural pathways we have in our brains, and how we can create new ones through repetition of a new thought or behaviour, and allow the old ones to fade away by repeatedly not giving our attention to them. At the moment, my pathway for the old story is extremely strong, cos I've had it for a long time and I use it pretty much all day every day. So, again, I need to be aware that this will take a while to shift and the shifts may be subtle. All this means is it's important to remain aware and document my progress. I suppose it's the same with the child, hey? People put up those star charts so the kid can track how they're going and can visually see the relation-ship between the new behaviour and the reward (or lack thereof!). Maybe I should make myself a star chart?! I could write down all my non-negotiables and give myself a star every time I do one, and then at the end of the week when I've done them all and accumulated enough stars I can reward myself with something excellent, like a massage or pedicure, or even bank them and work towards something bigger like a weekend away. Oooh yeah, that definitely makes me feel more motivated to do it – I might just bloody do that!

Okay, so in order for me to change my story, and therefore my life, I need to repeat my new story out loud ten times in the morning and in the evening as part of my daily routines. First I do my breathing session and/or meditate to get my body into a calm state and make my subconscious more accessible, and then I feed it the new info. I then sit for a couple of minutes and visualise a scenario that represents my life when I'm living by the new story, but visualise it as if it's now and it's already the way I'm living. As Ellie said before, the brain doesn't know the difference between real and perceived, so by visualising it as now, the brain thinks that's just the way it is and seeks to make it the same in my external world. I must make sure I really tune in to how good it feels in my body – just like I learned in the visualisation process back in my goals session. Ellie said this visualisation, coupled with the feeling, is the key to changing my story successfully. Just saying the new story is not good enough – I need to believe it. Apparently this is when my spiritual element will come into play again too, because it will shift my energy and perception, or interpretation, of the outer world so it's aligned with my inner world. When I come out of this routine, I should resist temptation to reach straight for my phone or rush about, and give myself a few easy minutes to allow that visualisation to stick.

In the evening, repeat this process and document three pieces of evidence from that day that prove my new story is true.

And every time I notice myself thinking and behaving according to the old story, I simply say, 'That was old Debs; new Debs doesn't roll like that anymore'. I can even have a chat with the old story, and thank it for showing up – I can say, 'Thank you old story, I know you're here because you're trying to keep me safe, but I now know that I feel safe when I'm being my true self and serving my values and goals, so I'm afraid you're either going to have to move on by or come along for the ride. I don't mind which, but holding me back isn't an option anymore.' I feel a bit silly having a chat with myself like that, but fuck it – if that's my ticket to the red pill, I'm all in baby!

Ellie gave me a great analogy, actually – she said imagine my brain is like a train platform, and there's a network of trains (thoughts) whizzing by me all day. I have the choice of which train I get on – in other words, the new story or the old one. Sometimes I'll board the right one (the one that takes me towards the destination I desire), and sometimes I'll take the wrong one (the one that keeps me stuck on my current track). That's okay, though, because it's unrealistic to think I will always board the right train, but the trick is to remember that I have the power to step off that train whenever I want. So as soon as I notice I'm on the wrong train/old story, I just step right off by reminding myself of the new one. Ellie said it's not stopping the thoughts that matters, it's what I do with them that does. I can't necessarily control which thoughts come up (or which trains go by), but I can always control how I deal with them (whether to get on them and when to get off). I like that, and think it's really helpful. I guess it's an extension of the notion that you should focus only on what you can control and let go of the things you can't. And along with that, focus only on what you want and let go of what you don't. I just need to keep my eye on the trains that will allow me to be myself and serve my values and goals, and let all the others just move on by. Ellie also said it's good to just stand on the platform and not board any trains when I can, too – just be present. Got it.

Okay, so covering that session took me a couple of entries but it was a pretty hectic session – it was a bit like a roller-coaster, actually. I laughed, I cried, I felt hopeless, I felt annoyed … but eventually I feel motivated and empowered that I now know what to do and how to do it. Fuck. Yeah.

October 7th

I'm just getting ready for my week ahead. I keep thinking about my session with Ellie – I still can't believe how one little belief could determine so much about the way I live my life. It's quite terrifying, really. I'm sort of starting to feel quite thankful that I hit rock bottom – otherwise, I may never have known about all this stuff, and I may have continued to be a slave to this belief. I do wonder how I'll be different when I change it, though. It's almost like that's my identity. If I'm not working my arse off and always trying to get to the top, then what will I do? I think I'm excited to find out the answer to that, but I'm also incredibly nervous. I feel like one of those middle-aged women in those novels where they find themselves and get a new lease on life – the only difference is they usually do it with the stunning backdrop of the Tuscan countryside or a Greek island, whereas I'm hoping it'll happen in between meetings. Ah well, at least I know what I'm doing will stick, I guess, since I'm able to fit it into my real, everyday life. I don't think I fancy throwing it all in and running off to become a yoga teacher or have an affair with an Italian waiter anyway – my life isn't actually that bad, it just needs a few adjustments.

October 8th

Shit, I just realised I've been forgetting to document my evidence that my new story is true. I've been repeating and visualising it in my morning and evening routine, though, so that's good. Anyway, I don't have much time because I have an event today and tomorrow, and of course all the conference packs are still inside the delivery van which is stuck in traffic, so I need to go and sort that shit out. So I just wanted to note that in here to remind me to start tomorrow. Bye.

October 9th

Still not much time cos the day session ran over, so a quick change and then off to the evening dinner. But I said I'd write my evidence, so here goes:

1. The conference packs didn't show up in time for the start, but instead of completely freaking out and having an anxiety attack because I was worried everyone would think I was incompetent, I got up on the mic and made a joke about it. I mean don't

get me wrong, I was still shitting myself that they'd think I was incompetent, but I just thought what the hell? Either way the packs won't be here, and either way they could think I'm incompetent, so why don't I just try dealing with it in a different way and see what happens. Anyway, everyone really appreciated my honesty, so it actually gave me a confidence boost and put me in a good mood for the rest of the day.

2. Michelle emailed me through a gift voucher for a massage with a lovely message saying, 'I haven't seen you in a while, assume you're busy, so thought you could do with a little you time'. It made me cry when I read it. I guess that shows she loves me for who I am, though, right? Because she has no idea whether I'm doing anything good right now or not. Plus I know she's dealing with a lot of shit in her own life at the moment, so to remember me amid all that is pretty fucking special. In fact, that reminds me – I must touch base with her and see how she's getting on. The time seems to have run away with me since we last had a good chat, and every time we've tried to catch up one of us has had to cancel.

3. One of the girls from sales complimented me on my outfit. She usually intimidates me, actually, cos she always looks so well put together and she's got an amazing figure. And, funnily enough, I was feeling quite self-conscious at the time because I was sure my muffin top was on display. But she seemed genuine, and she had nothing to gain by saying it if it wasn't true, so I'm going to take that.

Okay, bye!

October 10th

I don't have much time again today, but I want to summarise all this belief stuff. I know Ellie said I'll probably have more come up, so I want to make sure I'll be able to easily repeat the process.

Journal

☐ 1. **Track how you're doing:**
- What have been your top three wins for the week?
- What have been your top three challenges?
- What are three ways you've served your values this week?
- Next week, what will you stop, start and keep doing in order to serve your values better/more?
  - Stop:
  - Start:
  - Keep:
- Once you've decided on your new story, write three pieces of evidence that it's true (do this one daily).

Action

☐ 2. **Write down what life was like for you growing up.** Use the following questions to guide you. Remember to try to write from the perspective of your child brain, and how you may have perceived things back then. The key to doing this successfully is to commit to being 100 per cent honest with yourself and allowing yourself to be calm and open, so the words and thoughts can simply flow out. Ask yourself:
- What was the dynamic between you and your parents?
  - Did you feel like you got all the love and recognition you wanted and needed as a child?
  - Did you feel like no matter what you did, it was never quite enough (for one or both of your parents), or did you feel like they were proud of you no matter what you did?
  - Were both of your parents physically around as much as you wanted and needed them to be?
  - Did you feel like your parents were emotionally there for you? Did you talk about how you were feeling, or were feelings avoided?
  - How did your parents show their love? Was it through their emotional support, or more external means like providing and doing things for you?
  - Who did you feel you needed to be for your parents?

- What was the dynamic like with your sibling(s)?
    - Did you feel equal to them in terms of ability, talent and attention from your parents? Or was there an imbalance?
    - Did you have a loving and respectful relationship with them? Or did you fight a lot?
- Did any other people play a significant part in your life when growing up?
    - What was your relationship like with them?
    - What significance did they have in your life?
- Are there any significant events that happened during your younger years that stand out in your mind?
    - What were they?
    - What impact did they have on you?
- What was school like?
    - Were you a good student or naughty?
    - Did you think your intelligence was above or below average?
    - What social group did you fit in to? Were you a cool kid, a nerd or somewhere in between?
    - Did you get bullied? Were you a bully?
    - Did you have a core group of friends?
    - Did your friendships change as you went through school?
- What was your first significant romantic relationship like?
    - What was good about it?
    - What was bad about it?
    - Did you feel loved and like you got everything you needed?
    - What was your behaviour like? Did you behave like yourself, or did you change to fit with your partner and the circumstances?
- Have any significant events happened in your adolescent or adult life that have had an impact on you?
    - What were they?
    - How did they impact you?

☐ 3. **Now work through your childhood memories using the following:**

- Identify if you resonate more with the Golden Child or Forgotten Child scenario – were you constantly praised and recognised for your achievements as a child (Golden), or did you feel like you didn't get the recognition you wanted/needed, and like you often hadn't done enough or like your parent(s) thought you could do more (Forgotten)?

- Do you feel like you're constantly trying to prove yourself? Are you trying to hold people to a certain level of love and respect, or do you feel like you're constantly trying to gain it?

- What do you fear will happen if you don't have people's love and respect in the way that you want it? E.g. is it that you'll be rejected, or not fit in or belong?

- What behaviours have you enlisted throughout your life to try to avoid this from happening? For example, self-sabotage (over/under eating, over-working, perfectionism, alcohol, sex), reluctance to commit, avoidance of issues (putting your head in the sand), anxious tendencies (distrust, suspicion).

- How did this show up throughout school and in your friendship groups? For example, were you naughty or very good, did you over- or underachieve, did you have a solid friendship group or did you bounce between friends?

- How has this shown up in your intimate relationships? For example, a constant worry that your partner will cheat or leave you, an inability to talk about issues, or tantrums and being stubborn?

- How has this shown up in your relationship with your family? For example, arguments, tension, overly accommodating, avoidance.

- When you peel off all the layers of all the things you've identified here, what do you think is the underlying fear? For example, fear of failure, fear of success, fear of not being liked/loved, fear of not being good enough, fear of rejection?

- How has this fear shown up in your subconscious thoughts? Now you know what you know, what story do you think you've been telling yourself? For example, I'm not good enough, I'm not worthy.

- Is this story working for you? If not, what's a different story you could replace it with that will allow you to be your true self and serve your values and goals consistently? For example, I'm good enough just the way I am, I'm worthy, I'm loved for who I am.

4. **Complete the possibilities process to identify what your life will be like if you continue to live by the old story versus if you live by the new one.** Draw a line down the middle of a piece of paper and directly compare the two scenarios. Include all the main areas of your life: health, finance, work, family, intimate relationships, overall wellbeing.

5. **Decide which scenario you want to run with from now on and set non-negotiables to add the following to your morning and evening routine.**
   - **Morning:**
     - Do your breathing and/or meditation session.
     - Say your new story out loud ten times.
     - Visualise a scenario that represents you and your life while living with this new story. Make sure you visualise it as if you're there now and you have that life already, noticing all the little details and particularly the feeling in your body. Sit with this for three to five minutes and finish with a big deep breath and sigh. (*Note:* ensure the visualisation is the same every day so you're constantly reinforcing it and the brain is getting the same information.)
     - Avoid rushing around or reaching for your phone for a few minutes after your visualisation to allow it to embed into your subconscious.
   - **Evening:**
     - Repeat the same process you followed in the morning but also document three pieces of evidence from that day that prove your new story is true.

Remember

6. **You have lived with the old story for most of your life, so changing it will take some time.** Making the morning and evening routines non-negotiable, however, will help to accelerate the change.

7. **Reality is bullshit.** You have the power to make your reality whatever you want.

WHO DO YOU SEE?

October 13th

Wow, it's been a hectic week. I did manage to keep up some of my stuff, like the morning and evening routines, but pretty much everything else went out the window. I just didn't have a chance to even think about stepping back or preparing food, but I didn't lose my shit, so I think that's a win. Normally during a week like that, and particularly with a big event, I would have eaten everything and anything that was bad for me, and had hardly any sleep – which, of course, then would have made me extra exhausted, stressed and hard on myself. But I actually slept fairly well (though there were a few short nights while I was preparing for the event), and although I ate desserts at the evening dinners and had a muffin at one of the morning teas, I managed to stay pretty well on track. Steve, bless him, packed me some little snack packs to see me through, so I was munching on nuts most of the day.

I definitely still do not believe my new belief, but I'm sticking with the daily routines, and staying vigilant for the evidence, so I think it is helping me to respond a bit differently to things. I still have a way to go with that one, though, I reckon.

Anyway, on to my latest session with Ellie. Now that I've got a better understanding about how I perceive the world, she said the next step is to understand how I perceive myself. I immediately felt a sense of dread come over me when she said that. I know I've done it a bit more lately, but I still hate talking about myself and my inner feelings. I knew that I had to keep being as open and honest as I could if I was to get the most out of the session, but it made me feel so completely exposed – like I was stood in the middle of a football oval with a full crowd, completely naked.

Ellie could see how uncomfortable I was, so she said it was the perfect time to talk about the concept of vulnerability. She asked me to define what vulnerability means to me, so I described my image of the football oval, and explained that to me vulnerability is being completely exposed, weak and leaving yourself open to hurt and/or danger. So, most definitely something I would like to avoid. She then asked me to give her some examples of what makes me feel vulnerable. Clearly talking about myself and my feelings is a big one. Also getting things wrong, and not being able to do something. Oh, and people knowing about that. The thought of people knowing that I don't know what I'm doing makes me feel really vulnerable. That's why I've worked so hard to build up this image of being strong and capable, and I protect that at all costs.

Her next question was a good one and made me laugh when she asked it: 'So how's that working out for you?' Well, in fairness, it has allowed me to move up the career ladder pretty quickly, because it's motivated me to work hard and outperform my peers. But, yes, I see how working my arse off to essentially avoid being vulnerable and exposed has probably not worked in other areas of my life. As Ellie pointed out in her summary of my beliefs, I probably figured from a young age that it's just not okay to show your feelings and emotions, because growing up in our family we didn't talk about anything, and everyone seemed to try and hide it when they were upset. In my mind, I probably decided that if you do open yourself up, it makes you vulnerable and at greater risk of possible rejection and therefore abandonment. The fact that I used to hide away when I was upset would reinforce that. Actually, thinking about it, I think I've always seen open emotion as something that makes you vulnerable. If you're upset, you're open to attack because your defences are down. And even openly showing love and affection makes you vulnerable because it shows your weak point and leaves you open to hurt. It's like in those classic superhero movies – the baddies always capture the girlfriend of the superhero, because they know that will lure him into their trap; they know it's his weakness, his vulnerability.

Ellie then asked how operating in this way has affected me. I suppose, in a way, it can make me feel a bit lonely at times, because I always keep a bit of distance between me and others. I only show them what I want them to see, and keep the rest locked away nice and safe. I guess it makes me feel like I'm always a little bit on the outside. Even though I've got a great friendship group, whenever we're together I often feel like I'm watching the interactions, I'm never fully in them. It's always bothered me in the back of my mind, but I've never really thought to figure out why. Is this the reason? But I don't see why I should have to share my deepest, darkest thoughts and secrets with people, just to feel like I belong. Ellie said that belonging and indeed being vulnerable are so much more than just words. The reason I feel that way is because I'm always hiding. My belief of having to show the world how good I am in order to be loved means I'm constantly trying to figure out who or what I need to be for the world, so I'm never just me. I'm always second-guessing myself and my actions, so I'm never fully present. I feel like I need to hide the real me because I fear the real me is not good enough. According to Ellie, being vulnerable means being me, the real me and nothing but the real me – it means being Uppy. Apparently, staying true to this will make me feel safer and more protected than I ever thought possible, because it opens me up to real connection, real belonging, real courage and real happiness.

That all sounded great, but I still didn't fully understand what Ellie's definition of vulnerability was. So she reiterated it for me: being vulnerable is being you, the real you and nothing but the real you. It's showing up 100 per cent as yourself, and standing strong and present in that space no matter what.

She said that the changing of my fundamental 'I'm not good enough' belief will most definitely achieve this, so the next step is to make sure that the way I see myself is in line with it too. Before we got cracking on that, though, she asked me to think about how my relationship with Steve would change if I allowed myself to be more vulnerable with him. Gosh, now there's a thought. I'm not sure I'd even know how. Every time I try to open up with Steve, I freeze. I guess when I think about it, the reason I find it so difficult is because I get worried that he'll think I'm crazy, or weak, or I'll say something that will make him stop loving me. Oh SHIT, did I actually just say that? That's my belief right there – I'm worried that he'll withdraw his love and abandon me. LIGHTBULB. And you know what the really ironic thing is? Me being like that actually pushes him away anyway … so the things I'm doing to try and prevent this are actually making it happen. How fucked up is that? Ellie's right – I'm always thinking about who I should be in the relationship, and trying to be what I think a 'perfect' wife should be, so I'm not fully showing up as myself, and therefore I'm not fully connecting with him, which makes me feel less secure, which is the very thing I was trying to avoid in the first place. So why the fuck am I still behaving that way?!

As I started to get irritated, Ellie told me to take it easy on myself. She reminded me that until very recently I had no idea that this was how I was operating, and I'd had no reason to question it because I didn't know there was another way. I've been unconsciously incompetent until this point, but now we've uncovered it, we can start to move me to the unconsciously competent phase – where I will always show up as myself without even having to think about it.

Right, so the next part – my self-image. My first thoughts were: fat, lost and out of control. Something told me this probably wasn't going to be the right answer!

Ellie started by explaining a concept called 'labelling'. She gave me another little handout on it, because she said it's quite an abstract concept so she wanted me to be able to go back over it and make sense of it in my own time before we moved on to the strategies about it in our next session. So I've pasted it in here.

LABELLING

The human brain labels things in order to make sense of the world. The labels are like shortcuts and allow us to define the things around us. For example, a vertical rectangular structure that must be pushed inward or outward in order for you to walk through a wall is labelled a 'door'. In reality, however, this is not a door; it's actually a bunch of molecules, atoms and energy formed in a particular way. To describe it in this manner, however, would make it impossible to make sense of the world, because everything is in fact a bunch of molecules, atoms and energy, so we would have no way of differentiating between all the different things.

We're given these labels as a child, so we never think to question them or what they're really defining; we just believe them to be the truth. But since the labels are only a description of the thing and not the actual thing itself, surely that means they're not the truth – they're just a version of it. And, therefore, we can create a different version, if we want to.

Now I'm not suggesting you go around and start changing the names of things, and start calling a 'door' a 'rolling pin' – that would just get incredibly confusing. For the most part, these labels work and allow us to function efficiently in society; however, we also apply labels to ourselves – and this is when changing them can come in handy, particularly if they're not allowing us to be our true selves and serve our values and goals.

For example, if you constantly label yourself as 'fat' or 'lazy', it's only a matter of time before this starts to become the truth for you. And as we know, your brain likes your internal and external worlds to be aligned, so if your internal label of yourself is that you're fat, your external actions and behaviours will want to validate that, so your brain will filter all the 2 million bits accordingly and guide you towards poor lifestyle choices.

So if we can understand how you're labelling yourself, we can continue to understand the internal blueprint your thoughts and behaviours are trying to align with, and therefore we can change what's not working for you and continue to re-design your blueprint so it does indeed allow you to be the real you, focus on what really matters and what you really want, and, ultimately, live a healthier, happier and more fulfilled life.

This process of uncovering and changing labels has four parts:

1. Define the label – for example, 'I am fat.'
2. Ask, 'Is that really who I am, or is it just a definition or label that I've accepted until now?'

3. Ask, 'Is it allowing me to be my true self and serve my values and goals?'

4. If not, create an alternative label and definition – for example, 'I am kind to myself and my body.'

Can you see how this new label and definition will guide you towards different thoughts and actions? If you're 'kind' to yourself and your body, you won't want to harm it by feeding it unhealthy food and keeping it sedentary; instead, your brain will seek ways to look after and nourish it.

Again, remember that this is all happening on a subconscious level. So you may not consciously be aware of this shift in perception, but your brain will naturally guide you towards better choices in its bid to align your internal and external worlds.

Holy fuck, this was a head fuck!!! I've read over it a number of times now and I think I'm getting it. So basically, what Ellie is saying, is that without knowing it I'm labelling myself, and these labels are driving my thoughts and behaviours, and could be preventing me from being who I want to be and having what I want. These labels, though, are not the truth – they are simply my perception of the truth, which means I have the power to change them and create a new version of the truth. A truth that will serve me and what's important to me in a much greater way.

I'm pleased she gave me this info to go away with and mull over between sessions, because it has taken me a while to grasp it, but now I have I'm fully on board and SO ready to change my labels. Now let me see: I'm amazing, gorgeous and a fantastic lover … yeah, I reckon that would work!

After we went over all the vulnerability stuff, we spent the rest of the session reviewing where I'm at. Ellie said it's good to check in as we progress to track how we're going and identify if and where we need to focus and make any changes. For the most part, it's going really well and we're both really happy. But we did agree that I could be more diligent with my daily habits. Ellie asked me what was preventing me from doing all my non-negotiables every day. To be honest, there really isn't anything major getting in the way, except the usual busyness of my life; I guess I still just need to prioritise it a bit more. I've definitely bumped them up the to-do list, but I still think they could be higher. We identified that it would be a lot easier if I scheduled absolutely everything so I could take not remembering off the table as an excuse. I do think that will help.

Ellie also offered up another suggestion that I wasn't too sure about so am mulling it over. She asked if I thought it would be helpful to have some extra accountability. Of course I said yes, because we know how I hate to let people down, so that would definitely motivate me to do what I'm supposed to do. I thought she was talking about having extra accountability with her, but she wants to introduce me to a private Facebook group she runs that's specifically for professional women and female business owners, and focuses solely on personal stuff. Eeek! That makes me really uncomfortable. What if someone on there knows me? I'd die if they found out how useless I am with all my personal shit. As Ellie said back at the start, though, when you have specific people to be accountable to, you get much better and quicker results because it leverages the power of community and belonging. She said she hasn't mentioned it to me until now because she knew it would freak me out too much, but she believes I'm now at a stage where I could be ready to step up and admit that it's okay to ask for support, and in doing so I could even empower others to do the same. I guess I did always wonder where people go for help with this sort of stuff, and I won't be working with Ellie like this forever, and lord knows I'd like to get all the results as quickly as possible. Plus it would be pretty awesome to be able to make such a powerful difference in other people's lives. So I am considering it, but I'm still on the fence at the moment. To be continued …

October 15th

How the hell is it Monday AGAIN? Okay, so I have been really good with doing all my routines and non-negotiables, but I still need to be better with documenting it in here – especially my evidence. I know I feel better when I pay attention to the evidence, and I know it'll make a difference to changing my beliefs more quickly, but I'm still not doing it. Maybe this accountability thing might be a good idea after all. It's the busiest time of year coming up at work so I'd like to get all this happening more naturally before then, cos I just won't have the time or headspace to be consciously doing it all. I think I'll chat with Ellie about it in our next session. I can see how the group space makes sense but I'm still nervous of people thinking I'm crazy.

Oooh, I went back to the naturopath again today too. She said that all of my results were still in the same ranges they were when I saw the doctor before, but a couple of them were at the higher end of the range, so it's likely that there's some stuff going on that couldn't be detected by regular blood tests, hence why they weren't picked up by the doctor (she called these subclinical symptoms). As she said on my last visit, she believes that most of my issues are in response to stress. Of course, the polycystic ovaries are there, so we can't necessarily get rid of them, but we can certainly reduce the symptoms I experience, like my crazy PMT and water retention. Yes, water retention. That's why I sometimes get on the scales and I've put on up to 2kgs out of nowhere – I knew I couldn't possibly have put that weight on in one day, but until now I had no other explanation for it. Still a massive headfuck though, to see the scales go up like that when you know you've been good with your eating.

She also thinks that the size of my 'girth' is probably more as a result of excess cortisol, so she suggested I consider coming off the pill and medication from the doctor and using natural supplementation to manage my periods and belly fat. She said I can chat about it with my GP before making a decision, but to be honest what she's saying makes far more sense to me, and I don't feel any better from taking that medication, so I think I'll just go with what she says. So for now she's supplementing me to help get my periods more regular and reduce my PMT symptoms, and to help my system calm down and deal with stress better, so that I can reduce the amount of excess cortisol in my body. And once we've done that, we can look at the other systems and organs, and see what still needs help to be restored. She reiterated how important it is, though, to remain diligent with all the stuff I'm doing with Ellie, so that I can calm the body from within. Otherwise, the work with her will still ultimately be a bandaid approach. What I do with her is meant to accelerate the physical restoration of my body, but the work with Ellie is to instil it at my core. Okay, okay – I've got it!

October 18th

You'll never guess where I am today – at a freaking spa! Since my appointment with the naturopath the other day I've been thinking a lot about my health and the state my body is in. I can't believe I'm essentially like this because of the way I've been thinking … and that all along I've had the power to change it. I think now about all the people around me in my life, and realise they're probably going through similar things to me too. All of them have something going on – whether it's a health complaint, issues with their work, relationship problems, or a lack of general happiness and fulfilment in life – but they all just keep on keeping on. It's really quite sad that we all just accept this shit as normal and we fuck around trying all these different quick fixes to make ourselves feel better, but it never usually gets us any further forward in the long term and so we get stuck in these cycles of mind fuckery and live sub-optimum lives … and then inevitably pass all that shit down to our kids. Anyway, there's nothing I can do about that now, I need to focus on myself, but I really do hope that someday I might know enough to help other people too.

So long story long (oh how I love to do that!) I decided to take the day off and book myself in to get some pampering and very much needed rest and relaxation. I also wanted to take the opportunity to read back over all the info Ellie gave me about the stress response so I can make sure I fully understand what's happening inside me – I'm finding that having this knowledge is making me more motivated to do my actions and non-negotiables, because I understand the direct impact they are having on my health, and therefore my life. Likewise, I know the impact it will have if I don't do them. So that's all I'm writing for today – I want to try to switch my brain off for a bit if I can.

October 19th

Back to normality today – I felt a bit more chilled after my lovely day out, but then halfway through my two hours of power this morning Jenny from HR burst into my office to tell me she needed to talk to me about trimming down the size of my team as a result of restructures in the company. There's nothing like the prospect of having to make someone redundant and ruin their life to kill your buzz, I can tell you that. My initial reaction was anger, frustration and anxiety, but after Jenny had left and I sat for a bit, I managed to talk myself round and remind myself that even though I couldn't control the situation, I could control the way I respond – so I got my notepad out and started to create a game plan, which thankfully calmed me down a lot.

Anyway, all that shit will go on for a while so I'm sure you'll be hearing a lot more about it. For now, let me tell you how my session with Ellie went this week – we got stuck into the strategies around self-image and labelling. She basically took me through that four step process mentioned in her info sheet, but she made it a little easier for me by getting me to do it for the different personas in my life. She got me all relaxed with some breathing so I could access my subconscious more easily, and told me to just say the first things that came into my head as she asked me about each persona, and not to filter them in any way (just like I did with the mind-mapping). So here's how the process basically went for each persona:

As a leader I am:
Busy, strong, dominant, hard-working, dependable, winging it

As a team member I am:
Dominant, hard-working, loyal, anxious, dependable

As a wife I am:
Insecure, loyal, hard-working, well-meaning, uncommunicative, boring

As a daughter I am:
Selfish, distant, guarded, childish, uncommunicative

As a friend I am:
Selfish, flaky, loyal, well-meaning, insignificant

I'm Debs and I am:
Tired, lost, insecure, fat, busy, worried

A few surprised me – I thought it was interesting that 'insignificant' came up when I thought about myself as a friend, and 'childish' came up for me as a daughter. Well, on the face of it, I guess that doesn't seem too out there since I am the child, but I'm realising that my behaviour when I'm with my parents is still very much that of a child rather than an adult. In fact, I'm now even wondering if it's exclusively when I'm with my parents. I mean, when I think about it, the way I act with Steve is very childish – stomping off when things don't go my way or they get a bit hard, and expecting him to constantly give me recognition and validate me and what I do. Maybe that's why I feel so lost a lot of the time – I look like an adult living in an adult world, but inside I still feel like a kid who just wants to fit in and be loved. Hmmm, interesting. Hopefully when I can change this bloody belief I'll feel differently. Maybe that's the link to my childhood that's keeping me in child mode?

Anyway, so after we'd uncovered those labels we went through the other three steps of the process to decide if they're true, if they're working for me and, if not, how I can change them. I was pleased to see that some of them were working, and they weren't all bad – I'm taking that as a win, thank you very much. I'll write one of them here so I can remember the process. I've taken the 'insignificant with my friends' one since that jumped out at me. So here goes:

I am insignificant.

Is that really who I am, or just a label that I've accepted as the truth?
Well, no, I suppose that's not who I really am. I've just decided that because I don't feel like I have the connection or sense of belonging I would like with my friends.

Is it allowing me to be my true self and serve my values and goals?

Not at all. When I feel insignificant, I either try to find ways to get noticed more, or I retreat into myself and resolve that no-one will notice if I'm not there or present anyway (ironically making me feel even more insignificant). This means I don't have a strong network of people around me with whom I can be my true self, which is a massive value for me. And it makes me feel insecure, which resonates into other values and areas of my life – I'm not as confident or motivated to do the things that are important to me, like look after myself, be present and connected with Steve, and have fun … so ultimately I'm a whole lot more unhappy.

So what's an alternative label?

I am significant. Ha, that sounds so obvious, but I couldn't think of anything better! I can see that if I think that rather than thinking I'm insignificant, I'll feel like I have more of an impact on the people who matter to me, so I'll be more motivated to show up as the best version of myself I can be … which of course, is just myself without restrictions. And I can see how this will make me feel more secure and more empowered to be myself in other areas of my life, which will in turn inspire me to look after myself and serve my values and goals better.

After we'd gone through all the personas, and changed all the labels that weren't working for me, Ellie and I identified the top three new labels that would make the most difference to my life if I lived by them. They are:

- I am significant.

- I am present.

- I am secure.

As well as the benefits I've already mentioned with 'I am significant', being present will remind me to let go of unnecessary worries and thoughts, because these stop me from showing up as my true self. Telling myself I'm secure will remind me of my new belief – that I'm good enough just the way I am – and it will again empower me to do what I need to do, to be able to show up as my true self … to let go of the mind fuckery and unleash my Uppy!

Yeah, I like that: I'm Debs and I'm significant, present and secure.

So now all that's left to do is convince my subconscious that this is who I am – easy fricking peasy!! Well, in theory it is I suppose – I just need to add it to my daily routine with my new belief, visualise the fuck out of it, and look for evidence that it's true. I'm so happy it doesn't require me to make a massive addition to my to-do list. ☺

Oh, I spoke to Ellie about the Facebook group too. She suggested I just get on there and check it out. She said I don't have to post or make any comments until I'm comfortable, but at least if I go on and have a look I can make an informed decision about whether or not I think it's right for me. That sounded fair, so she's added me to it – I'll check it out over the next few days.

October 20th

I finally got the courage up to try that restorative yoga last night. It was such a nice end to the week, and made a lovely change to drinking too many glasses of wine with my colleagues and spending the rest of the weekend worrying that I did or said something wrong. It's funny that I usually drink wine to chill me out, but that feeling completely pales in comparison to how I felt after the yoga. I was so relaxed and calm it was like I was stoned – like I was floating out of the room on a big fluffy white cloud and everything around me was just drifting on by. I felt like nothing could affect me, and if anything tried, it would just bounce right off the force field of calm I had all around me.

Don't get me wrong, it was frustrating as all hell for most of the class – because we were holding the poses for three to five minutes each time, I had three to five minutes to think about everything that was humanly possible to think about. I was getting pretty agitated at first, but then I said to myself, 'Show me your Uppy', which reminded me of my new belief and labels, and of course my values and goals, and I realised that it was much better for me if I just gave in, stopped resisting and chilled the fuck out. So I tried to keep my attention on my breathing, and every time my mind wandered off I just brought it back to that. Even though I was constantly having to bring my attention back, by the time we got to the last five minutes where we just lie down and do nothing, I definitely felt more calm than I did the last time I tried yoga – so for me, that's a win. I even ended up buying a pack of classes at the end – I thought that would give me even more motivation to go again. Ha! One embarrassing thing did happen though – about twenty minutes in we were doing some sort of twisted move on our backs, and my stomach gurgled so loud I'm pretty sure the people out on the street could hear it! Luckily no-one in the class acknowledged it but I know they must have heard it – it just came out of nowhere! Ah well, I guess it was better than letting out a fart – there would be no coming back from that! Oooh, I just thought – perhaps that was my parasympathetic nervous system coming out to play. I remember Ellie's info sheet saying that when it's activated often your stomach will gurgle, and I most definitely did have my foot on the brake at that point. Oh my god, I totally think it was my body resting and digesting. Fuck yeah!

Last night was also a great opportunity for me to properly catch up with Michelle – we went for dinner after yoga and had a really good chat. I don't know whether it was the fact that the yoga had chilled me out, or the work I've been doing with Ellie lately that gave me more confidence, but I actually opened up a bit to Michelle and told her what I've been up to with Ellie. Even with all the calm, the terror got through as I started to talk, but I'm so happy I pushed on and did it anyway. Ellie mentioned something about that actually when we were discussing fear – she said the trick is not to eliminate all fear, because that's impossible, but to just do what you want to do anyway, and either let the fear come along for the ride or allow it to move on by and go about its business somewhere else. I guess that's what I did? WIN!

And the outcome of that was better than I ever could have imagined – Michelle gave me a massive hug and said she was so unbelievably proud of me. Bitch made me cry in public! It was lovely though, and such an awesome piece of evidence that I am indeed good enough and loved just the way I am. She even said later that I'd inspired her to seek some help and support herself, to help with the whole Phil thing. She still isn't sure what she ultimately wants to do, but she's decided that for now she's not quite ready to give up on their marriage. She said that after talking to me and hearing about my journey, she realises that maybe they do have a chance, and maybe they just both need to figure out some shit – together and independently. Most of their lives have been dedicated to their work, and then their kids, and so I think their priorities have become confused and they've lost their identities, both individually and as a couple. It seems they too have become stuck in this cycle of mind fuckery. It's easy to see why divorce rates are so high nowadays – I think this situation is extremely common, but most people just don't know it's possible to make a change another way, rather than just cutting and running.

Listen to me! I sound like I'm an expert now after working with a coach for a few weeks. It's funny, though – even in this short time, I really do see the world very differently, and I'm starting to notice just how much mind fuckery is constantly going on all around us, and how most people have no idea that there's a way out from it. Well, at least now maybe there's a way out for Michelle. I actually thought she'd be all over this shit, given that she's so in to yoga and health, but I guess that just shows how important it is to get the mind on board with it all too – and I think that's the piece she's been missing. Anyway, I'm going to collect another win here – for inspiring another woman to ask for help. I am killing it right now!

After all that, I also decided to look through that Facebook group. I have to say, it was quite liberating. I've always thought all the things I think and do are crazy, and I've always been terrified of people finding out. But looking through a lot of the conversations on the page, it turns out that I'm not crazy, I'm just a woman. I swear most of the threads could have been written by me – there was chat about muffin tops, sleeping in separate rooms from your partner, dealing with PMT and even secret internet shopping. I think I may have found my people!!! There was some technical advice on there about managing and overcoming some of these things, but to be honest I think the most value is in the normal conversations between the women, and the sharing of their experiences and practical solutions. Ahhh, it's so nice to know I'm not the only one going through all this. It's still going to be difficult to pop my cherry and get involved, but this is what I've been craving – a support network of people who get me. And who knew it was hiding right here on the internet this whole time!

October 21st

I really think I'm starting to get myself a pretty good-looking blueprint together now. I've laid the foundations with my values and goals, so I know what's important to me and what I want, and I've unlocked the major things that have been holding me back by creating a new story and labels. I know I've not nailed it yet and I need to stick to my routines and non-negotiables to make my subconscious believe that this is how I roll now, but I can totally see how this blueprint is going to change my thoughts and behaviours, and ultimately my life. God that sounds wanky. But I actually think it will.

Anyway, let's back that up by doing one of my non-negotiables, shall we?

Evidence that I'm good enough just the way I am, and I'm significant, present and secure:

1. Had a great evening with Steve that ended in a bit of sexy time. ☺ He told me he loves it when I get on top – so I guess my belly isn't an issue for him after all, and my body is indeed good enough as it is?

2. I wasn't thinking about my belly while we were having sex – so I was present for a change.

3. Sarah called, who I haven't seen in ages, and told me she misses me and would love to get together – she has no idea what I'm up to at the moment or if I'm doing good things, so I guess she must like me for who I am, and I must be significant to her, right?

October 22nd

Evidence that I'm good enough just the way I am, and I'm significant, present and secure:

1. I started doing a meditation app this morning – I've never wanted to do it before because I couldn't deal with all the thoughts that came up as soon as I shut my eyes, but I got through it. It was hard, but I stayed as present as I could with it, and all in all it did make me feel more connected to what's important, and so more secure in just being me.

2. My old, old boss from years ago sent me an email to ask how I was getting on, and to say how much he used to love working with me. He had no need to do that, he didn't want anything. He just said that he thought of me and wanted to check in, so I guess I'm significant?

3. I presented to the board and didn't get as flustered beforehand as I usually do, worrying about what they'd think of me or if they'd make any comments that would make me feel small. So I think that means I was present and secure, knowing I'm good enough as I am?

October 23rd

Evidence that I'm good enough just the way I am, and I'm significant, present and secure:

1. Steve called me randomly in the afternoon to tell me he loves me.

2. Rob made a comment during the team meeting that usually would have pissed me off because it would have made me feel like he was trying to make me look stupid, but instead I turned it back on him and everyone saw that it was a pointless comment and ignored it.

3. I mindfully ate my entire lunch!

I think I'm finally starting to get this evidence documenting thing. Man, it feels good! It's funny, because a lot of those things probably would have happened anyway, but up until now I would have either not paid attention to them or I would have perceived them in a more negative way. I'm definitely starting to notice that I'm behaving differently. I'm more calm and a lot of little things that would have bothered me before just seem insignificant. I think it's really helped as well, actually, that I've been looking at my values and goals, and doing my visualisation every day, so I've always got everything at the forefront of my mind. I guess that helps my brain know how to filter the information more efficiently, right, so that I see the things that help me to serve them? Hey, I think I'm getting it?

Right-o, let's summarise this self-image stuff before I move on to the final section with Ellie.

Journal

☐ I. **Track how you're doing:**

- What have been your top three wins for the week?
- What have been your top three challenges?
- What are three ways you've served your values this week?
- Next week, what will you stop, start and keep doing in order to serve your values better/more?
  - Stop:
  - Start:
  - Keep:
- What are three pieces of evidence that your new story and labels are true? (Do this one daily.)

Action

☐ 2. **Complete the labels process for all personas in your life:**
  - Define the label – for example, 'I am fat'.
  - Ask, 'Is that really who I am, or is it just a definition or label that I've accepted until now?'
  - Ask, 'Is this label allowing me to be my true self and serve my values and goals?'
  - If not, create an alternative label and definition – for example, 'I am kind to myself and my body'.

☐ 3. **Identify the top three labels that will make the most difference to your life and your ability to be your true self and serve your values and goals.**

☐ 4. **Add these to your morning and evening routine along with your new belief and document evidence that these are true also.**

Remember

☐ 5. **Be before you are and you will become.***

☐ 6. **Being vulnerable is being you, the real you and nothing but the real you. It's showing up 100 per cent as yourself, and standing strong and present in that space no matter what. This will give you the ultimate feeling of security because it will open you up to real connection, real belonging, real courage and real happiness.**

* I forgot to write about this in one of my regular entries, but Ellie said this to me during my session when I was getting a bit impatient about making all this unconsciously competent, and it really helped. Basically she said that if you just think and behave in the way that you want to be, and visualise (and feel) that it's that way already, eventually you will become it. Simple, hey?! It's a nice reminder of the importance of consistency, and how if you just stick with it, you will indeed become and have everything you want. Nice.

TAKE THE REINS

October 24th

Gosh, I can't believe I'm at the final topic in my work with Ellie already. I definitely thought there'd be more to this sorting your shit out business. Don't get me wrong; it has definitely been (and still is) challenging, in terms of staying true to what I know is right when all my brain wants to do is stick with what it's always done, but Ellie was right – the actual strategies and concepts behind it all really are quite simple.

So the last thing Ellie wants us to cover right now is communication. To be honest, I've always considered myself pretty good at communicating, but I've realised during this process that I'm actually only good on the surface level. I can build great relationships up to a point, particularly in business, but if the chat starts to get too deep and anywhere close to the 'me' I'm trying to hide, I put my barriers up and run for the hills. Ellie reckons this kind of communication will naturally get easier anyway, when I become more comfortable with letting the real me come out to play, but she wanted to share a couple of concepts and strategies that would give me even more confidence, and make my interactions with myself and others even more meaningful and fulfilling.

She said this final part will help bring everything together, because it's the vehicle for everything we've discussed and learned. We need to know how to communicate effectively with ourselves and those around us in order to live out our life blueprint (our values, goals, new beliefs and labels) effectively and stay true to who we really are. She explained that the first and most important part to this process is understanding that we can always control the way we respond to things and therefore control the way we feel. This had come up a few times throughout the process – that the only thing we can ever truly control is ourselves – so it wasn't a new concept for me, but now was the time to learn how to really do that.

She started by reminding me again that reality is bullshit, and how nothing is 'the' truth, it's only 'a' truth based on our perceptions and interpretations. She asked me to think of a situation that I had found stressful but someone else present had not. I thought of Steve the other day – I'd lost my car registration papers and needed to renew my insurance that day cos it was about to run out, and I couldn't remember my online login details so I sat on hold for over 40 minutes only to be told that I had to wait for new papers to be sent out, so I couldn't drive my car for a few days until they arrived. If I was measuring my stress on a scale of one to ten, I would definitely have been at eleven by that point. Steve, however, was super bloody calm – so calm in fact that it was stressing me out even more. I couldn't understand it because it actually affected him the most – he was supposed to be using my car to go up the coast for a few days to see his mates, which he'd been really looking forward to, so this meant he either had to fuck around getting different trains and buses to get there, or not go at all. That would have totally sent me over the edge, but he just calmly got onto the internet and started to figure out his options. Argh, just talking about it with Ellie was pissing me off again! Anyway, Ellie said this was a perfect example – Steve and I were both in the same situation, in that we were inconvenienced by not being able to use the car, but we each responded and felt very differently – therefore, our perceptions and interpretations of the situation were very different.

So … if different interpretations of a situation can produce different feelings, and the interpretations are not 'the' truth but simply 'a' truth, then if we change our interpretations and therefore the truth as we see it, we can change the way we feel. I wasn't computing this, so Ellie gave me an example.

She told me to imagine that it had started to rain. At that time, she said, since I was inside and had no intention of going out, it was highly unlikely that the rain would have any impact on me or the way I felt, because it didn't affect me or what I was doing in any way. If I was a farmer, on the other hand, and it hadn't rained for a really long time, this rain would make me feel happy and relieved because it would mean my crops could grow and, therefore, I would be able to sell them and make money to support my family. Another interpretation would come if I were a bride on my wedding day – the rain would likely make me feel upset and angry, because I'd been waiting for this day my entire life and now in my eyes it was going to be ruined.

So the same situation was happening to all three people but they all interpreted it in a very different way and, therefore, all felt a different way. The physical rain didn't make them feel anything – it was the interpretation, or meaning, they gave to it that did. Ellie stated that:

> *It's not the situation or person that makes you feel a certain way; it's the meaning you give to it.*

So if you change the meaning, you change the way you feel, and ultimately you change your life – because you are always in control of the way you feel.

She went on to state:

> *You are the creator of the meanings, so you are the creator of how you feel, and therefore you are the creator of your life.*

Mind. Blown.

So getting back to the car registration example, Steve had probably given the situation the meaning of, 'That's inconvenient, but I'd really like to go so I'll find another way.' Whereas I'd given it the meaning, 'That's so fucking inconvenient, I've already got so much to do and now this is going to make everything even harder.' Giving it that meaning didn't change the situation in any way, it just made me feel more stressed and pissed off, and did indeed make it all seem harder.

Hmmmm, so how could I use this in my daily life? Ellie took me back to the concept of the stress response. She asked me to remember all the things that happen with my mind, body and behaviour, as a result of my brain thinking I'm in danger. God, I didn't even know where to begin with my answer to that, there's so much – low energy, weight gain, poor digestion, bloating, PMT, irregular periods, brain fog, anxiety, erratic moods, shitty sleep, bad eating, no motivation, low confidence, over-working, procrastination … I think that should be enough for the purposes of this exercise! She then reminded me that this response, for the most part, happens because of a perceived danger and not a real one. And that perceived danger is there because of a meaning I've given to something, which has then caused me to worry, panic, stress and so on (for example, if I fuck this report up my boss is going to think I'm incompetent and lose respect for me … therefore I risk being rejected and abandoned, and therefore my survival is at risk). So if I can give different meanings to situations, I'll create less perceived dangers and, therefore, reduce or even eliminate the amount of times the stress response is triggered unnecessarily. So then all my systems and organs will function better in my body, I'll have more energy and feel better about myself, my mood and brain will be clearer and more able to operate proactively and logically, I'll be able to make better decisions, and I'll be more likely to think and behave according to my values and goals, and stay true to who I really am…so, ultimately, I'll be healthier, happier and more fulfilled – just from changing the way I communicate with myself by changing a few meanings. Holy fuck – is that true?!

So then how the hell do you change these bloody meanings, I of course asked. Ellie said, through the work I've done already with my blueprint, and particularly with changing my beliefs and labels, I'll naturally start to create different meanings for situations because the information I'm using to form them will be different. Ahhhhh interesting, I said to Ellie – this reminds me of that thing you told me a little while ago, about how we can only make choices based on the information and resources we have. So through this process you've been building up my resources so that I have more available to allow me to make different and better choices … and therefore different meanings, I guess? Absojollylutely, was her response – she told me that's exactly why I need to take it easier on myself and give myself time to go through this process and embed the changes. I've always been making the best decisions and choices I could with the resources I had, which is the best and only thing I could do. But now that I have more resources I'll be able to do that in a much more efficient way, one that allows me to stay more true to who I really am and what I really want.

So the next resource she gave me was a process of questioning that I can work through in the moment to create these changes to the meanings I give things. She said, when I find myself feeling or responding to something in a way that doesn't serve me, I can ask myself:

- Is this feeling I have right now allowing me to be myself and serve my life blueprint?

- If not, what meaning am I giving to this situation?

- What is a different meaning I could give to this situation in order to serve me better and therefore make me feel better?

Logically this all makes sense, but I'm just not sure how well I'll be able to work through that process in the moment when I'm stressed. Ellie again reminded me of the stages of learning, and said that this is just another case of building a habit and remaining consistent until it becomes unconsciously competent and my natural way of operating. So I may not do this successfully every time, but as long as I keep doing it when I can, eventually I'll start to do it more and more, until ultimately it becomes my go-to thinking.

She said I can make it easier by being proactive about my thinking and coming up with some different meanings to common situations now, so I don't have to create them in the moment. Once I have them ready to go, I can just reach into my toolbox of meanings and strategies, and pick the most appropriate one when I need it. Here's a few we worked through together:

I'm stressed because one of my team members hasn't done what I wanted them to do.

The meaning is probably linked to my belief that if they fuck up, it'll make me look bad and so then I won't be able to show how good I am and I'll lose respect from my superiors and peers ... and trigger my fear of rejection and abandonment.

Another meaning could be: 'Everyone's doing the best with the resources they have'. So then I can ask, 'What's the reason they haven't delivered what I expected?' Did they understand what they had to do? Did they have all the information and resources they needed? Do I need to give them more? Or did they just not want to do it? This puts me into my logical/problem-solving brain and makes me feel calmer and more motivated to find a solution to prevent it from happening again, rather than getting stressed and annoyed, and allowing it to impact me personally.

I'm angry because Rob is undermining me.

The meaning is probably again linked to my belief that I'm not good enough just the way I am. He's preventing me from showing how good I am and, therefore, putting me at risk of rejection by my other team members and colleagues.

Another meaning could be: 'I can't control the way other people think and behave, but I can control the way I respond to it'. And then I can get logical again and ask, 'What's Rob's story?' What does he believe that's making him respond this way? Is there any validity in his comments that I can learn and grow from? Or is this just his shit and it has nothing to do with me? This one makes me feel calmer even now.

I'm annoyed and I feel lonely because Steve isn't giving me what I need.

The meaning is probably AGAIN linked to my fear of being rejected – if he doesn't want to understand me or respect how I feel, maybe he's withdrawing from me and he'll abandon me.

Another meaning could be: 'We all have different versions of the world, and I respect that.' It will remind me that my version is very different to Steve's … and that he's probably never going to understand that on his own. So then I can ask, 'What can I do to help him understand my version and let him know what I need?'

Initially this new meaning made me a bit irritated, because it still feels like another thing I need to do and I still feel like Steve should just know how to respond to me by now, given that we've been together for so long. But then I remembered what Ellie said a while ago about how I'll only get closer to this ideal scenario if I first give Steve more resources to help him get a better understanding of my world and how I see it, and then stay calm and consistent with this while he moves through the stages of learning and becomes more unconsciously competent and therefore intuitive to my needs. Thinking about it in this way does make me feel a bit better – knowing that I've got the longer-term game in mind. So I've decided that, rather than getting annoyed because Steve doesn't know everything, I'll just remain present and figure out what I can do in that moment to give him some insight into what I need. Wow, how's that for a different meaning? That's so grown up of me! Now I just have to do it.

Actually, Ellie shared an awesome exercise with me that I can do with Steve to help with that last point A LOT – I'll write about it later once I've finished on this bit, though – otherwise, I'll do another one of my famous digressions!

Now I've gone through that exercise with Ellie and learned how to make changes to my self-communication, I can see a clear pattern – usually my meanings are linked to my belief of not being good enough and so I end up feeling pissed off and stressed because I think every-thing that happens could result in me being rejected and abandoned, and therefore is essentially a threat to my survival. I can also see that usually the way I feel is a result of me trying to control the uncon-trollable. I actually think that if I just have my default meaning as, 'I can't control what happens around me but I can always control the way I respond to it', I'll always be able to get a handle on my feelings. It will kick my arse into problem-solving mode and remind me to get logical and curious – which is something Ellie told me about right at the beginning. That way, I can remain in control of the meanings and therefore in control of my feelings, and therefore in control of my life … because I've been in control of creating it all. Actually, maybe my default meaning should just be, 'I am the creator of my life'. That seems to sum up and encapsulate everything very nicely.

Okay, done. I'm Debs and I am the creator of my life.

This whole meaning thing will also allow me to have more empathy towards others and not take things so personally, because it will remind me to try and see things from their perspective. I can ask myself, what meaning have they given to that situation? If I feel it's appropriate, I can ask questions to try and understand, and then help them to change the meaning by giving them more resources or getting logical with them, but if not it will simply help me to remain calm because I'll know that it's just their perception of the truth I'm experiencing, and not 'the' truth.

Ellie said that the way I communicate with myself is incredibly important, because this is all the brain knows as the truth. As she's explained a couple of times, the brain doesn't know the difference between real and perceived – she said to me, 'Don't think of a pink elephant', so of course I thought of a pink elephant. She said this is an example of how the brain just takes everything as very matter of fact. So if I'm constantly telling it negative things – like I'm fat or I'm not good enough – it will take them on as the truth, and use that information to filter what I consciously see and experience in my life, and indeed how I create meanings and how I feel. So, of course, by feeding it the good stuff – my values, goals, new beliefs, labels, meanings and visualisations – I'll consciously see more of the good stuff and therefore experience and feel it too. Happy, fucking, days.

Well, on that note, I'm going to shut up shop for the evening and go on my date night with Steve – we're trying this new Vietnamese place his colleague told him about down a random tiny alleyway in the city. Apparently it's super-authentic and delicious – can't wait!

October 25th

I've got one word to say about that Vietnamese place – holy fuck. Oh whoops, that's two words! Oh my god it was so bloody tasty, I'm definitely going back … perhaps every night if I can. ☺ It was a lovely night with Steve too – he only had to say 'Show me your Uppy' once, and the rest of the time it really felt like we were just there with each other, and nothing else mattered. It was great. It gave me an opportunity to bring up this whole relationship blueprint thing with him too, and explain all about it before we actually sit down and do it – that's right, I pre-framed that shit baby! And it worked – he's totally on board with doing it (although I think that's probably largely because he hopes it'll make his life easier)! Ah wait, I just realised I haven't written about the relationship blueprint yet so you're probably wondering what the hell I'm going on about. I'll explain it now …

So, obviously, Ellie has been banging on about my life blueprint a lot, and how important it is to understand it fully and change anything that prevents me from serving it, so that I have a solid foundation to guide me in everything I do. But in our last session she told me that's actually just one blueprint of many. Apparently we have a blueprint (a set of guidelines, standards and rules) for pretty much every situation in our lives – what it takes to be a good wife, a bad wife, a loyal friend, an unreliable friend, an inspiring leader, an oppressive leader, even an efficient waiter or an incompetent waiter … I think you get the idea. To help me understand the role that these blueprints play in my life, Ellie asked me to think about one of these scenarios and identify my blueprint for it. I went with the good wife one.

A good wife:

- takes care of her body
- looks nice for her husband
- is hard-working and contributes considerably financially
- has a nice home that is tidy and organised
- ensures her husband has everything he needs in the home – cooking, washing and so on

- is always honest
- communicates openly with her husband
- buys her husband thoughtful gifts
- makes her husband feel special
- is faithful
- satisfies her husband sexually.

How interesting is that?! We stopped there because we had enough stuff for the purposes of the exercise, but I'm gonna come back to it cos I can see now that I have shit loads of rules and standards, and I want to uncover them all! I couldn't believe I hadn't known about them before now, but Ellie said that's because they've mostly been constructed subconsciously, based on what my version of the world is (that is, my experiences, beliefs, labels and so on) so I haven't been consciously aware of them. So, basically, all day every day I'm sub-consciously measuring myself and my behaviour up against all these guidelines, and then I put all this underlying pressure on myself to adhere to them, and if I don't, I beat myself up and resolve that I'm a shitty wife. Oh, and this is only ONE blueprint, so I'm also doing the exact same thing with hundreds of other blueprints and scenarios at the same time. Urgh, I'm freaking exhausted just thinking about it!

Looking at this, it's no wonder I often feel insecure and constantly worried that I'm not being a good wife, because I'm not adhering to most of my rules and standards. I was quite surprised at some of them too – a good wife looks nice for her husband and ensures he has every-thing he needs in the home? Are we in the fucking 1950s?? I've always considered myself to be a strong, independent woman, but clearly I've picked up some old-fashioned beliefs that don't align with that. Ellie reminded me that we create these blueprints and our versions of the world based largely on what we see and experience as children, predominantly from our main caregivers. So I would have picked up some of these guidelines and rules from my parents, who would have picked theirs up from their parents, who were indeed raised in an era where the belief was still very much that the role of a man is to work and provide, and the role of a woman is to keep the house and take care of the children. We're not actually that far on from those times, so our thoughts and beliefs have not completely evolved yet to be those of true equality. So it seems I'm operating with both mindsets – that, as a modern woman, I must be equal to my husband and work and provide, while at the same time fulfilling my traditional role as a female by taking care of everything domestically too. It's no wonder I'm constantly busy and stressed – I believe I have to be everything to everyone and do it all … which, of course, is not possible. So then I believe I'm failing, which adds even more pressure and stress – and so the cycle of mind fuckery continues.

So by uncovering what my blueprints are, and changing any parts of them that don't align with my fundamental life blueprint, I'm able to take even more control of the way I feel and therefore of my life, because everything is working towards a common goal … which, of course, is the goal of allowing me to be who I truly am and serve what I truly want. Understanding the blueprints of those around me is also helpful, because it allows us to align with each other much better and get the most out of our interactions together. Ellie said we don't have to understand all of the blueprints for everyone, just those necessary and relevant to that relationship and scenario. So, for example, I don't need to know what Rob's blueprint is for being a good lover, but it would be handy to understand what standards and rules he's measuring me up against in terms of being a good leader for him. With that in mind, she shared with me a worksheet she's devised for couples to go through, to help uncover each other's blueprint with regard to being in a relationship. Ellie said that a lot of the problems in relationships come from not understanding each other's individual needs and expectations (and indeed not understanding them for ourselves either), so going through this series of specific questions and laying all the cards out on the table gives you unbelievable insight into what you fundamentally need and allows you to create a game plan to be able to give that to each other. She advised that Steve and I fill them out separately first and then come together to discuss. After getting the go ahead from Steve last night to do this I emailed him the worksheet this morning, and we've agreed to do them over the next couple of days and chat about it together on Sunday. I've made a start on mine but I'll finish it later and stick it in here tomorrow – I need to run now as I've just realised I need to confirm a meeting for tomorrow and I'm almost at my technology curfew for the night! See ya.

October 26th

I gave myself a cheeky afternoon break today to finish off my relationship blueprint – it's so interesting I just couldn't wait to finish it! Anyway, here it is:

Relationship blueprint

What has to happen for me to feel loved?

I need to feel like I'm being listened to when I talk, I need physical displays of love (through words, thoughtful actions, gifts or treats), I need to feel like I'm the most important thing to him, I need to be respected and appreciated (value my opinions, treat me as equal, be honest and faithful), and I need to be shown when he's proud of me.

What must not happen for me to feel loved?

Don't judge me, don't be unreliable or lie, don't ignore me or make me feel like I'm being stupid, don't shut me out.

How do I like to show love?

Doing nice things together, buying thoughtful gifts, helping him achieve what he wants, being there for him.

How do I like to be shown love?

Thoughtful actions (like spontaneously organising something for us to do together), saying nice things about me and/or what I'm doing, understanding what I need, being there for me no matter what.

What are the top five things I love about you?

You're reliable, kind, calm, up for doing things, and you put up with me and my shit.

What are the top five things I find challenging about you?

You're up for doing things but you never come up with the ideas (it's always down to me), sometimes you're too steady and chilled so you're content with the same things (which can get a bit boring), you're not very ambitious, you don't always understand what I need, you leave your fun-size chocolate bar wrappers on the couch every night!

What three things do I love most about our relationship?

We have a strong mutual respect for each other, I do feel like it's solid and it does fundamentally give me a level of security, and you seem to love me even when I'm being crazy!

What three things do I think we could work on in our relationship?

Deeper communication, more quality time being present with each other, get a bit more of a plan for our future in place.

What do I wish we had more of in our relationship?

Sex! Fun, deeper conversations.

What do I wish we had less of in our relationship?

Unnecessary tension.

What am I passionate about?

Arrow word puzzles, puppies, the ocean, my health, learning and developing.

What pisses me off?

Lies, selfishness, not being listened to, noisy eaters.

What is my idea of a perfect date?

A delicious dinner (starting with a yummy cocktail or two at a bar) on the waterfront, followed by gelato and a walk along the water, finished off with passionate sex surrounded by candles and music.

What does my ideal day look like?

Lie-in together talking about anything and everything, a nice brunch in a funky café, a stroll along the coast, chill out by the water, early evening cocktails by the water and then a nice long dinner together.

I'm looking forward to finding out how Steve has answered all these questions, and if any of his answers are even close to mine. I still haven't chatted about our goals with him yet actually – maybe this can be the warm up for that. I guess it'll be helpful to understand our fundamental needs first and then we can formulate a plan that includes all of those too? Or maybe I'm still putting it off because I'm scared of the awkward conversation we'll have to have if we want different things? Oooh, did I just say that out loud? Anyway, whatever – at this point I think it's better just to know. I can't keep worrying about all these things I have no control over, it's tiring me out. Talking of, I'm off for an early night tonight – I want to go into the weekend with as much energy as I can so I don't waste another one moping around and feeling guilty because I can't be arsed to do anything fun. Plus I really want to spend a bit of time in the kitchen this weekend experimenting with some new recipes so I have some yummy food for the week – I'm going to try making a Thai curry, a frittata and some bread that's not actually bread but just a whole heap of seeds and nuts … YUM. Night.

October 28th

Had the relationship blueprint chat with Steve tonight. It went really well, actually, although there were a few times when I went a bit quiet and got a bit agitated, particularly when he was talking about the bits he finds challenging about me and what we can work on in our relationship – I kept telling myself this was constructive feedback (that I had asked for) and not a personal attack, but it was still difficult not to take it personally and feel insecure about it. Ellie did warn me that this might happen. She advised me that if it did, to take a step back, breathe and remind myself of the overall goal of the conversation – which was to understand each other better and therefore take our relationship to a deeper level and make it even stronger. She reminded me that I'd said this is what I ultimately wanted all along, and that me getting defensive could prevent us from achieving it, so I must always keep in mind the bigger game plan and choose my responses according to that. This was helpful – I could feel my blood pressure rising and my cheeks start to get hot and turn red, but as Ellie's words popped into my mind I managed to catch my reaction by taking a deep breath and imagining that photo of the old couple with their backpacks holding hands. I realised that if I didn't suck down my own insecurities and work together with Steve, I'd never be that couple – and I want that more than anything.

Anyway, let me summarise what we uncovered.

It seems that in order for me to know that Steve loves, respects and is there for me I need validation through him being genuine and present with me – I need him to give me his undivided attention when I talk, be open to understanding my needs and be 100 per cent with me on a deeper level when we're together. When I feel like I'm the centre of his world and he truly gets me, I feel completely loved, secure and content. Don't you think it's funny, by the way, that this deeper stuff is the key to my heart, since that's something I've always tried to avoid? Makes sense though why I've always felt quite insecure, because I've always had the door shut to what truly matters to me. Steve, however, prefers physical validation, which he gets through things like cuddles, loving smiles, holding hands and even a cheeky tap on the arse! Since I'm not a very touchy-feely person and he's happy just bobbing along on the surface of life, properly meeting each other's needs has clearly been an issue for us that we were never even aware of. I often feel insecure or question if everything is okay because I'm craving a deeper understanding that he has no idea about, and he often feels neglected because I'm rarely proactive with the physical stuff – I usually wait for him to come to me. So even though we think we've given the other person what they need, we've actually been missing the mark on the most important stuff – so it's therefore gone unnoticed and unappreciated. How freaking dumb is that? Now we know this, however, it's so easy to fix – I just have to make sure I'm more proactive with my hugs and bum taps, and Steve needs to give me more focused and engaged attention … which, of course, I need to teach him how to do. Ellie said that an important part of the process once we've uncovered everything is to set expectations that we both agree on, so we can help each other to embed the new behaviours and make them unconsciously competent. So we agreed to speak up if we feel the other person isn't giving us what we need, and agreed not to get shitty when this happens (and if we do, we have permission to call each other out on it). It's funny, because I've always been annoyed that Steve doesn't just know what I need, but it turns out it works the other way too. Okay, so here are our initial expectations. To overcome some of the things I find challenging, Steve agreed to sit down with me for 15 minutes every night and give me his undivided attention. He's also going to take charge of at least one date night per month and organise everything. Plus he said he will try to be more spontaneous and adventurous, push himself out of his comfort zone more often, and take the time to properly understand our goals together and create a plan for the future … oh, and he'll put his chocolate wrappers in the bin! He gave me permission to pick him up on any of these things if he failed to do them, or didn't do them properly.

For him, the most challenging things about me were: of course that I don't give him enough physical attention, I'm too pre-occupied with work all the time (obviously), I often say derogatory things about myself and my body (which makes him uncomfortable), I rarely relax and allow myself to just be, I always talk about doing things to take care of my health but never follow through (and then moan), oh and I never empty the dishwasher (I freaking HATE doing that by the way!)

Anyway, with all that in mind, I've agreed to be more proactive with my physical touches, stick to all my non-negotiables and daily rituals/strategies, always communicate what these are to Steve so he can help keep me accountable and support me, focus on the positive things about me and my body, accept compliments when Steve gives them rather than shutting them down – and, of course, take turns in emptying the dishwasher. I too have given him permission to pick me up on all these things if he needs to.

To be honest, I was quite pleased with the outcome because I'm already doing a lot of the things so it didn't add much on to my to-do list. I think the important thing that came out of this, however, is how much difference me doing these things will make to my relationship, as well as myself – so it's extra motivation for me to do it. The other important thing it highlighted was how crucial it is to communicate with each other and create a safe space in which to do so. Now that we've laid everything out and given each other permission to say the things we're often scared to say, it's like a massive weight has been lifted and the gigantic elephant has left the room. It's also made me appreciate that this relationship business is a two-way street – I thought I knew Steve's version of the world better than he did, but it turns out I have some things to learn too. ☺ The final few questions on the worksheet regarding passions and ideal day and so on were just FYIs, to give us the opportunity to articulate a few extra nuggets of info for each other if we didn't know already.

Right, so before I head off for our Sunday chill night let me just summarise this blueprint stuff so I can get it straight in my head. We all have different blueprints for all the different people, things and situations in our lives. In order to truly understand ourselves we must understand all the rules, standards and guidelines that make up these blueprints, and identify how they impact our overarching life blueprint. With this insight, we then have the power to change the elements that aren't working so we can align them with who we truly are and what we truly want. It's then important to share the relevant blueprints with the relevant people according to the situation, so everyone can understand each other and their expectations. With this information you can then create a new set of mutual expectations that allow you to align your blueprints and work together using a common set of rules, standards and guidelines, making the process a lot more efficient and a damn sight more enjoyable. The key to doing this successfully is to allow open communication without judgement or attachment to anything except the ultimate outcome, so personal feelings and insecurities don't get in the way.

Got it. I'm looking forward to uncovering some more of my blueprints – I think it'll be super interesting to find out what my rules and standards are with regard to my health and my body, and also with regard to work and being a leader. If I can uncover who it is I think I need to be, I can start to change it to be more in line with who I actually am and want to be. I also want to turn this into a training session for my team so we can uncover some of their blueprints, particularly around leadership and teamwork – I can see how doing something like that will really unite us and help us to get even more shit done, both individually and as a collective. Game, set and match.

BYE.

October 29th

I'm working from home today – I didn't have any meetings scheduled so figured I may as well make the most of that and have a braless day, plus it's a great way for me to show Steve that I'm serious about all the blueprint stuff and making changes to strengthen our relationship. I thought I'd prepare a nice dinner for when he gets home too (well, heat up some of the curry I made at the weekend … it was still prepared by me, just not today – so that still counts, right?)

Anyway, I wanted to write about the last thing Ellie taught me before I forget. She talked about the notion of rapport and understanding people so I can communicate effectively and get the most out of my interactions. She said this is important because, as she said when she introduced the communication topic, communication is the vehicle for everything. Since the purpose of all this is to get me to always be my real self and nothing but my real self, I need to understand how to manage people to ensure that can happen, and I can have the confidence to stand strong in that space no matter what. I need to be able to make myself understood as well as understanding others, so this next part will help me to read behaviour and communicate at a much deeper level. Bring it on, I said!

So, apparently rapport is essentially when you have a strong connection with someone and you're both kind of 'in-sync'. You have a mutual understanding of how each other feels and communication flows easily. I asked Ellie how long it takes to build this kind of relationship, cos it sounded to me like it would take years – and I just don't have that kind of time to put in with everyone. She reckons, though, you can be in rapport almost immediately … especially if you know what you're doing. She asked me if I'd ever had a situation where I'd met someone for the first time and then within 10 minutes I felt like I'd known them for years. Funnily enough, I'd had that exact scenario the other day when I went to one of our PR agencies to meet our new account manager. I have to admit, I was expecting her to be a bitch – I figured she'd probably fluff her feathers and piss all over her territory to show me who was boss, but in reality she was bloody lovely. As soon as I walked in, I felt comfortable – she seemed to have this magical way of making me feel like I was actually important and that she valued everything I was saying. I've never seen anything like it – usually in those scenarios the interaction is just one big power trip, and while the other person is talking all you can think about is taking off your shoe and stabbing her in the eye with your stiletto. But this was quite the opposite.

Ellie pointed out that this wasn't actually magic, it was rapport – and clearly this other woman was a master at building it. Heck yes she was. Rather than leaving the meeting with the usual bitter taste in my mouth and heightened blood pressure, I felt motivated and even empowered, which then carried through to the rest of the day. We talked freely about our upcoming campaigns, and the current issues we had as a result of the previous account manager, and together we came up with outcomes I'd never even considered – we collaborated rather than trying to outdo each other and constantly fight for the spotlight, and in the end we both came out winning. It's funny, because I hadn't actually thought about the whole thing in much detail – I knew it was a great meeting but I hadn't taken the time to break it down and figure out why. Ellie said this was a perfect example of what she calls an accidental mentor. She said that people and things will pop up in my life from time to time to teach me whatever it is I need to know.

They may be subtle and completely random, but if I remain in my mindset of always being curious, I'll be able to extract the learnings that I'm supposed to get. This woman, Georgina, was my accidental mentor for building rapport – she'd shown me what to do and the impacts it can have, and now that I was consciously aware of it, she'd opened up a new door for me and a new realm of possibilities.

Of course by this point I was champing at the bit to acquire this rapport building skill. It seems like it could become my secret weapon. Not only can I create better outcomes for everyone involved, but I can also inspire and motivate people in a much greater way, and actually enjoy myself at the same time. Hell. Yeah. Anyway, why don't I just crack on with the details?

So Ellie said that the majority of rapport occurs on a subconscious level. In fact, words make up only 7 per cent of the communication process. Most of it happens through our physiology (like facial expressions, blinking, gestures, posture and breathing) and our voice (like the speed, pitch, volume and quality of it). So by learning how to pay attention to these elements, you can use them to create a subconscious 'common ground' with the other person, and then to notice shifts that indicate a change in the way that person is feeling. Let me tell you about this subconscious 'common ground' thing first. As Ellie has mentioned multiple times throughout this process, the main objective of our brains is to keep us safe, and it will naturally guide us towards the thoughts and behaviours that it believes do that most effectively. One easy way to ensure survival is to maintain a level of certainty and stick with things that are the same as us or what we already know – that's why we feel so much more comfortable and calm when we're in our normal surroundings or doing something we've done many times before. I get that – I'm always so nervous or apprehensive when I go somewhere or do something for the first time, and I can see now that a lot of the time it's just because it's the unknown, because usually after a little while, or after the next time, I feel much more at ease. I always figured this was because I'm a control freak, but it makes sense that it's actually my survival mode kicking in.

Anyway, Ellie went on to explain that when it comes to rapport we can use these survival instincts to our advantage. If we know that people feel safer when things are the same as them, then if we just make ourselves as similar to them as possible, we can create instant comfort … and therefore instant rapport. I was a little confused with this idea – how can I possibly make myself the same as other people? In my head, I was imagining myself carrying around a suitcase full of different wigs and outfits, and doing quick changes in the corner like a magician – it just didn't seem that practical to me! But Ellie reminded me of all the subconscious elements she'd mentioned a little earlier, and said that the similarities required are much more subtle than physical appearance. You simply observe how these elements are playing out for the other person, and essentially just copy them. In NLP they call this matching and mirroring.

For example, if they are talking loudly and abruptly with lots of hand gestures and sitting on the edge of their seat, you do the same. You come to their level. In this scenario, if you were to behave differently and talk quietly and softly while making little movement and reclining back into your chair, the other person would most likely feel uneasy and become consumed with trying to figure you out, rather than relaxing and allowing the interaction to naturally move towards one of mutual understanding.

Of course, that doesn't mean you have to stay at their level for the whole time – the key is to copy them for just long enough to get them comfortable and then you can start making subtle changes back towards your level, and allow them to follow. So, for example, you could bring the volume of your voice down a few notches and modify your posture to a more relaxed position in your chair. When you do this, however, you must keep observing what they do – if they don't follow, then you need to go back to their level and build more comfort. But if they do, then you know you're in rapport and they feel safe and at ease, so you can start taking the interaction and conversation forward. Once you do proceed, Ellie said it's important to keep observing to notice any shifts – if they all of a sudden sit back up in their chair or raise their voice, it's easy to tell something is probably wrong, but you can also look for more subtle signs – like a colour change in their cheeks, for example, or a slight narrowing of the eyes. This indicates a mismatch with you – maybe they've become confused, angry or afraid – so you can set about making them comfortable again or exploring what has made them feel that way.

I found this all so incredibly interesting, but I couldn't quite see how relevant it was in terms of pulling together all the work we'd done. So Ellie suggested flipping the scenario around. Let's say you go into a meeting with your new boss, your natural reaction is to feel completely intimidated because you feel inferior to him, so your brain sets about trying to find ways to make you feel safe. Its initial response is to create certainty and make things the same, so you start to change your behaviour to be more masculine by being more direct and assertive, and you try to be what you think he wants you to be, so that you're the same as his expectations (even though in reality you have no idea what they are). Within seconds you've completely lost all sight of the real you and all the hard work we've done together has gone out the window. Imagine, however, if you went into the scenario with the intention of building rapport with your boss and making a safe zone based on the subtle physiological and vocal cues we've talked about today, so your brain doesn't feel the need to go into survival mode. Yes, so you may change yourself initially to match and mirror him, but you're doing it consciously and with control, and solely with the intention of creating an environment that allows the real you to flourish. By doing this, you not only make him feel at ease, but you do that for yourself too, which then does indeed allow you to stand strong in your space and stay true to the real you, which in turn allows you both to be more open and willing to engage in a mutually beneficial interaction.

Then Ellie went all hippy on me again. She said this also works on an energetic level – another opportunity for my spiritual element to come out to play. She said if I go into an interaction feeling self-conscious and stressed, the other person will subconsciously pick up on that energy and start to copy it, putting them in a similar state – and, as we'd already talked about, when in that state we're operating from our emotional brain, which makes it extremely difficult to think logically, so this of course is not an ideal state to take the interaction into. She gave me a good example actually – she asked if I've ever walked into a room and, without even seeing the other person's face, I've just known that they were in a bad mood. Pretty much every day, I said, with one team member or another! Ellie asked, how can you know they're in a mood if you haven't seen or spoken to them? That was a good question, and one I'd never really thought about before. Ellie had told me a while ago that we're all actually just bundles of energy that come together in a specific way to create our physical, mental, emotional and spiritual bodies, and now she went on to tell me that our hearts emit an electromagnetic field. So when we're in close proximity to one another we can pick up on these different energies, and that's how we can understand how other people are feeling without needing any physical cues. So with that in mind, if I go into that same meeting with my boss having given myself a few minutes beforehand to breathe and visualise myself standing strong as my true self, my heart will emit a confident and calm energy that will then be picked up and copied by him, and allow us to create a connection, or rapport, much more easily and quickly because we'll be the same on an energetic level – the ultimate level of the subconscious.

Faaaaaaaar out. So I can influence the way someone feels just with my energy? That's some crazy shit. Actually, when I think about it, though, I often feel instantly calmer when I see Steve. I guess that's probably because of both of these things – I feel safe because I know him and he gives me certainty, but also he's calm and chilled out about 90 per cent of the time, so maybe my energy picks up on that and moves towards it? Gosh, his energy must be strong to be able to take charge of my crazy energy and bring it to his level!

So, obviously, after Ellie had explained it all like this it made much more sense. In order for me to stay true to who I really am and what I really want, I need to create safe spaces for myself and others that allow us to connect and feel at ease on a subconscious level, so we can stay true to who we really are, remain focused on getting the most out of our interactions and therefore create win–win scenarios for all involved. And I can do this by observing, copying and changing the physiological and vocal cues, as well as the energy. And when I notice shifts in these things in myself, it's a sign that I don't feel comfortable so I can take that as a cue to either make a change to restore safety, or to remain vigilant and ensure I don't start to move away from who I truly am. Got it!

October 30th

I tried the rapport building thing with the new girl in sales today. I actually think she was shit scared of me initially, because when I went up to introduce myself, she looked like she wanted the ground to open up and swallow her whole. Anyway, I took note of that and brought down the strength of my power handshake, and spoke more softly than I usually would (particularly when meeting a new person). I realised through this process that I do the exact thing I was moaning about the other day – I try to exert my authority over people and show them I'm powerful by cutting off the blood supply in their hand when I shake it and being quite abrasive in the way I speak. Ha, if only they knew it was all just an elaborate act.

Anyway, I figured that me being able to build quick rapport and make this girl feel comfortable was probably a far greater sign of power than her continuing to be terrified of me. And guess what? It bloody worked! I could see in her face at first that she was a bit surprised by my manner, but I ensured I maintained eye contact and took a genuine interest in what she was saying, as Georgina did with me, and I stayed down at her level by softening my demeanour and minimising my movement. It was like I could almost see her energy change right before my eyes. I noticed that her shoulders dropped and she started to breathe more slowly and deeply – she'd obviously been tense and anxious at first. A couple of times I forgot myself and reverted back to my assertive manner, but I could see her face and shoulders tighten up immediately each time, so I brought it back down again and watched as she relaxed. Later in the afternoon she sent me an email to say how lovely it was to meet me and she's looking forward to working with me – I've literally never had that before. So that was a great first go. I think she was quite an easy one because she's young and clearly quite impressionable, so it'll be interesting to see how I go with the miserable old bastards on the board!

It was awesome evidence too though to show that I am indeed liked and good enough just as I am. I dropped the act and just showed up as myself, and I got a much better reaction than I ever have before. Other evidence, by the way – Michelle decided to take my advice and has asked Phil to have a chat with me about what I've been doing with Ellie, to see if he can get some similar help too. The shit bit about that is I have to have a really open and honest conversation with him … about me … which will be challenging to say the least, but if Michelle values me and my opinions enough to let me help her save her marriage, then I guess I can suck it up and deal with the uncomfortableness – after all, as Ellie said, uncomfortableness isn't permanent, right?

Ah, and I managed to work through that whole meaning thing, fairly successfully. I had a bit of an argument with Steve over the phone because he hadn't told me that he'd be away for the night on a work thing. Initially my reaction was, he's obviously up to something and that's why he'd kept it from me until the last minute, and I started to feel angry and upset. I figured he'd finally had enough of me and had decided to go out and get someone better, someone who will treat him the way he deserves. Anyway, as I started to go down the black hole of despair in the space of about 2.5 seconds, I managed to force myself to take a step back and ask myself what was actually going on here. I realised that the situation was triggering my belief of not being good enough and my fear of abandonment, and I also realised that this probably wasn't a helpful meaning.

So I decided to change the meaning to: Steve's version of the world is different from mine and he probably had no idea that telling me late would be such an issue, because it wouldn't be for him. So I could let him know how it had made me feel and ask him to be more mindful in the future to keep me informed. As soon as I started thinking in that way with that new meaning I felt SO much better. My chest released itself from the knots it had tied itself up in and I started to breathe again (I think I actually held my breath for a little while there). And Steve really appreciated that too. He apologised for not being more aware of how I was feeling and said he would communicate his movements better to me in the future. Check me out … I'm like an actual grown up now!

Anyway, so that was the end. What an amazing way to finish this process – it tied everything together so nicely. Ellie and I ended our last session by going back over the Uppy scale and reviewing how I've gone. You won't bloody believe it, but my Uppy score had gone from 37/100 to 74/100. That's RIDICULOUS – in just a few weeks. Of course, there's still room to grow, but I do feel like I now have all the tools I need to be able to live the life I want and be the real me, so I'm sure that the more I continue to apply them, the higher my score will become.

Ellie said she was super-pleased with how I'd gone as well. She was really grateful to me for being so open and receptive to everything she taught me, and she has no doubt that I will continue to grow and change as I continue to employ all these strategies and make them a natural part of my life. She wanted to finish by summarising the key points for me to remember:

- Always stay true to my values and goals, and use my life blueprint to guide me in everything I do.
- Stay present and live in the moment.
- Focus only on what I can control and let go of the things I can't.
- I'm good enough just the way I am.
- I'm significant, present and secure.
- I am the creator of my meanings, therefore I am the creator of how I feel, therefore I am the creator of my life.

If I live by these things, and do what I need to do to make them my reality, I'll have everything I could possibly need to live a truly healthy, happy and fulfilled life.

HELL YEAH!

Okay, let's wrap this last section up with my reminders.

Journal

☐   I.   **Track how you're doing:**

- What have been your top three wins for the week?
- What have been your top three challenges?
- What are three ways you've served your values this week?
- Next week, what will you stop, start and keep doing in order to serve your values better/more?
  - Stop:
  - Start:
  - Keep:
- What are three pieces of evidence that your new story and labels are true? (Do this one daily.)
- What meanings have you changed this week and how have they changed the way you felt?

Action

☐   2.   **Complete the relationship blueprint worksheet, and ask your partner to do the same:**

- Come together and discuss what each of you has written. Remember to keep the ultimate goal in mind – to understand each other better and deepen your relationship.
- Identify three key actions each that you can do to serve each other's needs.
- Set expectations around fulfilling these and picking each other up when they're not done or done properly.
- Review each month and build upon the actions.

☐   3.   **Prepare some new meanings in advance for situations and people that typically cause you to feel in a way you don't want to feel.**
Ask yourself the following (and remember these questions for in the moment too, when you feel your mood changing):

- Is this feeling I have right now allowing me to be myself and serve my life blueprint?
- If not, what meaning am I giving to this situation?
- What is a different meaning I could give to this situation in order to serve me better and therefore make me feel better?

245

☐ 4. **Practise building rapport with people.** Notice the following about them:
  - Physiology
    - Posture
    - Gestures
    - Breathing
    - Blinking
    - Facial expressions
  - Voice:
    - Speed
    - Pitch
    - Volume
    - Quality
  - Energy

☐ 5. **Copy what they do at first and come to their level, and then try to change elements to bring them to your level.**

☐ 6. **Continue to observe throughout the interaction to notice if anything changes.** If so, come back to their level to regain the comfort and rapport.

Remember

☐ 7. **The brain's main priority is to keep you safe, so set up your surroundings and interactions with others in a way that communicates to your brain and others that your survival is not at threat.**

☐ 8. **You are the creator of your meanings, therefore you are the creator of your feelings, therefore you are the creator of your life.**

HELLO AGAIN

February 3rd

Dearest journal, I'm so sorry I've neglected you. Ironically, actually, I think if I'd had you by my side I would have made it through this shit storm much faster than I have, and potentially without having such a massive meltdown. I don't know why I didn't think to pick you up. To be honest, you didn't even enter my mind. After forgetting to take you away with me to that stupid week-long conference in November and then getting crazy busy at work before Christmas, I just got out of the habit. I was tracking things in my phone for a while, but then this all just hit me with such an almighty bang I didn't even know which way was up. But then you did come back into my life, dear journal, and somehow you knew exactly what I needed. I can't even remember what I was looking for when I went into the bottom of my wardrobe – it must have been something important, though, because I never venture down there unless I really have to. I'm sorry you ended up in the land of mismatched shoes and old handbags; you're so much better than that.

Even just the sight of you made a wave of calm wash over me. It genuinely felt like I was being reunited with an old friend I hadn't seen in a long time. I know this sounds really sad, but you are my friend. In fact, you may possibly be the best friend I've ever had. I've never told anyone as much as I've told you. Actually, that's probably why I did hide you away in the depths of the wardrobe vortex, because I didn't want to risk anyone else finding you and seeing how crazy I was. But how did you know which page to open at when I picked you up?

By that point I'd spent weeks trawling the internet looking for answers. I needed to know why this had happened to me. I know it's my fault that I've not looked after my body for years, but I didn't realise I'd fucked myself up that much – to not even be able to keep a tiny foetus alive. I mean, seriously, how much can something that small even need to survive? And I can't even give it that. I know I still wasn't sure if I even wanted kids – believe me, no-one was more surprised than me when those two lines showed up on the test – but to have the possibility and then get it so cruelly ripped away like that, without a choice, was brutal. I guess old Debs came out to play. And she did everything she could to destroy new Debs, including ignoring you journal. I felt like the ultimate failure. So, of course, the perfectionist in me went crazy and became obsessed with figuring out what was wrong with me and how I could fix it.

But then I found you again. I opened you and Ellie's words jumped out and gave me a massive slap across the face: *You're not broken and you don't need to be fixed. You are exactly where you need to be.*

At first I just yelled out, 'FUCK YOU' and broke down crying. How could this possibly be something that needed to happen? Why did I need to be mind-fucked harder than I'd ever been mind-fucked before? No-one should have to go through that. No-one needs that. But then all these thoughts started rushing into my head. I could hear Ellie's voice and see the words I'd written in you: *stay true to your values, they will guide you. Focus only on what you can control and let go of the things you can't. You are the creator of your life.*

I realised at that point that I did have all the answers. I did have everything I needed. My quest for answers on the internet was actually me living at Effect – I'd been looking for something to blame my pain on, instead of owning it, and in doing so I'd completely lost control. Steve and I were hanging on by a very loose thread, I'd considerably dropped the ball at work, and apart from going to work I hadn't left the house in weeks. I was ashamed to face the world. Ashamed that it would finally see how truly useless I really was. It felt like I couldn't hide this one. I couldn't just keep calm and carry on, or fake it till I made it. There wasn't enough war paint in the world to cover up this unbelievable fuck up, so I'd figured it was just best to retreat.

I didn't just do that physically, though, I also did it mentally – especially from Steve. I just felt so guilty for letting him down, I couldn't face him. He kept saying we should talk about it, but I just couldn't. I mean, what was there to talk about? We created a life and then I lost it, end of. Talking about it wasn't going to bring it back. I realise now how incredibly selfish that was. I'd made it all about me, but not in the good way. I'd completely disregarded the fact that Steve was hurting too, and perhaps talking about it was what he needed to get through it. I guess I'd taken on full responsibility for the situation – because it was my body, I'd decided it was my problem – and so I felt like I had to bear the whole burden. I didn't think Steve would understand anyway, since he hadn't experienced the physical loss. He would never know how it feels to be doubled over in pain with cramps so strong they make you feel sick. He would never know the fear you feel when you see blood that shouldn't be there. Or the feeling of complete and utter helplessness when you know you can't do a damn thing about it. No, unless you've experienced this, you wouldn't be able to understand how it's possible to hate yourself and your body so much, you just wish you could run away from it and never look back.

After finding you though journal, I realised that I had to get over myself and talk to Steve. The atmosphere in the house had become unbearable, and because I never left, Steve was going out most nights to 'give me space', which made me feel even worse and my anxiety go off the charts, because in my head I'd decided he'd found some-one else. I remember writing in here ages ago that I'd never felt so alone, but that didn't even come close to how lonely this had all made me feel. Thoughts of 'what if?' kept going around and around in my head, and they were pushing me even further into my hole – 'What if I hadn't pulled all those late nights at work?', 'What if I hadn't spent so many years abusing my body with yo-yo diets and stupid exercise regimes?', 'What if I'd never met Steve?' Again, I was totally living at Effect and looking for things to blame, rather than just owning it.

It took me a while to pluck up the courage to actually have 'the chat', but once I did it was like the flood gates opened and years of shit just poured right out of me. I found myself bringing up things from my relationship with Dan I'd never spoken about before (not even to you). I talked about how I never feel good enough in anything I do, and my fears around having children. I'd never really thought about that consciously before, but I realised as we talked that the main thing that had been causing doubt all these years was my fear of fucking it all up. I was terrified that if I did have children I'd get it all wrong. So I'd figured that before I even made the decision of whether to have them or not, I needed to build a safety net. I needed to ensure I'd made enough money to set us up financially, with a nice house and enough savings to send them to private schools and take them on nice holidays whenever we wanted. Then if I did fuck them up, at least they'd be comfortable during the process. But I now see that was all just a convenient excuse to keep me safe – to prevent me from having to make a decision and face potential (or inevitable, as I saw it) failure.

Steve shared that he was terrified too. He was scared that he wouldn't be inspiring or fun enough for the kids, and worried that our relationship would never be the same again. He also said, however, that he'd resolved that if we did have children he would just have to deal with all this, if and when it came up. He realised that he was worrying about something that may potentially never happen, and he knew deep down that he'd be able to handle whatever came up, and that our relationship is strong enough to deal with the changes – changes that might even make it stronger, if we let it. He revealed that over the last few years he'd started to change his mind about wanting to be a parent, but he didn't want to bring it up and add even more pressure to my already crazy life. I'm not sure if that's honourable or just plain stupid. Was he really willing to miss out on such a massive part of life, just because he didn't want to upset me? Does that make him an amazing human being, or a fucking idiot? The jury's still out on that one. Anyway, it was really nice to know that he had fears too, and quite inspiring to see how he was dealing with them in such a practical and matter of fact way. We talked for hours and hours, and eventually came to the conclusion that maybe we would give this parenthood thing a crack. Although this whole ordeal has been horrific and I'm terrified it'll happen again, it has made me realise that when I peel back the fears, the desire to be a mum is there.

After this conversation with Steve, I felt more connected to him than I ever had before. And I felt light. It was like I'd finally released whatever it was I've been holding on to all these years. It was almost like I could see and hear more around me. It's weird, it's hard to explain, but it was kind of like I'd finally lifted my head out of the water and I could breathe. I finally felt free.

And holy fuck, it's amazing how much more shit you get done when you feel free! I was like a greyhound being released from the traps. Whereas before I was running around all over the place (and often in circles) trying to prove how good I was compared to everyone else, this time I had my eyes firmly fixed on the 'lure', and I knew that all I had to do was chase that and I'd win. The lure, of course, was my values and goals, my life blueprint. I got myself re-connected with that and created a plan that ensured I would only focus on what's important to me and what I really want. I realised that this self-deprecating mindset I'd fallen back into and the destructive pattern of behaviours wasn't serving my blueprint in any way. Clearly my health was going to shit because I was regularly binge eating, I'd stopped doing any exercise at all, and the negative self-talk was out of control, so I was back in full-blown fight or flight mode. I didn't have any sort of security in my life, because I'd lost all sight of who I was and shut out anyone who might be able to remind me. Fun was a distant memory that I felt like I didn't deserve. I didn't care to grow or develop, I just wanted to shrink into the shadows and fade away. And, of course, I was disconnected from all the people I loved and not present in any way – in fact, the idea of being present terrified me. I just wanted to be as far away from me and my situation as I possibly could. Hmmm, it's no wonder I was feeling so shit.

I can see now that I was in complete survival mode. Feeling like I had no control over anything (not even myself) was the most vulnerable and exposed I've ever felt, so naturally my brain wanted to wrap me up in cotton wool and protect me from the big bad world that was making me feel this way. The problem was, though, it couldn't protect me from the big bad world because it wasn't the big bad world making me feel that way – it was me and the meanings I'd given to the situation that were. I'd taken all my beliefs about not being good enough and superglued them on to the situation, along with my fears of being rejected and abandoned. My own child had rejected me for fuck's sake … or at least that was the meaning I'd decided to run with.

Once I managed to pull my head out of this ultimate cycle of mind fuckery, however, I realised that this meaning was controlling all of my feelings, and if I didn't change it then it would continue to control my life and make me a bitter, miserable and lonely woman. So I created a new meaning. I decided to believe that this was actually just nature doing its job – one of the things my copious amounts of internet research did teach me was that miscarriage is actually really common (like one in four common), and even more so if you have polycystic ovaries. And the reason it happens is usually not the woman's fault at all, but because of an abnormality or defect, so it's basically just natural selection doing its thing. It's a nice reminder that we're all part of something much greater, so I should keep my eye on the bigger picture and allow myself to ride over the waves of shit that come up along the way.

Anyway, that meaning helped me to jump back into my logical brain and get practical – I can't control nature but I can give it a help-ing hand and make the best of everything I can control … which, of course, is myself. I think I'd become a bit complacent after finishing my work with Ellie – I thought that cos I'd done her program I knew everything and so I'd nailed it. This situation has given me a good kick up the arse, though, and reminded me of what Ellie told me all along – that this is an ongoing process and in order to be successful (that is, be able to stay true to who I really am and what I really want, and live a happy, healthy and fulfilled life) I need to remain consistent and make it my way of life. I realise now that this is not something I learn, it's something I am.

So I put my organisation hat on, which is one that looks really good on me, and I got my shit together. Thank God I'd written in you with so much detail, because I had a ready-made guide book for what to do. Not only because of the things I did with Ellie, but also because I could see the things I was thinking and doing when I was stuck in the mind fuckery. It showed me what to look out for, and what I most definitely should not do. It helped me to see what my natural survival mode has been and what my go-to meanings were, so now I can get proactive and create new meanings before these situations even think about coming up again. So here are my non-negotiables to get me back in the game. I'm writing them in here because I need your help to keep me accountable. You got me out of my hole before and I know you can do it again. Here goes:

- I will nourish my body daily by eating real whole food, moving, breathing, and giving myself moments throughout the day to step back, reflect and communicate to my brain that I'm safe and everything is okay. I will go back to my naturopath and find out what I need to do to prepare my body for motherhood.

- I will nourish my mind daily by continuing to work on myself and my own personal development. I will do my morning and evening rituals of breathing/meditating, repeating my new beliefs and labels, and documenting evidence in here that they are true (as well as consistently writing my other thoughts and feelings down, as I've done so well before). I will visualise daily everything I want my life to be, and visualise it as if it's now, concentrating on the feeling it gives me.

- I will always have my values and goals visible and refer to them in the moment for everything I do.

- I will re-connect with the people I love and value, and make plans to spend quality time with them regularly.

- I will commit to being open and honest with these people, and asking for help and support when I need it.

- I will re-schedule a weekly date night with Steve.

- I will do something I love every week.

And, most importantly:

> *I will always be me, the real me and nothing but the real me.*

I am Debs. I am good enough. And I am the creator of my life. Let's bloody do this!

Don't forget, you can access and download all the worksheets and resources Debs mentions throughout the book at:

www.uppy.com.au/unfaked

www.ingramcontent.com/pod-product-compliance
Lightning Source LLC
Chambersburg PA
CBHW061205220326
41597CB00015BA/1497